MW00330787

The Fragrant
Companions

For a complete list of books in the series, see page 339.

The Fragrant Companions

A Play About Love Between Women

Li Yu

TRANSLATED BY

Stephen Roddy and Ying Wang

Columbia University Press

New York

GEISS HSU
FOUNDATION

This publication was made possible in part by an award from the
James P. Geiss and Margaret Y. Hsu Foundation.

Columbia University Press wishes to express its appreciation for
assistance given by the Pushkin Fund in the publication of this book.

Columbia University Press
Publishers Since 1893
New York   Chichester, West Sussex
cup.columbia.edu

Library of Congress Cataloging-in-Publication Data
Names: Li, Yu, 1611–1680?, author. | Roddy, Stephen, translator. |
Wang, Ying, 1955 December 26– translator.
Title: The fragrant companions : a play about love between women /
Li Yu ; translated by Stephen Roddy and Ying Wang.
Other titles: Lian xiang ban. English
Description: New York : Columbia University Press, [2022] |
Includes bibliographical references and index.
Identifiers: LCCN 2021050624 (print) | LCCN 2021050625 (ebook) |
ISBN 9780231206280 (hardback ; acid-free paper) |
ISBN 9780231206297 (trade paperback ; acid-free paper) |
ISBN 9780231556408 (ebook)
Subjects: LCGFT: Lesbian drama.
Classification: LCC PL2698.L52 L4713 2022 (print) | LCC PL2698.L52
(ebook) | DDC 895.12/48—dc23/eng/20211222
LC record available at https://lccn.loc.gov/2021050624
LC ebook record available at https://lccn.loc.gov/2021050625

Columbia University Press books are printed on permanent and
durable acid-free paper.

Printed in the United States of America

Cover design: Milenda Nan Ok Lee

Cover image: 明陈洪绶花卉 (flower painting by Chen Hongshou
[1598-1652]). Photograph by Jiahuan He 何家欢.© Sichuan Museum

CONTENTS

INTRODUCTION: WOMEN IN LOVE AND THE BUSINESS OF MEN IN LI YU'S *CHUANQI* DRAMA

YING WANG AND STEPHEN RODDY

he Fragrant Companions is the product of a particularly tumultuous era in Chinese history. Just seven years prior to the play's completion in 1651, the Ming dynasty (1368–1644) was violently replaced by the Manchu-led Qing (1644–1911), a transition precipitated by the traumatic fall of the capital to peasant rebels and the suicide of the reigning emperor. The play's author, Li Yu 李漁 (*hao* Liweng 笠翁, 1611–1680), navigated these turbulent waters relatively smoothly, thanks in part to his talent for channeling his prodigious literary gifts into profitable ventures in theatrical production and publishing. *The Fragrant Companions* (*Lianxiangban* 憐香伴, literally "Companions Who Love Fragrance," also known as *Meiren xiang* 美人香, "The Fragrance of Beauties") was Li's first play in the *chuanqi* 傳奇 genre. He went on to write a total of nine others, which, along with three collections of short fiction, form the core of his literary oeuvre. He also accrued considerable fame from the manuals and essays he wrote or inspired others to create about painting, horticulture, cuisine, and various elegant pastimes that he cultivated as a flamboyant bon vivant. In his lifestyle and his writings he challenged long-held conventions regarding historical events, public morality, literary expression, or other arenas. His irreverent contrarianism won him popularity and commercial success. But it also provoked disdain, causing him to be seen as an opportunistic *bangxian* 幫閒 (literally "aiding idleness," meaning a hack writer who caters to the whims of the rich and powerful for financial gain). Such condescending epithets continued to dog his posthumous reputation until well into the modern era, when writers like Zhou Zuoren 周作人 (1885–1967) began the process of rehabilitating him from the disrepute to which he had long been consigned.

While Li's short stories were first translated into English as early as 1815, the longstanding neglect of his work within China apparently impeded the full range of his writings from reaching foreign audiences. This began to change in the 1960s, when Helmut Martin worked with collaborators in Taiwan to edit and publish Li Yu's collected works (1970). It picked up pace in the 1980s: two critical biographies were published in the United States, and Patrick Hanan followed his award-winning *The Invention of Li Yu* (1988) with his translations of *The Carnal Prayer Mat* (1990), an erotic novel attributed to Li Yu, and selections from Li's two short story collections, *A Tower for the Summer Heat* (1992; original title Twelve Towers / *Shier lou* 十二樓) and *Silent Operas* (1996; *Wusheng xi* 無聲戲). Hanan did not apply his prodigious talents to Li's plays, however, and though *The Lively Plays of Li Yu* (1980) by Eric Henry does focus on Li's theatrical corpus, it translates only a handful of extended passages. Non-Chinese readers had to wait until 2020 for the first English version of an entire play, *A Couple of Soles* (*Bimuyu* 比目魚), to appear in print. *The Fragrant Companions* is thus the second of what we hope will eventually be Li's entire dramatic oeuvre rendered into English as well as other languages.

The Fragrant Companions tells the story of two young gentry ladies who fall in love with each other after exchanging poems in a nunnery, and who then overcome a series of obstacles to come together through a legitimate marriage—with the same husband. The romance starts with the newly wedded Cui Jianyun 崔箋雲 going to burn incense in the Rain-Flower Nunnery in Yangzhou. At the nunnery she meets Cao Yuhua 曹語花, who has stopped there overnight with her father on their way to the capital for the triennial metropolitan civil service examination. Jianyun is first captivated by Yuhua's alluringly fragrant bodily scent and natural beauty, while Yuhua reciprocates with admiration for Jianyun's stunning looks and elegant manner. It is love at first sight.

But the emotional bond between the young women goes even deeper after they discover their shared interest in and talent for writing poetry. Their mutual affection grows so strong that they conduct a mock wedding ceremony at the nunnery and hatch a plan to spend the rest of their lives together by having Cao Yuhua marry Cui Jianyun's husband as a second wife. The marriage proposal is rejected by Yuhua's father, however, then further stymied by the machinations of another suitor, and yet further postponed by Jianyun's husband, who suffers from slander and mistreatment as an indirect consequence of the ladies' infatuation. Jianyun and Yuhua are forced to part, but three years later they fortunately meet again, in the capital. This time, through a well-contrived scheme and some good luck, Jianyun becomes Yuhua's literary companion while her husband comes under Yuhua's father's tutelage through the palace examination. In the play's grand finale, the two young women are able to fulfill their wish to live together in a ménage-à-trois marriage.

The relationship between Jianyun and Yuhua goes through a complete cycle of free love that is typical of standard heteronormative Chinese romantic tales—falling in love, pledging to marry without parental permission, longing and becoming lovesick when separated, and eventually achieving a joyous reunion and sharing a life together. Despite its conclusion in a heterosexual marriage that seems to reaffirm the norms of the Confucian-based gender hierarchy, polygamous marriage, and the patriarchal social order, the heart of the play lies in its portrayal of the two women's genuine love and passion for each other, their mutual longing when separated, their efforts and resourcefulness to surmount social biases and impediments, and the triumph of their love—even if partially compromised—over social mandates and expectations. The play is not without flaws, but it is indeed a remarkable and rare sympathetic treatment of a subject that historical and literary writings rarely broached over the long span of imperial Chinese history.

Although brief descriptions of the plot of *The Fragrant Companions* can be found in Hanan's and Henry's respective studies, close familiarity with its complex story has remained relatively limited outside of—and even to some extent within—China. While sharing much in common with the style and themes of Li Yu's nine other plays, *The Fragrant Companions* can be distinguished from them in several respects. First, as in many of his plays, the examination system features prominently. But as the locus of (at least temporary) injustice, nepotism, ineptitude, and sheer malice, the range and intensity of its satire toward this institution is unequalled by any of Li's other works of drama or fiction. Second, the play includes a subplot set in an exotic overseas location—the Ryukyu Kingdom—whose king sends a delegation to China and in turn receives an imperial envoy from Beijing. Third, *The Fragrant Companions* is written in an elevated and markedly more allusive style than *A Couple of Soles* and most of Li Yu's other later plays. And finally, it is one of the very few literary works of premodern China to treat the theme of female same-sex love in detail. These and other features contribute to the rich complexity and contemporary relevance of the play, and they have earned it the attention of the foremost scholars in the field of Li Yu studies. As a jewel among Li's artful and invariably delightful plays, *The Fragrant Companions* has long deserved to be made accessible to readers and theater audiences beyond China, a task we have undertaken with both humility and considerable pleasure.

LI YU'S LIFE AND WRITINGS

Li Yu was born into a well-to-do gentry family of the Jinhua-Lanxi district of Zhejiang Province in 1611, where he received a classical education in preparation for the official examinations typical of young men of his status. The wars, rebellions, and banditry that marked the dynastic transition at first interrupted and then permanently ended Li's aspirations to pursue an official career, forcing him to seek an alternative means of making a living. Fortuitously, the rapid increase of literacy, the booming publishing industry, and the relaxation of Neo-Confucian ethics in the late Ming and early Qing all created a sociocultural milieu and market conducive to the growth of opportunities for professional writing. Li Yu became one of the first and arguably the most renowned professional writer and artist of his kind, and he maintained a relatively opulent lifestyle at his Nanjing villa by publishing and selling his writings, running his bookstore, touring the empire with his private theatrical troupe, and engaging in other types of artistic business ventures.

Implicitly and often explicitly dubious toward the strict etiquette of Neo-Confucianism embedded in the curriculum of the examination system and widely shared among the elite, Li Yu emerged as a witty and iconoclastic writer who was obsessed with novelty, ingeniousness, and virtuosity. As Patrick Hanan has put it, Li's literary works demonstrate "his individuality, his expression of self, his concerns with the close-at-hand, and his rejection of the authority of tradition."[1] Some of Li Yu's choices of subject matter and artistic strategies seem strikingly "modern" even in this day and age. For instance, in his fiction and plays, he ridicules the Confucian rules governing women's conduct, such as the promotion of chastity and strict limits on women's education; he also writes about same-sex eroticism not only in *The Fragrant Companions* but in two short stories and one other play;[2] and, he uses parody throughout most of his fiction and plays to make fun of literary stereotypes and tiresome conventions.

Though recognized for his impressive literary talent, Li Yu's pursuit of profit through writing and patronage resulted in the aforementioned epithet of "hanger-on." His notoriety as the author—even if perhaps spuriously—of an erotic novel, and for allegedly "immoral behavior" such as enlisting his two concubines to perform in public with his family theatrical troupe, further contributed to his ill repute. In spite of his partial revival in the early twentieth century, Li Yu's writings continued to suffer from neglect or, even if they were noticed, bore the brunt of bigoted and uninformed criticism and prudishly motivated censorship. His fiction and dramatic works were often judged to be lacking in historical significance or moral seriousness and castigated for dwelling on "trivial" subjects; *The Fragrant Companions* is the most representative example of this persistent neglect. It is said that the play was seldom performed even during Li Yu's time, and hardly at all before the twenty-first century. When it was finally staged in its entirety by the Beijing Opera Company in 1957, it was reconfigured as a heterosexual romance, completely stripped of its homoerotic dimensions. While Li's iconoclasm may have benefited the play during the early years of the People's Republic of China, its theme of women in love with one another evidently could not be faithfully rendered in a public performance until the dawn of the twenty-first century.

By the time Li Yu wrote *The Fragrant Companions* in 1651, the *chuanqi* drama already had more than a century of history behind it as an elite art form. Originating from *nanxi* 南戲 (Southern Drama) in the Song dynasty (960–1279), *chuanqi* is a type of sung drama; it is often handled in translation as "opera," like other traditional Chinese theatrical forms that consist of both singing and spoken parts and alternate between prose and verse. Whereas the actions and dialogues advance plot development, the singing parts reveal the inner states and emotions of the characters.[3] A *chuanqi* play is quite lengthy, containing thirty-plus scenes, and it usually interweaves two or more story lines together, with a romance in the foreground and some political intrigues and military affairs in the background. As Cyril Birch indicated, "the traditional Chinese stage used no sets, and so there is complete freedom of movement and much scenic description (vicarious stage-setting) in dialogue and songs."[4] Role type is another factor that determines and contributes to the theatricality of *chuanqi* plays. The role types were devised to incorporate a fixed-role system consisting of four main categories of actors, *sheng*, *dan*, *jing*, and *chou* (male, female, painted-face, and clown). These four categories are subdivided into more specific role types according to age, social standing, and profession. Unlike Yuan *zaju* ("variety plays") that were mainly products of professional playwrights and troupes, the *chuanqi* dramatists before Li Yu were mostly amateur writers with official careers, and their plays were typically performed by household troupes owned by wealthy bureaucrats or merchants. By Li's time, such amateurism and elite taste had pushed *chuanqi* toward formulaic monotony in musical and narrative structure, cumbersome verbal embellishment, and hackneyed subject matter and generic conventions, all of which often emphasized literati sentimentality and aesthetics at the cost of theatricality. Li Yu is representative of a nascent reaction against these trends, and of the emergence of both professionalism in and popularization of the genre. The plays by Li and many of his contemporaries were generally better suited to performance and also more agreeable to the tastes of a wider social spectrum of audiences than the literati elite.

Li's approach to dramaturgy is best reflected in his *Xianqing ouji* 閒情偶寄 (Casual Expressions of Idle Feeling, 1671), a collection of essays on the cultivation of taste amid "idleness." The first two sections, "The Composition of Plays" and "The Production of Plays," are probably the most important theoretical discussions of theatrical art in all of premodern times. Concerning *The Fragrant Companions*, the central conception discussed in these two sections is Li's (re)interpretation of *qi* 奇 (the marvelous or extraordinary). As indicated by the name *chuanqi* (transmitting marvels), *qi* is the essential subject in this theatrical art. But in the hands of many of Li Yu's contemporary playwrights, *qi* verged on the bizarre, outlandish, and absurd. Conversely, some of the subjects and plots typical of the genre, such as the love between *caizi* 才子 (a talented man) and *jiaren* 佳人 (a beautiful woman), and the *caizi*'s success in the civil service examination, became so clichéd that they simply lost their freshness and failed to evoke the proper dramatic responses of excitement and surprise.

Li Yu addresses these problems in two entries in *Xianqing ouji*—"Tuo kejiu" 脫窠臼 (escaping hackneyed conventions) and "Jie huangtang" 戒荒唐 (swearing off the ridiculous or absurd)—to explain how he understood and manifested the concept of *qi* in his plays. To Li Yu, *qi* means to seek newness in writing and producing a *chuanqi* play. As he puts it:

> In people one seeks only the old, in things the new. Newness is a term of approbation for everything in the world, but doubly so for literature. This is what the statement "striving to rid one's writing of clichés—oh, how hard it is!" refers to. And in the art of drama, newness is twice as valuable again as in the other literary genres. Not only is the work of past authors now obsolete, there is a gulf even in my own writing between what I wrote yesterday and what I am writing today. Yesterday's work has appeared, while today's has not, and if we regard what has not yet appeared as new, we must accept what has already appeared as old.[5]

If newness or novelty is the best realization of *qi*, one needs to find it in normal human situations, and not search for it in the fantastic realm. Li Yu reasons that plays that expound on human feelings and portray events that conform to the normative workings of nature will be appreciated for generations to come, whereas those that are frivolous, incredible, ridiculous, and weird will be forgotten within the lifetime of the playwright. The best way to seek novelty, or *qi*, according to Li Yu, is to make the ordinary extraordinary, the familiar unfamiliar, and produce surprising and novel effects. Li Yu further explains:

> It is said that everyday events have been exhausted by writers of the past and that even the most minute and extremely obscure incidents have been fully explored. That is why contemporary writers seek what is strange and bizarre. But I beg to differ. Not many extraordinary events happen in the humdrum world, but the principles governing human emotions are infinite. As long

as the relationships between rulers and subjects, fathers and sons, exist for one day, there will be feelings and concepts of loyalty, filial piety, chastity, and righteousness. Human nature manifests itself in novel ways with the passing of time. There are certainly events of the past left for writers of a later generation to explore and to depict more sensitively, thus improving on what has been done by one's predecessors.[6]

This desire to bring out fresh aspects or explore new sensibilities of old subject matter is manifest in Li Yu's works known as *fan'an wenzhang* 翻案文章 (inversion or table-turning essays), literally, meaning "essays written to reverse a previous verdict." This idea is remarkably close to the Western concept of parody and, like the latter, usually involves two texts: a previous historical story or a legend and a later rewriting that undermines or totally reverses the previous text. From the late Ming onward, the notion of *fan'an wenzhang* became very popular and began to be used as a rhetorical device in both writing and judging history and literature, ranging from Zhang Zhupo's 張竹坡 (1670–1698) commentary on the vernacular novel *Jin Ping Mei* (*The Plum in the Golden Vase*), to Wang Shizhen's 王世貞 (1526–1590) essay on an episode of pre-Qin history, "Lin Xiangru wan bi gui Zhao lun" 藺相如完璧歸趙論 (A Discussion of Lin Xiangru's Restoration of the Jade Disk to Zhao), to Li Zhi's 李贄 (1527–1602) provocative reappraisal of the An Lushan Rebellion (756–763) in his compilation *Cangshu* 藏書 (A Book to Be Hidden Away).[7]

Li Yu's own collection of essays on historical events and figures, *Li Yu lun gu* 李漁論古 (Li Yu Discusses the Past), completed in 1664, can be seen as an entire collection of *fan'an wenzhang*. In Patrick Hanan's words, it "was a genre that gave the writer of iconoclastic temper the opportunity to *fan'an*, that is, to overturn an accepted historical judgment."[8] The technique of inversion is even more pronounced in Li Yu's literary writings, including plays as well as fiction. Li Yu's fiction and drama, which closely overlap thematically and structurally, share the same set of themes: the proper role of sexual love, domestic moral issues, and the doctrine of karmic cause and effect—themes that are popular across *chuanqi* drama, *huaben xiaoshuo* 話本小說 (vernacular short stories), and *caizi jiaren xiaoshuo* 才子佳人小說 (scholar-beauty fiction). But Li Yu deliberately reversed or reconstructed these stock themes in order to subvert the conventions and norms that are generally upheld in earlier texts. In dealing with the subject of love or sexuality, for example, the transcendent power of *qing* 情 (love, desire, and feelings) and the obsessive romanticism best exemplified by Tang Xianzu's 湯顯祖 (1550–1616) four "dream plays" is devalued in Li Yu's play *Shen luan jiao* 慎鸞交 (Be Careful in Love) and a closely similar short story "He gui lou" 鶴歸樓 (Homing Crane Lodge) in favor of a more rational, practical, reserved, and controlled kind of love. But Li Yu's works do not affirmatively adhere to the realistic presentation of sensuality or the didactic and aesthetic conventions of this theme that are characteristic of *huaben xiaoshuo*. Like the tales in Boccaccio's *Decameron*, Li Yu approached sensuality in an almost purely comic mode. To Li, sensuality is something amusing, to be laughed at or even satirized rather than celebrated or condemned. For Li Yu's young lovers, as seen in his short story "Cui ya lou" 翠雅樓 (House of Gathered Refinements) and his novella *Rouputuan* 肉蒲團, no matter what kind of relationship they are involved in—lawful or illicit, heterosexual or homosexual— the emotional satisfaction of *qing* and the claims of honor or religious devotion appear irrelevant. Instead, Li treats the sexual fulfillment of its young lovers irreverently, with gusto and humor rather than seriousness. The formulas of scholar–beauty fiction are invariably inverted and mocked in Li Yu's dramatic works, but in *The Fragrant Companions* this takes an even more unusual form: the relegation of marriage to a strategy for achieving the protagonists' desire for a same-sex union.

THE PARODY OF THE "SCHOLAR-BEAUTY" ROMANCE AND FEMALE SAME-SEX LOVE

Given how Li Yu understood the concept of *qi* as bringing out newness from the old and his consistent use of the rhetoric of *fan'an* throughout his writings, it is logical to read *The Fragrant Companions* as an intentional inversion or parodic retake of the stereotypical scholar–beauty romance of Chinese drama and fiction. Such a romance is best represented by *Xixiang ji* 西廂記 (*Romance of the Western Chamber*) and *Mudan ting* 牡丹亭 (*The Peony Pavilion*) of the late-Yuan and late-Ming, respectively, and during Li Yu's lifetime, by the genre of novellas known as scholar–beauty fiction. *The Fragrant Companions* follows the outline of this tried-and-true-formula: the protagonists possess dashing beauty and peerless talent, their match was made in heaven, the rendezvous occurs in a temple or garden, and the love quest is tested by obstacles (including the objection of family elders) and challenged by villains, until the final consummation of matrimony is ensured by the scholar's victory in the civil service examination and blessed by the emperor himself. Several scenes of the play are even reminiscent of *Xixiang ji* and *Mudan ting*: scene 5, "Guidance from the Gods" (Shen yin 神引), reminds us of the episode of the flower spirit ensuring Liu Mengmei's 柳夢梅 tryst with Du Liniang 杜麗娘 in *Mudan ting* (scene 10), whereas scene 24, "Interrogating the Maid" (Kao bi 拷婢), invokes Madame Cui's questioning of Hongniang 紅娘 about her mistress's affair in part 2, act 4 of *Xixiang ji*. Li Yu seemed to have the thematic mode of "the talented scholar and his beautiful mate" in mind when he wrote *The Fragrant Companions*, but he subverted it and told an entirely different story by switching the gender of the talented scholar from male to female.

This gender transformation is significant in several ways. First of all, the fairy-tale formula of the scholar–beauty romance between a man and a woman has been decentered and even upended. The dramatic climax or the happy finale of the standard scholar–beauty play is usually summarized in this couplet: "when the candles are lit in the wedding chamber, his [the male protagonist's] name is listed on the gold registry of examination passers" (洞房花燭夜，金榜題名時). Such double success in marriage and in officialdom best represented and certainly satisfied an elite male's desires, which were also assumed to be a woman's ideal as the vicarious beneficiary of his temporal successes. Instead of the typical ending of such works in the wedding of the protagonists, *The Fragrant Companions* begins with one: Cui Jianyun, one of the two female protagonists, enters the household of a talented and handsome scholar, Fan Shi 范石, with whom she enjoys the first taste of matrimony. What more could she desire? Only through a chance meeting at the Rain-Flower Nunnery with Cao Yuhua, a fifteen-year-old of peerless beauty and talent, does she realize what is missing from her otherwise fulfilling life. In a scene that mimics the clichéd chance meeting of lovers, the two compose matching poems to display their respective poetic talents, turning the stock storyline upside down and challenging the gendered desires encoded in previous plays. For Jianyun, her marriage to Fan Shi seems not to satisfy her desire for a deeper affection. To Yuhua, love and happiness need not be achieved first and foremost by wedding a successful male scholar; in the denouement, her marriage to Fan Shi serves as an expedient ploy to bring her together with Jianyun.

The hero's rescue of his beauty is a typical episode in the conventional scholar–beauty play. In *Xixiang ji*, Zhang Gong 張珙 saves Yingying 崔鶯鶯 from the clutches of the bandit ringleader Sun Feihu 孫飛虎, and in *Mudan ting* Liu Mengmei 柳夢梅 raises Du Liniang 杜麗娘 from the dead. Li Yu's own more conventional play *Shenzhong lou* 蜃中樓 (The Illusory Tower) assigns the male protagonist the task of extricating the dragon princess from an abuser.[9] In *The Fragrant Companions*, however, the rescue is accomplished by none other than Cui Jianyun, the talented female scholar. She is the one to hatch the plot to save Cao Yuhua from lovesickness by entering the Cao household under the guise of "poetic companion," a scheme to which Fan Shi passively agrees but plays no role in carrying out. Thus, the masculine role of savior is assigned to a woman; the inversion retains a conventionally fragile and vulnerable young woman, pining away for the object of her affection, as a beneficiary of the rescue. More important, in *The Fragrant Companions*, "the talented woman" is given agency to not only decide her own fate in love and marriage but also to drive the dramatic plot forward.

Although female characters with literary talents were repeatedly portrayed in previous Chinese theater, including *chuanqi* drama, Li Yu was probably the first to turn the convention of a pair of male-female protagonists into a female duo. The image of the "talented woman" is endowed with dual form through both female protagonists, Cui Jianyun and Cao Yuhua. Both women are gorgeous in appearance and attract each other physically: Jianyun stands out even among the women of Yangzhou famous for their beauty, and Yuhua, born with an intoxicatingly fragrant body scent, possesses a natural charm without need of makeup. But shared by both and appreciated most fervently between them is poetic talent, described as unequaled by their contemporaries, male as well as female. Such talent is problematic in a male-dominated society; as Yuhua's father sternly warns her, "Women should not show off their literary talents, and write poetry only to entertain themselves. . . . For women, to lack talent is a virtue."[10] The quotation of the well-known phrase, "for women, to lack talent is a virtue" (女子無才便是德) can hardly be taken at face value, and the two women's elegant, learned repartee is an example of just the sort of inversion that Li Yu practiced in all of his writings. We can detect a definite similarity with the celebration of female talent in seventeenth-century scholar–beauty fiction, but in *The Fragrant Companions* the two female protagonists are more down-to-earth and believable than the formulaic super-geniuses created in the *caizi jiaren* fiction of that period. Under Li Yu's pen a woman's talent (literary or practical), intrinsically worthy of praise, becomes an asset in love and happiness as well as the catalyst of the unfolding drama: the talented woman is loved and loving, and she is empowered—whether emotionally, practically, or both—to fulfill her desire and pursue her love. Li Yu's generation witnessed the emergence of a group of female talents, particularly in the affluent Yangzi (Chang) River delta of Jiangnan 江南 where Li Yu lived. A number of women even sought and acquired teaching and writing careers. Li Yu associated with some well-educated and well-versed women himself, and two of his plays were prefaced by Wang Duanshu 王端淑 (1621–after 1701) and Huang Yuanjie 黄媛介 (seventeenth c.), two talented women of the time.[11] From this we can see that the rhetoric of inversion was not only a literary device, but also an effective tool with which Li Yu viewed and reflected his contemporary reality more sensitively than most of his predecessors had.

Though he has been displaced by a "talented woman" and relegated to a subsidiary position within their triangular relationship, the "talented scholar" Fan Shi retains his overall prominence

as the play's male lead or *sheng*. (Beginning in scene 23, however, he is called Shi Jian 石堅, so we refer to him hereafter as
Fan/Shi.) Indeed, in keeping with *chuanqi* convention, the
second scene consists entirely of good-humored banter among
Fan/Shi and his male friends celebrating his wedding. The phrase
from the aforementioned scholar–beauty couplet, "the gold reg-
ister of exam passers," concludes this play, too: not only Fan/Shi,
but most of the male protagonists—his father-in-law Cao
Gechen 曹個臣, Cao's fellow provincial graduate Wang Zhongxiang 汪仲襄, Fan/Shi's cousin-in-law Zhang Zhongyou 張仲友,
as well as his arch-rival, Zhou Gongmeng 周公夢, aspire to and
mostly achieve examination success.

But as with the inversion of the conventional heteronormative romance, the play's portrayal of the examination system also
overturns the standard plot lines. Although examination foibles,
injustices, and mishaps are hardly unknown in *chuanqi* plays,
very few can compete with *The Fragrant Companions* in turning
the entire examination system, from county-level licentiates and
their "teachers" to the solemn precincts of the Confucian temple in Beijing, into a sustained farce.

At the climax of this burlesque, scene 29 "Searching the
Crack" (Sou jia 搜挾), begins with body searches of candidates
entering the metropolitan examination hall; this leads to the
hilarious exposure of Fan/Shi's nemesis Zhou Gongmeng as he
attempts to smuggle in notes by tucking them into his anus, and
the subsequent descent into an extended burlesque at the expense
of whatever dignity remained in the examination process. This
scene might be read as a parodic inversion of scene 41 "Delayed
Examination" (Dan shi, 耽試) from *Mudan ting*, where Liu
Mengmei, the young male lead, not only clinches top honors in
the metropolitan examinations, but in the process demonstrates
his scholarly aptitude and political acumen, with the inferior

essays and strategies of three prior examinees serving as his foils. In *The Fragrant Companions*, by contrast, Zhou Gongmeng, the villain of the play in the painted-face role, displaces Fan/Shi as the protagonist of the entire scene. This role reversal between the painted-face role (usually portraying a boorish and unsophisticated character) and the young male lead frames the travesty of the whole situation: if in *Mudan ting*, the examination hall is where important national policy is discussed and the most capable men are recruited for government service, in *The Fragrant Companions* the hall is turned into a theater of the absurd with a body cavity search that resembles the treatment of criminals in detention,[12] and the depravity of Zhou Gongmeng's deeds both within and beyond the examination precincts. In the theatrical highpoint centered on Zhou's antics, Li Yu relegates Fan/Shi and two other law-abiding examinees who enter just prior to Zhou to the function of secondary "props," thereby reversing the *chuanqi* convention of treating examinations as a reasonably fair arbiter of talent, as exemplified by *Mudan ting* and numerous other plays.

The denouement in heteronormative matrimony brings us full circle to recall Jianyun's wedding night in scene 2, now overshadowed by the love of the two women who have eyes only for each other. At a number of points in the play, but especially in scene 5 ("Guidance from the Gods"), scene 10 ("A Joking, Bantering Alliance"), scene 21 ("Sealing a Sorrowful Letter"), scene 23 ("Accompanying a Husband to the Capital"), and scene 27 ("Surprising Meeting") the intimations of sexual attraction and even the consummation of physical relations between the women are only barely disguised, if at all. Though many readers recognize and acknowledge these homoerotic innuendos, debate over their significance has nonetheless persisted. Some critics in China have slighted the physical dimensions of their bond, even insisting that their affection is based on and entirely confined to the literary—namely, the mutual appreciation for the abundant poetic talents each possesses. This reluctance to acknowledge physical attraction may be more prevalent among scholars of the older generation, yet in a narrow sense their point is not without merit. Admiration for literary talents lies at the heart, so to speak, of the women's mutual attraction; if anything it grows ever more ardent as they exchange lovelorn verses and finally reunite as "poetic companions," thanks to Cao Gechen's inadvertent intervention. But we should note that intellectual entente is a staple and even a sine qua non in the scholar–beauty tradition. Beauties are of course beautiful, and scholars at a minimum dashingly good-looking. But their mutual attraction is generally ignited and sustained by the poetic exchanges that take place without physical contact, let alone illicit or lewd behavior, until the consummation of marriage. Jianyun and Yuhua's relationship is much less constrained by such strictures, but it too is still predicated on some degree of sublimation of their raw physical desire. Indeed, the power of Yuhua's "scent" or "fragrance" (*xiang*) to ignite Jianyun's "love" (*lian*) appears to foreground their physical attraction. The traditional association of fragrance with books (*shuxiang*) as well as with moral probity and literati values in general, however, points to the multivalence of this olfactory motif embedded at the very heart of the story. In fact, Yuhua emphatically deprecates her own scent in favor of the fragrance (also *xiang*) of ink that she detects on Jianyun, further reinforcing the centrality of their literary tie (scene 6). And it is this olfactory complementarity between the two protagonists that has led us to render the play's title in the plural (*The Fragrant Companions*), unlike previous versions (*Fragrant Companion*, for example) where the singular noun suggests a focus on only one protagonist.

THE SIGNIFICANCE OF THE PLAY FOR QUEER STUDIES OF CLASSICAL CHINESE FICTION AND DRAMA

Voluminous descriptions of (and commentary on) male same-sex relations go back as far as the Zhou dynasty (1046–256 BCE) and can be found in histories, poetry, fiction, drama, and prose notes (*biji*). But historical and literary writings were almost completely silent about female same-sex desire over the more than two millennia of imperial Chinese history. The treatment of female same-sex love is so rare in premodern sources that the scholarly probing of this subject is confined to only a few examples. Aside from *The Fragrant Companions* and Pu Songling's 蒲松齡 (1640–1715) classical tale, "Feng Sanniang" 封三娘, the other oft-mentioned examples—such as Shen Fu's 沈復 (1762–after 1803) *Six Records of a Floating Life* and Cao Xueqin's 曹雪芹 (1715?–1763?) *The Dream of the Red Chamber* (or alternatively *The Story of the Stone*)—only deal with female same-sex desire in a peripheral manner or touch on the subject in passing.[13] "Feng Sanniang" tells of a beautiful female fox fairy, the titular character of the story: she falls for an equally fine-looking young lady of gentry class and helps her marry a promising young scholar, but she refuses to join the couple in a heterosexual polygamous marriage. Although similar to *The Fragrant Companions* with its clear allusion to the female protagonists' same-sex desire and love, the abjection of one of the main characters as a nonhuman, and her rejection of a triangular relationship, generate some variables that contrast with Li Yu's play. These two works written within a few decades of one another are widely considered to be far and away the best representatives of female same-sex desire and love portrayed (respectively) in premodern Chinese fiction and drama.

In addition, there are a few literary works by female writers
believed to demonstrate "the woman-preferring woman"[14] desire
while not taking female same-sex love as their primary theme.
One such example is Wang Yun's 王筠 (1784–1854) play titled *A
Dream of Glory* (1769, *Fanhua meng* 繁華夢). This play deals primarily with a woman's frustration at not being able to exercise
her talents at the imperial examination and in the court; in a
dream she imagines herself transformed into a man who enjoys
a glorious official career and marries three beautiful women.
Despite the claim that this play has "quite a few female same-sex
love overtures,"[15] and that the female-turned-male protagonist is
attracted to women exclusively, it still depicts a man-centered
"polygamous utopia"[16] in which the main character's gender
switch does not challenge the patriarchal status quo.

To scholars of queer studies and lesbian love, the dearth of
literary works on the subject of female same-sex love in premodern China is puzzling and challenging. The scarcity of such references in the written record may suggest that the issue "did not
constitute a significant source of anxiety for men,"[17] who authored
the vast majority of historical and literary writings in premodern times. It could also simply be that since female same-sex
relations in premodern China is an understudied or overlooked
field, we must dig more broadly and deeply to locate relevant and
useful materials. Whichever the case, this vacuum tells us how
extraordinarily significant it is that Li Yu, whose many works
provide ample evidence of an interest in gender issues, not only
selected such a subject, but also treated it as the main theme of
the play. The centrality of female same-sex love in this play, and
the rarity of this theme in premodern Chinese literature as a
whole, make *The Fragrant Companions* an indispensable work for
those who are interested in gender relations, same-sex desire, and
queer studies of premodern China, as scholars in recent years
from both China and the West concur.

In both China and the West almost all recent studies of female same-sex love before modern times treat *The Fragrant Companions* as an invaluable source in dealing with the subject and agree that despite *The Fragrant Companions'* denouement in a polygamous marriage, the play is in essence the story of two women in love. In highlighting this aspect, the nunnery scenes that testify to the protagonists' love were the first sections of the play to be translated into English: Dongshin Chang translated scene 6 "Xiangyong" 香詠 ("Praising the Scent in Verse") and published it in *CHINOPERL Papers* in 2011; Mark Stevenson and Cuncun Wu included their English translation of scene 10 "Mengxue" 盟謔 ("A Joking, Bantering Alliance") in their edited volume *Homoeroticism in Imperial China: A Sourcebook* (2012).

Published English-language critical studies that are emphatically unequivocal on this point include Laura Wu's article on the subject of lesbian love in Ming-Qing literature, where she states that the intimacy established between the two female protagonists in the play "is not purely sentimental *qing* 情 but is charged with sensual passions and even carnal cravings."[18] In the article titled "Transgender Performance in Early Modern China," S. E. Kile comments that "the most obvious difference between Li Yu's *Women in Love* [an alternative translation for *The Fragrant Companions*] and other stories of cross-dressing women is that one woman's love, and her desire for another woman, is the starting point of the cross-dressing. Li Yu's depiction of their love points to the possibilities within contemporary literati culture for gender performance by a female person."[19] In her monograph, *The Emerging Lesbian: Female Same-Sex Desire in Modern China*, Tze-Lan D. Sang states: "For the reader, doubt is momentarily cast over the viability of bigamy as a practical solution for gentry women's passion and adoration, as Cao's father's objection to his daughter's becoming a mere concubine indicates. But this objection to bigamy is overcome by the strong love between the female protagonists, their resourcefulness in outwitting Cao's father, and their willingness to be of equal status in marriage."[20] To Sang, "the connection that Li Yu makes here between an all-female ascetic establishment (the nunnery) and female-female desire is provocative."[21]

A significant number of research articles with a focus on the female-female relationship in *The Fragrant Companions* have been published in Chinese periodicals and journals, although no major studies on female same-sex desire and love have been produced in China in recent years. The relevance of *The Fragrant Companions* to contemporary discussions of queer studies was further confirmed by its 2010 adaptation to the Kunqu opera form, which the internationally acclaimed Hong Kong–based LGBTQ director Stanley Kwan (Ch. Guan Jinpeng 關錦鵬) was invited to direct. Kwan interpreted the play's female–female infatuation as having an unambiguously lesbian character as well as a protofeminist undercurrent, while downplaying the heterosexual relationship in the original play. Resonating with Kwan's interpretation, Li Yinhe 李銀河, a famous Chinese sociologist well known in China for her work on homosexuality and as an advocate of marriage equality, has made much of the implications of this seventeenth-century play celebrating love between two women and has led cultural discussions on female same-sex love in premodern China.[22]

As a play focused on gender relations and performance—issues that are very much au courant in contemporary society as well as in academia—*The Fragrant Companions* has the potential for new theatrical adaptations both in and outside of China. In fact, recent productions of this play in Mainland China have demonstrated its possibilities of cross-dressing and chrono-crossing. For instance, the 2010 Kunqu performances featured gender-straight artists (female actors playing female characters) and cross-gender actors (female impersonators playing female characters). The Zhejiang Spoken Drama Troupe created a new experimental version of *The Fragrant Companions* in 2015, incorporating elements of Kunqu opera. This latter adaptation juxtaposes three different frames of space-time, from the Qing dynasty to the Republican period, and then to contemporary China; it emphasized the characters' psychology and the deep feelings of two women in love. As an avant-garde offering, *The Fragrant Companions* contains many interesting modern and multicultural elements. In 2016 a young actor, Zhang Peng from the Northern Kun Opera House, staged a new version of the play featuring other young Kunqu opera performers in which he emphasized the theme of the women as soulmates. He adopted a retro Qing dynasty–style of theatrical costumes and customs and enhanced the authentic Kun opera musical style by catering to the presumed tastes and preferences of a modern audience. These recent revivals and reworkings demonstrate how *The Fragrant Companions* resonates among contemporary Chinese and other audiences and readers, attesting to its increasing prominence as a precedent for modern discussions of the diversity of sexual expression.

CIVIL SERVICE EXAMINATIONS, IMPERIAL DIPLOMACY, AND THE BUSINESS OF MEN

In *The Fragrant Companions*, Li Yu realistically reflects two developments of the civil service examination system at his time: the loss of the educational function of dynastic schools and the manipulation of the levers of promotion and demotion to keep the lower degree holders in line. According to Benjamin Elman, the civil service examinations "engendered a dynastic school system down to the prefectural level during the Song and further down to counties in the Ming and Qing dynasties."[23] But despite initial success of these schools as an empire-wide educational network, the amount of actual teaching that took place in them gradually decreased over time: "they simply became quota-based way stations for students to prepare on their own for civil service examinations and receive stipends for their efforts."[24] Li Yu satirizes the dysfunction of the dynastic schools in *The Fragrant Companions* by having the character Wang Zhongxiang complain that no students visited him during non-exam times, leaving him dependent on his meager teacher's salary. Thus Wang's own fate reflects the failure of the dynastic schools: demoralized by his inability to rise in examination rank, he has little interest in anything except squeezing more money out of his students in the form of gratuities for his virtually nonexistent "guidance."

In deflating the idealized image of scholars as a whole, Li Yu does not spare his male protagonist, either. In Fan/Shi, we find few of the faults of his tormentors and rivals, but the romantic flair of a conventional young male role is somewhat hollowed out: he is neither the lovesick Scholar Zhang from *Xixiang ji* nor the daring Liu Mengmei, who rescues his lover from the netherworld in *Mudan ting*. Content to take advantage of the two women's relationship to get himself another beautiful wife, he savors the pleasures of a polygamist but hardly takes the initiative. When presenting the marriage proposal to Cao Gechen runs into resistance, he is the first to want to back out. The audience can hardly blame him for such fecklessness, for although he is still cast in the male lead and successful in winning both female protagonists, Fan/Shi is no longer the love interest of either woman. Li Yu can be said to have written a variation of the standard love comedy, but one in which the conventional talented male scholar is forced to yield his romantic role to the female genius, the *cainü* 才女.

Although Fan/Shi may have ended up down he is hardly out of the picture, and to the degree that he fulfills the societal and familial duties normatively assigned to his gender, the play redeems his earlier humiliation at the hands of Cao Gechen and Wang Zhongxiang with a triumphant dénouement. The penultimate song in scene 36 alludes to the final expression of his comeback: his simultaneous impregnation of both Jianyun and Yuhua, ensuring their fulfillment of a stereotypical beauty's duty to bear her scholar's male progeny, thereby extending the lineage's prosperity into the future. And just prior to this conclusion (in scene 33, "Serving as the Imperial Envoy"), Fan/Shi leads a ritualistically charged mission that, while not entailing the rescue of a woman as in *Xixiangji* or the nation as in *Mudan ting*, nonetheless establishes his credentials as a scholar-hero fully deserving the special imperial dispensation he is granted to wed two wives. In that scene, where he is sent as an imperial envoy to confer vassal status to the Ryukyu Kingdom, Fan/Shi acquits himself with dignity and pomp, clothed in elegant attire, described in elaborate verbiage, all earning the awe of the king and his rustic subjects, and the gratitude of the imperial court upon his return.

The request for Chinese intervention in Ryukyu has arisen out of a debate portrayed in scene 11, where courtiers discuss how to defend their islands from predatory kingdoms to the north (Japan) and south (Siam). The king sides with his advisors, who argue for peace with China, and sends an embassy to make their request for conferral of vassal status. In scene 18, the Ryukyuan envoys barely evade a typhoon to make landfall at Cangzhou, where they fortuitously encounter Cao Gechen and enjoy a sumptuous banquet amiably hosted by Cao's brother-in-law (the local magistrate). Fan/Shi's acceptance on his father-in-law's behalf of this overseas assignment enables him to fulfill the role of dutiful son-in-law, thereby defusing Cao Gechen's lingering resentment over previous events. In short, the Ryukyu episodes of the play enact the Confucian utopia of bringing tranquility and ritual propriety across the entire range of human relations, from family to nation to "All-Under-Heaven" (*tianxia* 天下). Fan/Shi does not quell barbarians or bandits through force of arms—as Liu Mengmei or Scholar Zhang do in their respective romances—but his achievement is if anything even more impressive for having civilized piratical neighbors and ensured peace along the nation's borders through his display of charismatic cultural refinement. Such a role is mirrored in his negotiations with Jianyun and Yuhua, where he threatens them with punishment should they fall into the polygamist's nightmare: jealousy (over him). Given their feelings for each other, he may be too naive to realize how little he need worry on that score, but he nonetheless demonstrates the Confucian gentleman's requisite ability to calm any turbulence at home, just as he has abroad. Moreover, the parallel between his charismatic influence over Ryukyu and the authority he wields at home is further emphasized by the Ryukyuan girls he has brought back with him being assigned as maids to each of his two wives. After suffering the humiliation of being stripped of examination rank, his decision to revert to his birth name, Shi Jian—literally "Rock Solid"—mirrors his metamorphosis from helpless victim to first-tier metropolitan degree holder, favored courtier, and most of all, fearless and intrepid imperial envoy.

In conclusion, *The Fragrant Conpanions* stands out as a signally important dramatic work in several ways—as Li Yu's most representative work, as a parody of the scholar–beauty *chuanqi* romance, and as a peerless example of the sensitive and detailed treatment of female same-sex desire and love in premodern China. We are very pleased by the signs that *The Fragrant*

Companions, along with many of Li's other works, has attracted interest in contemporary China, where a more relaxed atmosphere in literary and artistic circles has opened up space for previously taboo works or topics. Not only was it included along with his nine other *chuanqi* in *The Complete Collection of Li Yu's Works* published by Zhejiang Classics Press in 1991, but a standalone edition with extensive annotations by Du Shuying was published by the Chinese Social Sciences Press in 2011. Moreover, the modern adaptations of *The Fragrant Companions* that have been staged in different theatrical genres in Mainland China are evidence of how this play has been revitalized after more than 370 years by inspiring and stimulating modern artists in multiple and thought-provoking ways.

It is our hope that this version of the play will spur stage adaptations for English-speaking audiences in the not-too-distant future. To that end, we have endeavored to convey the language, conventions, and context of the play as faithfully as possible, but with the overall goal of making it accessible to non-Chinese readers (and potentially theatergoers) by introducing some degree of creativity into this translation. This has not meant abridgement or outright rewriting, unfortunate habits of earlier generations of translators from Chinese, but it has sometimes led us to replace obscure idioms with phrases that capture the essence of the original language rather than its literal meaning. In order to make the play more readable and potentially less confusing, we have made two minor changes to the stage directions in the original.

First, we have identified characters by their names instead of only by their role types, as the original text does; and second, we have provided prompts ("says," "speaks," or "sings") to distinguish sung from spoken lines and words or phrases, whereas sung and spoken parts are indicated by different font sizes in the original script. In *chuanqi* drama, however, it is common to insert extra words or phrases within sung parts, as what are known as *chenzi* or literally "lining words." The singing lyrics of *chuanqi* (or *quwen* 曲文) need to follow the rules and forms, for instance with fixed tonal patterns and rhyme schemes. Thus the function of *chenzi* mainly allows a certain degree of flexibility by adding some free words while maintaining these rules and forms. *Chenzi* are usually indicated by using a smaller font in a classical Chinese play script. In this translated text, we have set these off from the rest of the song by reducing their font size (to 10 point), as in this example: I ask: Have the magpies already made a crossing bridge?

We hope that our efforts might serve as one basis for a future production that could bring the play to life and endear it to audiences beyond the Chinese-speaking world.

DRAMATIS PERSONAE

(The characters and their respective role types are listed in the order of their first appearance in the play)

Fan Shi 范石 / **Shi Jian** 石堅 **(courtesy name Jiefu** 介夫**), the** *sheng* 生 **role type (the young male lead)**

Fan Shi, who first appears in scene 2, is a young scholar in his early twenties, born as Shi Jian into the Shi family of Jiahe Prefecture in Zhejiang Province. (Before the play begins, Shi Jan was adopted by an uncle on his mother's side of the family who had no son and thus became that uncle's heir, changed his name to Fan Shi, and then moved to Yangzhou.) He reverts to his original name in scene 23 and moves back to his birthplace to take the civil service examination after being designated the "worst-behaved scholar," which had disqualified him from taking examinations in Yangzhou. Fan Shi marries Cui Jianyun in scene 2, later becomes the nominal love object of Cao Yuhua, and he eventually (as Shi Jian) marries her so that the two women can be together.

Cui Jianyun 崔篆雲, **the** *dan* 旦 **role type (the young female lead)**

Cui Jianyun, who first appears in a nonspeaking part in scene 2, is one of the play's two female protagonists. She is a young lady in her late teens or early twenties from a gentry family. Jianyun becomes the bride of Fan Shi / Shi Jian in scene 2, but she later falls in love with Cao Yuhua, the second female protagonist of the play, and comes up with a plan for her husband to marry Yuhua so that the two of them can be together.

Zhang Sanyi 張三益 **(courtesy name Zhongyou** 仲友**), the** *xiaosheng* 小生 **role type (the supporting young male)**

Zhang Zhongyou, a childhood friend of Fan Shi / Shi Jian and the cousin of Cui Jianyun, first appears in scene 2. He acts as the matchmaker for Fan Shi and Jianyun and is later entrusted with the task of attempting to broker a match between Fan Shi / Shi Jian and Yuhua. That plan fails, however, because of Zhou Gongmeng's interference and slander.

Jianyun's maid, Hualing 花鈴**, the** *chou* 丑 **role type (the clown role)**

She appears for the first time accompanying her mistress in scene 2. In the stage directions she is identified as Jianyun's maid, but other characters in the play address or refer to her by her given name.

Zhou Gongmeng 周公夢**, the** *jing* 淨 **role type (the painted-face role)**

Zhou Gongmeng, the villain of the play and the actual "worst-behaved" scholar, relies on bribes and cheating to pass examinations. He first appears in scene 2. Zhou also wants to marry Cao Yuhua and thus slanders Fan Shi / Shi Jian in order to block his marriage to her.

Cao Yourong 曹有容 (courtesy name Gechen 個臣), the *wai* 外 role type (the older man role)

Cao Gechen, as he is primarily called throughout the play, first appears in scene 3. He is an elderly scholar who passed the provincial-level examination in his twenties but failed multiple subsequent metropolitan-level examinations until finally passing it in old age. He is a widower with a young daughter, Cao Yuhua, but has no sons. At the beginning of the play, he is traveling with his daughter on his way to the capital to take the metropolitan examination and stops at Yangzhou to meet his old friend Wang Zhongxiang, who had passed the provincial examination the same year as Cao. In later scenes, as the result of slander leveled at Fan Shi / Shi Jian by Zhou Gongmeng, Cao opposes the idea of a marriage between the young scholar and his daughter, but he agrees to the marriage after Fan / Shi passes the metropolitan examination.

Cao Yuhua 曹雨花, the *xiaodan* 小旦 role type (the supporting young female role)

Cao Yuhua, the fourteen-year-old daughter of Cao Gechen, is the second of the two female protagonists of the play. She appears for the first time in scene 3, where she meets Cui Jianyun in the Rain-Flower Nunnery and falls in love with her. As a way to achieve her dream of living with Jianyun, her true love object, Yuhua agrees to marry Jianyun's husband.

Yuhua's maid, Liuchun 留春, **the** *tiedan* 貼旦 **role type (the assistant young female role)**

She first appears in the scene 3 accompanying Yuhua. In the stage directions she is identified as Yuhua's maid, but other characters in the play address or refer to her by her given name.

Jingguan 静觀, **the** *laodan* 老旦 **role type (the older female role)**

Jingguan, the abbess of the Rain-Flower Nunnery where Jianyun and Yuhua meet, first appears in scene 3.

Wang Zhongxiang 汪仲襄, **the** *fujing* 副净 **role type (the secondary painted-face role):**

Wang Zhongxiang first appears in scene 4. He and Cao Yourong (Gechen) are old friends who passed the provincial examination in the same year, making them "classmates." He is a teacher working for the local dynastic school that is helping *xiucai* or budding scholars prepare for the provincial-level examinations. He is miserably poor and relies on bribes he extracts from his students to make ends meet.

Sakyamuni Buddha, the *sheng* 生 **role type (the young male lead)**

Serving as one of four dei ex machina (see the others below) who conspire to ignite the passion between Jianyun and Yuhua and reward Fan Shi / Shi Jian with two worthy wives, Sakyamuni first appears in scene 5.

Mañjuśrī, Bodhisattva of Ultimate Knowledge, the *wai* 外 **role type (the older man role)**

Serving as the second deus ex machina who joins Sakyamuni in igniting the love between Jianyun and Yuhua, Mañjuśrī first appears in scene 5.

Samantabhadra, Bodhisattva of Universal Benevolence, the _mo_ 末 role type (the supporting male role)

Serving as the third deus ex machina who joins Sakyamuni and Mañjuśrī in bringing Jianyun and Yuhua together, Samantabhadra first appears scene 5.

Love Messenger, the _xiaosheng_ 小生 role type (the supporting young male role)

The Love Messenger first appears in scene 5, serving as the fourth deus ex machina, sent by the Daoist heavenly hierarchy to join Jianyun and Yuhua, which he accomplishes by sending a waft of Yuhua's fragrance toward Jianyun with his fan.

Shang Bazhi 尚巴志, the king of the Ryukyu Islands, the _jing_ 净 role type (the painted-face role)

As host of the Chinese visitors to the Ryukyus, he appears in scene 11; the king's effusive praise and appreciation for Fan Shi / Shi Jian adds further embellishment to the latter's brilliant achievements as imperial envoy.

Wei Kai 魏楷, the _chou_ 丑 role type (the clown role)

Wei, who doesn't appear until scene 32, is another unqualified scholar who passes examinations, including the highest (or metropolitan) level, by relying on family connections and pulling strings. He intends to ask for Jianyun's hand in marriage (after she has assumed a false identity as an unmarried woman), but she parries his proposal by revealing her prior betrothal to Fan Shi / Shi Jian.

THE RELATIONSHIP BETWEEN ROLE
TYPES AND CHARACTERS

The *Fragrant Companions* belongs to the genre of *chuanqi* plays in which characters are played by actors and actresses assigned to various role types. These role types include "the young male lead (*sheng* 生) and the young female lead (*dan* 旦); the supporting young male (*xiaosheng* 小生) and the supporting young female (*xiaodan* 小旦); the older male (*wai* 外) and the supporting male (*mo* 末); the painted-face role (*jing* 淨) and the clown role (*chou* 丑). Other minor roles include the older female (*laodan* 老旦) and the assistant young female (*tiedan* 貼旦), the latter often portraying a maid. Because *chuanqi* plays are rather lengthy, ranging from thirty to fifty scenes or acts, the casts typically include many characters, and more often than not one actor/actress of a certain role type is assigned to play more than one character. In addition, *chuanqi* plays often involve crossdressing or playacting, such as a man cast in a woman's role or vice versa. These generic conventions and stage prompts are usually clearly indicated in the source dramatic text. Here is one example of a stage direction from scene 2, "The Wedding:"

(CUI JIANYUN, *the young female lead, beautifully made up and riding in a sedan, enters with:* ZHANG ZHONGYOU, *the supporting young*

male role, wearing a scholar's cap and a round-collared robe; JIANYUN'S
MAID, *a silent part played by the clown; and* THE MASTER OF CER-
EMONIES, *a silent part played by a minor role actor. The chorus enters
to the sounds of flutes and drums, carrying wedding lanterns.*)

This stage direction clearly assign four different role types to
four different characters, and the "clown"—typically a male role
type—is assigned to play the maidservant of Cui Jianyun, one of
the female protagonists.

But in scene 5 ("Guidance from the Gods"), the young male
lead (playing the male protagonist Fan Shi), the older male role
(playing Cao Yuhua's father, Cao Gechen), and the supporting
male role (playing Cao Gechen's servant) each play a second
character:

(SAKYAMUNI BUDDHA, *the young male lead, appears on stage sitting
on a golden lotus seat in a five-colored-cloud carriage. He is accompanied by* MAÑJUŚRĪ, BODHISATTVA OF ULTIMATE KNOWLEDGE,
the old male role, riding a lion, and SAMANTABHADRA, BOD-
HISATTVA OF UNIVERSAL BENEVOLENCE, *the supporting male,
riding an elephant.*)

Role types originated in the *zaju* dramatic genre of Yuan
times, but they were standardized and further classified in Ming
chuanqi plays to incorporate a fixed-role system with four
categories—*sheng*, *dan*, *jing*, and *chou* (male, female, painted-
face, and clown)—that would assume "a more minutely descriptive definition of age, status, and occupation."[1] Although a young
actor or actress was encouraged to learn to play more than one
major role type in order to be able to meet any contingencies
that might arise, "specialization in a single role and its related

variations was the universal practice of everyone once launched on a professional stage career."[2]

Since a good number of *chuanqi* plays are romantic tales of "the talented scholar and beautiful woman," the leading role tends to be either a young male or young female. But whichever the case, their order of appearance on stage follows a conventional pattern—the young male lead makes his first stage appearance in scene 2 of the play, prior to the entrance of the young female lead. This is true for *The Fragrant Companions* and also for *chuanqi* masterpieces such as *The Peony Pavilion* (*Mudan ting* 牡丹亭), *Peach Blossom Fan (Taohua shan* 桃花扇), and *The Palace of Eternal Youth* (*Changsheng dian* 長生殿).

THE STRATEGIES FOR NAMING THE CHARACTERS

The naming of characters is often a rhetorical strategy in Chinese fiction and drama, one that translators tend to overlook. For instance, a pinyin (phonetic) translation alone of the characters' names in *The Dream of the Red Chamber* (*Honglou meng* 紅樓夢) loses their homophonic or punning qualities and thus their symbolic function: for example, pairing and contrasting two of its prominent family names, "Jia" and "Zhen," underscores the archetypal dichotomy of "unreal/fake/fictional" versus "real/genuine/truthful" running throughout the whole novel. Similarly, a pinyin translation of Jia Baoyu, Lin Daiyu, and Xue Baochai (a male and two female characters, respectively) misses the fact that the word *yu* (jade), contained in both Baoyu's and Daiyu's names, indicates beauty, purity, and aloofness from vulgar worldly concerns, whereas the word *bao* (precious), inserted in both Baoyu's and Baochai's names, points to their similar noble birth and wealth. These meanings are implied in the written Chinese but are obviously lost when names are rendered phonetically in pinyin, depriving English readers of this crucial dimension of the Chinese original.

In *The Fragrant Companions*, Li Yu uses a similar naming strategy for his two female protagonists, Cui Jianyun 崔箋雲 and Cao Yuhua 曹語花. While Jianyun means "letter cloud," Yuhua can be translated as "talking flower." Both names point to the intelligence and literary talents of the two women characters. Moreover, the nunnery—where they first meet, exchange poems, fall in love, and conduct a mock wedding ceremony—is also named Yuhua 雨花 or "Rain-Flower," which is a homophone to Cao Yuhua's name and thus puns. Reading the names in this way, then, one realizes that "talking flower" is actually "rain flower," which is matched with "letter cloud." Those who are familiar with Chinese culture will not fail to notice the word combination of "cloud" and "rain" (*yunyu*) as a euphemistic expression for sex. The implication here is that the relationship between Cui Jianyun and Cao Yuhua is indeed a lesbian love "with the bonds covering emotional devotion to, desire for, or the performance of sex with another woman or other women."[3]

The villain's name—Zhou Gongmeng 周公夢 (the literal translation is "the dream of Duke Zhou" or "the dream of Zhougong)—also carries considerable rhetorical weight. There are two allusions related to the name of Zhou Gongmeng. One involves the character Zhuangzi (whose full name is Zhuang Zhou) and his dream of butterflies ("Zhougong mengdie" 周公夢蝶 or "Zhuang Zhou mengdie" 莊周夢蝶). The story is told in "Qi wu lun" 齊物論 ("On Making All Things Equal"), a chapter from the ancient collection of texts titled *Zhuangzi*, where Zhuangzi describes that he has dreamed of himself transforming into a butterfly. When awakened from the dream, he is unsure of whether it was he who turned into a butterfly or it was the butterfly that metamorphosed into him. Through this parable, Zhuangzi questions which one is truer, the dream state or the waking state? To him, it all depends on how one views "things," and sometimes the dream state can be truer than the waking one. This viewpoint reflects the Daoist conception of "life is but a dream" or "life is but a play or an illusion." Li Yu might have chosen this name to allude to the play's fictionality or illusiveness, as in how dream is used by Cao Xueqin for his eighteenth-century fictional masterpiece, *The Dream of the Red Chamber*.

When the order of the name Zhou Gongmeng is reversed, it is read as "Meng Zhougong" 夢周公 (to dream the Duke of Zhou). This alludes to a famous line of Confucius from Book Seven of *The Analects* (*Lunyu* 論語), which reads: "The Master said, 'How I have gone downhill! It has been such a long time since I dreamt of the Duke of Zhou.'"[4] The Duke of Zhou, who was the younger brother of King Wu, assisted the king in pacifying his subjects and governing as a virtuous, capable, and benevolent minister of the Zhou state. Confucius was an admirer of the Duke of Zhou, and he promoted the "benevolent government" and rituals credited to the Duke of Zhou. This allusion not only reminds the audience what Confucius said about not being able to dream about the Duke of Zhou, but it also further indicates that the villain Zhou Gongmeng typifies the result of forgetting or abandoning the legacy of the Duke of Zhou. This certainly fits well with Zhou Gongmeng's character in *The Fragrant Companions* as an ignorant and immoral scholar.

The names of the other three male characters also have rhetorical functions. For example, the male protagonist's formal name is Fan Shi or Shi Jian, which includes the word "stone" 石 (an inanimate thing that has no feelings). But his courtesy (or style) name—which is a name bestowed upon a person in adulthood and used in addition to that person's given name—is Jiefu 介夫, which means "a mediocre man." Both of his names suggest the male protagonist is actually not the stereotypical "talented scholar" who is love-crazed about the female protagonist in *chuanqi* plays, as the true lovers of the story are its two talented and beautiful women. The formal name of Cao Yuhua's father, Cao Yourong 曹有容 (Cao, the tolerant), is ironic, as he turns out to be rather narrow-minded and intolerant, and he vents his anger toward Fan Shi through Wang Zhongxiang. Wei Kai 魏楷, who appears in scene 32, and whose name puns with words meaning "fake role model,"[5] is indeed a fake scholar who passed examinations by relying on family connections and pulling strings.

Li Yu also used characters' names to indicate their roles or functions in the play. For instance, the male cousin of Cui Jianyun is Zhang Zhongyou. The name *zhong* 仲 means secondary and *you* 友 means friend, thus indicating that Zhang Zhongyou is a friend of the male protagonist and also a secondary character in the play. The name of the man who graduated the same year as Cao Yourong—Wang Zhongxiang—also serves the same function: *zhong* 仲 means secondary, and *xiang* 襄 means "to assist."

NOTE ON EDITIONS
OF *LIANXIANGBAN*

For this translation, we have relied principally on Du Shuying's 杜書瀛 annotated edition, *Lianxiangban*, published in 2011 by the Chinese Academy of Social Sciences Press. Du Shuying's text is based on a Kangxi 康熙 era (1661–1722) version included in *Liweng shizhongqu* 笠翁十種曲 (Ten Plays of Li Yu) held in the library of the Academy of Social Sciences in Beijing; Du also consulted copies of two other Qing editions, as well as the modern edition published as part of Li Yu's collected works by Zhejiang Classics Press (1991). According to Du, the Kangxi text, published by Yishengtang 翼聖堂, was probably based on a version edited and printed by Li Yu himself. Copies of another edition from the Kangxi era, printed by the storied publisher of vernacular fiction and drama, Shidetang 世德堂 (located in Jinhua, Zhejiang), also exist in various libraries in China and elsewhere. Most of the extant Qing copies are included in the collected editions of his ten plays (variously titled *Liweng shizhongqu* or *Liweng chuanqi shizhong* 笠翁傳奇十種); a stand-alone copy of the play in the library of the Academy of Social Sciences may have simply been taken from a collected edition, though it is impossible to say with certainty.

LIST OF SCENES

The Fragrant Companions

SCENE 1

OPENING

To the Tune of *Xijiangyue* (Moon Over the
West River)

(The supporting male actor enters and sings)
When has a true beauty ever envied another?
Only a true genius appreciates her own kind.
Birds not of the same feather naturally suspect each other.
Why question something as self-evident as this?
Although the worst jealousy is found in women,
so too is love among hairpins and skirts the most precious
of all.
Turning jealous resentment into the seed of a tender
love—
that is not the sort of lovesickness one sees every day.

To the Tune of *Han'gongchun* (Spring at
the Han Palace)

The talented belle Jianyun
detects the fragrance of Yuhua,
and love sprouts up from poetry.

With a vow to wed in the next life—
their wishes turn true.
Promising that she will assume the status of a concubine,
Jianyun beseeches the matchmaker, and
upsets Yuhua's father.

In the yearly civil service exam,
Fan Shi is reported for deplorable conduct
and stripped of his titles.
Inexplicably, the two women pine after each other, but
their families move away,
and they lose all contact.

Her tears streaming down,
Jianyun follows her husband to the north;
separated [from Yuhua] by these circumstances,
it is impossible for her to approach her love.
But through the ruse of a contest for a talented maiden,
and concealing her true identity, Jianyun
steals her way into the gentleman's house.

Separated by the exam curtain,
a "teacher" meets a new "student,"
and the two families are reunited with a conjugal knot.

Making a match, the mischievous older sister disguises
    herself as the groom.
Willingly carrying her silk quilt, the besotted younger
    sister marries a female husband.
His resistance having come to naught, the dimwitted
    father-in-law falls into a trap, and
the clueless but very lucky lad ends up marrying both belles.

SCENE 2

~~~~~~~~~~

THE WEDDING

Prelude in the Mode of *Nanlü: Lianfangchun*
(Longing for a Fragrant Spring)

(FAN SHI, *the young male lead, enters with* THE SERVANT,
the supporting male role, and sings)
My looks compare with those ranked high on the Flower
  Registry,[1]
my aspiration rises to the clouds;
the vexations of poverty never crawl up my brows.
From all glamour and fortune,
and all worldly fame,
I shield my nose,
worrying only that the stench of vulgarity is hard to avoid.
Love-crazed by nature,
I only yearn to taste love's tenderness.
But it is not easy—
to find a fine flower,
I search among fragrant thickets the world over.

[*Zhegutian* (*Partridge Sky*)] (FAN SHI *recites*) Wielding the deer-tail,
  burning the incense, and stroking the stringless zither,[2] / my spirit is

untethered and carefree, surpassing even immortals. / Pan An was showered with gifts and attention from women, yet was plagued by slander. / Jiang Yan's talent bloomed early, yet was too splendorous to endure.[3] / [Unlike both,] I am a heroic knight among scholars, a Chan Buddhist among wine drinkers. / Can I ever be cured of my philandering ways? / This year I intend to imitate Zhang Chang. / The tip of my writing brush seeks a new wife's fine brows.[4] (FAN SHI *speaks*) My name is Shi Jian, with the sobriquet Jiefu. I am originally from Jiahe County of Zhejiang Province. My mother's maiden name is Fan, and her family has lived in Yangzhou for generations. Her brother had no male heirs, and thus he adopted me, his nephew, as his son. I, therefore, changed my surname to Fan, and kept Shi as my given name, retaining my sobriquet. My learning knows no bounds; my talents are beyond measure. When on occasion I sing "White Snow,"[5] people rush to praise my tone as unrivaled. Many times have I competed in the civil service exam, and never once came in second place among the licentiates. My late birth father served as a prefectural magistrate, my adoptive father as an officer of government recruitment. Although they left me little in the way of property, my inheritance is still enough to support my profligate habits for a lifetime. Unfortunately, my adoptive father passed away before settling my marriage. I have sought a mate for many years, yet true beauties are few and far between. Now I have asked for the hand of Officer Cui's daughter, whose name is Jianyun. The beauty of Yangzhou women is unparalleled in the world, and I have heard that hers reigns supreme in that city; moreover, her looks are only matched by her talent. Luckily for me, her cousin Zhang Zhongyou and I are childhood friends, and he went all out to make this ideal match for me. I am happy now that the Six Rituals of marriage[6] have all been completed, an auspicious wedding date has been chosen, and the poem urging the bride to don her makeup has been sent.[7] I now call my servant: today the young master Zhang is going to accompany the bride here, so get the banquet ready! (THE SERVANT *says*): Yes, everything is ready!

Passing Tune in the Mode of *Xianlü: Basheng Ganzhou* (The Eight-Rhymed Song of Ganzhou)

(FAN SHI *sings*)
The day of the wedding banquet has been set long before;
wary of the bride tarrying in dressing up,
I repeatedly urge her with poems:
the Milky Way is clear and shallow today.[8]
I ask: Have the magpies already made a crossing bridge?[9]

(*The drum and music are played offstage*)
(THE SERVANT *speaks*) I hear the sounds of drum and music coming from afar; it must be that the bridal sedan is arriving!

(FAN SHI *sings*)
Hearing the sound of music from afar,
my soul is carried away;
though I have yet to smell her warm fragrance,
I am intoxicated already.

(THE SERVANT *speaks*) Young master, would you please change into your wedding garb and wait for the bride? (FAN SHI *changes into wedding garb and sings*)

[I must] change clothes;
this blue robe is hardly a fitting match for her iridescent
rainbow dress.

(CUI JIANYUN, *the young female lead, beautifully made up and riding in a sedan, enters with:* ZHANG ZHONGYOU, *the supporting young male role, wearing a scholar's cap and a round-collared robe;* JIANYUN'S MAID, *a silent part played by the clown; and* THE MASTER OF CEREMONIES, *a silent part played by a minor role actor. The chorus enters to the sounds of flutes and drums, carrying wedding lanterns.*)

> (*To the same tune as before*)
> (*They sing in unison*)
> Graceful and fair, this lady weds today.
> In this season of peach flowering,
> the Sui dike is decked out in full red.[10]
> Her trousseau shows signs of scholarly elegance,
> such as ivory bookmarks and brocaded scrolls.
>
> (*Arriving at the gate*)
> The vermilion gate brilliantly decorated,
> and glowing with felicitous spirits,
> brightly lit candles and gauze lanterns
> in dazzling shades of purple.
> A marvelous pair,
> the groom and bride are a match made in heaven
> —his talents and her beauty.

(*Carrying out the usual wedding rituals,* JIANYUN *and* JIANYUN'S MAID *exit*)

(FAN SHI *speaks*) It is all thanks to your efforts that I have been able to find this perfect match. Allow me to kowtow to express gratitude. (ZHANG) This match was made in Heaven, so what credit can I claim? I should bow down to you in congratulations, but I am afraid of troubling you to do the same in return. Let us just exchange a casual salute, and leave it at that. (*They bow to each other*) (FAN SHI) Bring the wine! (FAN SHI *takes* ZHANG *to his seat*)

To the Tune of *Jiechengge* (A Song for Sobering Up)

[*JIESANCHENG* (THRICELY SOBERED UP)]

(ZHANG *sings*)
Bustling with life,
the whole house is filled with signs of auspiciousness;
brimming with joy,
both host and guest are elegant.
I see that though he has yet to drink from the nuptial wine
  cup,
his heart is already drunk with love.

(FAN SHI *speaks*) Cousin-in-law, please have a few more drinks!

(ZHANG *speaks*) I have already had too much.

(FAN SHI *sings*) You must drink to your heart's content;
please do not refuse.

(ZHANG *speaks*) On this, your wedding day, we should delay you no longer. I'll escort you, my brother-in-law, to your wedding chamber,
  but then I must be going.

(FAN SHI *turns his back to* ZHANG *and sings*)
Although the brief night of conjugal bliss cannot be
  lengthened,

isn't it also true that the friendship of host and guest is deep, and our drinking cannot be rushed?

(ZHANG *stands up and says*) Light the red lantern and take the groom to the wedding chamber. (*The crowd lights up the lanterns, following the groom with music and drums*)

[*PAIGE* (THE ROW SONG)]

(*They sing in unison*)

The shade of flowers turns,
the shadow of bamboos tilts,
treasuring the lovemaking that awaits.
He keeps asking what time it is.
Led by the lantern,
and followed by the wine,
he will take up another cup in the wedding chamber with
     his beloved,
her arm wrapped in his.

(*All exit stage*)

(ZHOU GONGMENG, *the painted-face role, enters and recites*) The Matrimonial Star does not shine on an empty chamber; / for twenty-four years have I remained a bachelor. / Under the thin quilt my fingers busy in vain; / I envy Fan for becoming a bridegroom at such a young age. I am Zhou Gongmeng. Today being the wedding of Fan Jiefu, it's only right that I crash his party and have a few drinks with him. (FAN SHI *and* ZHANG *enter as* FAN SHI *attempts to see off* ZHANG) (ZHANG) Cousin-in-law, please do not bother to see me out; I will bid you farewell here. (ZHOU) Hold it right there, someone is here to congratulate you. (FAN SHI *and* ZHANG *meet* ZHOU) (FAN SHI) Since Brother Zhou is paying us a visit, cousin-in-law, please have a few more. Bring some wine! (*They all sit down*)

> (*To the same tune as before*)
> (ZHOU *sings*) Brother Fan,
> you married into this prominent family
> without having to pay a penny,
> receiving both a beautiful young wife
> and a hundred taels of silver along with her.

(ZHOU *speaks*) I heard that not only is your new wife pretty, but she also has a huge dowry. How pleased you must be!

> (FAN SHI *smiles*)
> (Zhou sings) Look at him:
> smiling foolishly
> without uttering a word.
> You are drunk with joy.

(ZHOU *speaks*) Brother Fan, your body is here with us, but your mind has already left for the wedding chamber.

> (ZHOU *sings*)
> Your heart and body are now separated from us
> by layers of curtains.

(ZHOU *speaks*) Brother Zhang, it's time to take the groom to his wedding chamber, where we can take a peek at his new bride, and give him a few good punches while we're at it. We can leave once we've taken care of these rituals.[11] (FAN SHI) I've already taken the bride to the wedding chamber. Although teasing the bride and the bridegroom on their wedding night is an old custom, please do me a favor and let us skip it tonight. (ZHOU) How can we let you go without it? (ZHOU *sings*)

> Eager to pound the groom,
> my unruly fists are itchy;
> impatient to see the bride,
> my lusty eyes are hungry.

(ZHANG *sings*) Please moderate your teasing,
and do not lose your manners;
let us all empty our cups and call it a night.

(FAN SHI *sings*) Brother Zhou,
your wedding day, too, is not far off,
and when it comes
we swear we won't skimp on reciprocating your kind
    feelings,
as "peaches for plums."[12]

(ZHANG *gets up and says*) Let's go home.

Weisheng (Closing Tune)

(*They sing in unison*)
The water clock drips on,
the guests all are tipsy, and
the east-rising moon sinks down in the west.

(ZHANG *sings*) Brother Zhou, let's not you and I be boorish
    and
delay his beautiful dream.

(FAN SHI *sees them out and makes an obeisance, and then hurries off stage*)

(ZHOU *laughs and says*) Look at him, speeding off without looking back. This newlywed is so impatient, how should a bachelor such as me feel? (ZHOU *sings*)

> Tonight this stag's desire can hardly be reined in,
> under the moonlight
> I'm headed straight for a house of pleasure.

(ZHANG *sings*)
How can a convenient liaison deserve praise?
Only romantics like these become genuine couples.

SCENE 3

~~~~~~~~~~~~~~~~~~~~

RENTING A HOUSE

Prelude in the Mode of *Shuangdiao:*
Jinlongcong (Golden Chimes)

(CAO GECHEN, *the older male role, enters wearing cap, robe,*
and gray long beard, accompanied by his SERVANT) (CAO
sings)

I am forever rushing about on official business,
my carriage wheels stirring up the dust of the capital's
streets.
My hair so white,
as if it were snow frozen to my scholar's cap.
Yet even now I cannot bring myself to let go,
I heave up my aged wings trying to raise myself into the
lofty clouds,[1]
fighting against the ravages of time
with cosmic dignity.

(CAO *recites*) For whom do I busy myself with books and zither? /
Though I have yet to rise up the ranks into the lofty blue sky, my
hair has already turned frosty white. / Do not laugh at this hero's
sagging thighs; / jumping into the saddle, I can still ride like a young
lad. I am the scholar Cao Yourong, with the sobriquet Gechen, from

Shanyin County in Zhejiang Province. Though I passed the entry level examination at the tender age of twenty, even now, in my dotage, I have failed to progress beyond that. Because examination rank is important in officialdom, I have been unwilling to seek fame and fortune through other means, and despite having failed nine times in the civil service examinations, this has not dulled my fighting spirit in the least. My only regret is that my poor wife died young, leaving us without an heir. But she did bear me half a child—a daughter—and though a mere girl, she fully deserves the title of Master of the Confucian Five Classics.[2] Her childhood nickname is Jade, and her formal name is Yuhua [Talking-Flower]. She can compose verses extemporaneously, and recite a passage from memory after a single glance. (*Sigh*) Because she is altogether too clever, I go out of my way to protect her. Now past her fourteenth birthday she has yet to be betrothed. Next year is again the examination year, and I will have to go up north. I have no close relative to entrust my daughter to, except a brother-in-law Yang Yugong, who is an inspector in Shandong Province. How fortuitous that Shandong is on the way to the capital. I will take my daughter with me and leave her at her uncle's official residence, so that I can go on to the capital to take the examination. Today I have nothing special to do on the boat. Why don't I call her out from the cabin and give her some parental guidance? Calling to the servant, I say: while you're urging the boatmen to make haste on the journey, go to the rear compartment and tell the young mistress to come over here. (THE SERVANT *goes to call the young mistress*)

To the Tune of *Haitangchun* (Crabapple Spring)

> (YUHUA *enters wearing light makeup, accompanied by her*
> MAID, *and sings*)
> Life aboard a boat is nothing like the boredom of being
> cloistered in the female quarters;

placed alongside the water,
my zither and books take on a new luster.

(YUHUA'S MAID *sings*)
With my worries gone, the sails have grown light;
with my heart anchored, this floating house feels steady
and secure.

(YUHUA *and* CAO *gesture to each other*) (CAO *speaks*) Child, you spend your days writing verses and composing rhapsodies, never resting your pen. Although writing poetry is not what is expected of women, since this is something you naturally enjoy, I shouldn't put a stop to it. It is just that a woman should not show off her literary talents. Women write poetry only to entertain themselves, and not to share with others. They even need to keep their manuscripts well hidden, so that not a single word falls into the hands of others and leads to scandal. I am going to take you to your uncle's official residence to stay for a while. Although he is our relative, life at his place will be quite different from our home. You need to be careful. (CAO *sings*)

Passing Tune in the Mode of *Zhenggong: Shuazixu* (Brush Sequence)

Famed mountains have their own ways of
self-preservation.
[You must] close up your poetry satchel very tightly,
not leaving even a trace of your poems exposed.
Put away your incomplete manuscripts,
you can never be too careful in keeping them to yourself,
or simply burn your poems!
A woman without talent is a woman of virtue;

her name and her writing are both forbidden from leaving
the women's quarters.
You may be as gifted as Su Hui in weaving palindrome
verses, but
you still won't be the equal of the Weaver Girl,
who remained steadfastly bound to her loom.

(YUHUA *speaks*) Yes, father, thank you for your guidance. (YUHUA *sings*)

To the Tune of *Yan'guosheng huantou* (The Sound of Wild Geese Passing, Variation)

Hurrying out
to listen to father's esteemed advice,
I might as well follow his words,
for he is a learned gentleman.
There's no harm in sticking to women's ways like a
humble, clumsy turtle dove:
What's the good in being swift penned and sharp tongued,
amusing others with her cleverness, like an oriole?
(*An aside*)
But I wonder to myself:
If I meet a talented woman who can compose linked
verses with me,
how could I possibly conceal my superior artisanry then?

(CAO *speaks*) Where are we now? (THE SERVANT) We have arrived in
Yangzhou. (CAO) If you hadn't mentioned Yangzhou, I would have
forgotten this matter. A fellow student from my youth named Wang
Zhongxiang is now teaching at Jiangdu. He sent me a letter a few
days ago inviting me to go to the capital with him. Since the examination dates are still far off, why don't we stop here for a few days to

wait for him, so that he and I can travel together? I now call to the servant boy: tell the boatmen to moor the boat, then go ashore to search for some lodgings, and come back to report what you've found. (THE SERVANT *responds and exits the stage*) (CAO) Daughter, look at all the merchants gathered here, and hear the clamor of the horses and carriages. What an impressive wharf! (CAO *sings*)

To the Tune of *Qingbeixu huantou* (Bottoms-Up Order, Variation)

At the ford crossing,
[Yangzhou is] the meeting of waterways and land routes,
on the shores of both river and sea;
this southern land is peerless.
Local custom favors luxury and splendor;
beauty is in vogue,
imperial envoys stop here
searching for unrecognized talent;
Officials' canopies overlap like clouds.
Look at this late autumn scene:
Sui dikes covered in early frost,
willows all bare of their foliage;
yet people go about smiling
on painted yachts with flutes and drums,
as if still on spring outings.

(THE SERVANT *enters and says*) Thankfully, the lodgings are nearby, / we do not need to travel long and far. Master, there is a nunnery on the bank of the river, and it is both secluded and elegant. I have already made inquiries of the nuns there; they told me that we could rent some rooms from them. (CAO GECHEN) In that case, let's pack up our things and go there. (*The abbess* JINGGUAN, *the old female role*, *enters*) Holding a glazed lantern and a string of rosary beads, / on a prayer mat I meditate at night amid the sounds of the bamboo swaying in the wind; having long since shaved off my raven locks, I embrace idle melancholy. / I'm just an old servant of the Buddha, whose gentle ways tame wild elephants and lions. I am Jingguan, the abbess of Rain-Flower Nunnery. I heard that a young lady has come to seek lodging here; I need to go out to welcome her. (CAO *goes ashore with* YUHUA, *saying*) I want to find the schoolmaster, but first must stay at a temple. (JINGGUAN *receives them with a gesture of greeting*) (CAO) Your nunnery has flowers and bamboos in groves, with beautiful winding balustrades. The layout of this place is very unusual for a temple, and in fact, it rather resembles the study rooms of a household. (JINGGUAN) This was indeed formerly the cottage of a gentleman, Mr. Fan, that he donated to us. The rooms off the left corridor are the study chambers of his adopted son, Fan Jiefu. (YUHUA) This is indeed an elegant nunnery! (YUHUA *sings*)

To the Tune of *Yufurong* (Jade Hibiscus)

Flowers' fragrance wafts from Buddha's dais;
grasses cluster beside the rush prayer mat.
What need is there for dusting?
All is clean and immaculate,
without a speck of dust.[3]

(YUHUA *speaks*) Papa, my name is Talking-Flower [Yuhua] and this nunnery is called Rain-Flower [Yuhua]! What an unusual coincidence![4] (YUHUA *sings*)

Gautama[5] has already left a mark on my heart;
don't tell me that this was not caused by karmic seeds
planted in a previous life.

I should reflect on this and realize the emptiness of our
true natures.

Lost in thought, flower in hand, the Buddha suddenly
manifests in a girl's body.

(CAO *turns his back to* YUHUA *and says*) If the left wing is being used as
someone's study, how can my daughter stay in the right wing? (CAO
sings)

To the Tune of *Xiaotaohong* (Small Peaches Redden)

Suddenly plunged into uncertainty,
I regret that we have landed in a place of sordid
worldliness.

Given that a young man like Song Yu[6] dwells close by,
it will be hard to hide the sounds of scissors and rulers
[for sewing].

What if [my daughter] pokes out over the walls like an
apricot branch[7]
and stirs up a scandal that brings me humiliation?

(CAO *speaks*) Daughter, this place is busy and disorderly; we shouldn't
linger here for long. (YUHUA) Dad, since we'll only be staying for a
little while, let's just put up with it. (YUHUA *sings*)

To the Tune of *Zhu'nu'er* (Little Red Slave)

Although we "raise our thatched hut" in the human
world,

seeking out a temporary refuge does not require us to
leave the crowd behind.[8]

Simply by shutting the door,

I can create my own private mountain retreat,
and let go of the turbulent affairs outside.
Not to mention that our stay here is only temporary,
like duckweed floating on the water.
Now that we are here,
let's settle in for the time being.

(CAO *speaks*) We will only stay here for tonight. I will make other arrangements after seeing your Uncle Wang tomorrow.

Weisheng (Closing Tune)

(CAO *sings*)
Though fatigued by travel, streaked with frost, and bathed
    in dewdrops,
thankfully, we've enjoyed smooth sailing without many
    setbacks.

(YUHUA *sings*)
Who could have expected that I, who never before ventured
    beyond women's compartments,
have become a traveler in an unfamiliar land?

(YUHUA *sings*)
Staying in an inn we should not be too picky,
like a kitty wren that can make its nest anywhere, easily.

(CAO *sings*)
Though we have no close friends within a thousand
    miles,[9]
we have a host right here beside the Bridge of Four and
    Twenty.[10]

SCENE 4

A VISIT TO A STUDY

Prelude in the Mode of *Nanlü: Buchan'gong* (Pacing
Through the Frog's Lunar Palace)

(WANG ZHONGXIANG, *a secondary painted-face role, enters
wearing a cap and a robe with belt, accompanied by*
WANG'S SERVANT, *a clown role*) (WANG *sings*)
I am too old to wait for the Official Star to shine on me,
and grant me the black felt cap of officialdom.[1]
Those who are proud and aloof may laugh at us as two
    humble tribute students,
but their blue felt caps are even colder than mine.

(WANG *speaks*)This humble officer is an educational intendant at
Jiangdu by the name of Wang Zhongxiang. Though I passed the
provincial level examination quite early, success at the top level has
eluded me all these years. I am temporarily teaching in the dynastic school and waiting for another chance to advance. In my year
there were ninety-seven of us who passed. Some of them went on to
pass the highest level, some were given official posts, and some have
already passed away. Cao Gechen and I are the only two left behind,
forming a pair of seeds still waiting to sprout. Next year the exam
will be held again. Whether I pass it or not, this will be my last time.

When we old timers travel to the exam wearing our "snow cape" over our shoulders and carrying a "meat sack" on our backs,[2] those newly passed haughty young scholars make cutting remarks that really irk me! This is why I vowed to never again travel with those youngsters. A couple of days ago, I wrote to Mr. Cao inviting him to go north with me, but how is it that he has not yet arrived? (CAO GECHEN *enters, accompanied by* CAO's SERVANT, *and says*) Leaning on my cane I've come here in search of my old, dear friend; / carrying my books and zither with me, I also wanted to find a temporary abode. (CAO's SERVANT) Is there anyone at the door? Your same-year provincial graduate, Mr. Cao, has come to pay you a visit. (WANG's SERVANT *reports the visit*) (WANG *takes the guests in and bows to* CAO) It has been three years since we bid farewell at our lodgings in the capital. You look even more hale and hearty than ever.

To the Tune of *Taishiwei zui*
(The Grand Tutor Is Dead Drunk)

[THE INTRODUCTORY TUNE OF TAISHI]

(CAO *sings*)
Bamboos are quiet and calm, only when there is no
    wind,
withered leaves rustle and fall from their branches after
    the frost.

(WANG *speaks*) Sitting at home, even an old scholar can't bear the loneliness.

      (CAO *sings*) Although the plum puts forth blossoms in the
        quiet desolation of winter,
      it willingly bears the cold, thanks to its alliance with the
        pine and cypress.

(WANG *speaks*) Were you able to marry again and give birth to a son?

[*ZUITAIPING* (A DRUNKEN PEACE)]

> (CAO *sings*)
> Left alone, with neither iris orchids nor jade trees on
>   which to lean,[3]
> The courtyard of my house remains deserted and forlorn.

(WANG *speaks*) My concubine is a local Yangzhou woman. Why don't
I find you a concubine?

> (CAO *sings*)
> Even should the lucky star of love come close
> and grant me the embrace of a passionate vine,
> how could her tender stems stand my company,
> a withered old tree trunk with no strength to support her?

(CAO *speaks*) Old brother, I see you've become a bit gaunt.

> (*To the same tune as before*)
> (WANG *sings*)
> Cranes have a hard time plumping out
> because they are often sickly,
> with autumn winds constantly shearing off their
>   feathers.

(CAO *speaks*) You should take some medicine to boost your strength.

> (WANG *sings*)
> I can only come up with enough to buy a plate of alfalfa.
> How could I afford a restorative of ginseng and fungus?

(CAO *speaks*) Your sons must all be bringing glory to the family name?

> (WANG *sings*) Useless, they are like ordinary birds whose
> singing shames the household,
> undeserving of praise fit for the phoenix.

(WANG *speaks*) I am burdened with quite a few sons and daughters. If
I do not pass this next examination, I will be forced to seek some
other employment.

> (WANG *sings*) I have no choice but to hurry;
> in my old age of withering elm and mulberry,[4]
> like a tired bird, sick of flying,
> I hurry to find a perch in the forest.

(CAO *speaks*) Elder brother, when do you plan to go north? (WANG) I
earn a small salary of a few taels of silver, but in order to make a bit
of interest, I have loaned it all out to the licentiates in this county. I
have to wait until winter to be paid, and only then will I know how
much I'll have left for my travel. I will have to trouble you to wait for
me for a while. (CAO) Because I have no close relative to entrust with
the care of my daughter, I have brought her with me. She now
lodges at a nunnery, and it is very inconvenient. I need to find her
another place to stay before I can relax and wait for you, to begin our
journey together. (CAO *sings*)

To the Tune of *Sanxueshi* (Three Scholars)

> This father and his daughter have been uprooted and cast
> adrift,
> like wrens in search of a branch;
> we rely on [others'] help.

Although we are but temporary lodgers,

I insist that no uninvited guests come knocking at our
     door.

Elder brother,

I urge you to hurry up and pack your bags.

With my family here,

it's difficult for me to wait much longer.

(WANG *speaks*) A director of discipline in my school has been promoted
   and moved to another posting, leaving his former residence unoc-
   cupied. Brother, you can move into his place. (WANG *sings*)

(*To the same tune as before*)

How fortunate that

there is an empty abode close by,

and hence no need for you to search high and low for a
     place of residence.

Please do not say that this meager fare of mine shows a
     lack of hospitality—

tomorrow I shall fete you with the meat for sacrificing to
     the Lord of Scholars.[5]

Although I cannot be responsible for both "firewood" and
     "water,"

I would like to help you with one of them.

With firewood as pricey as laurel wood, and rice as
     expensive as pearls—

this promise may be difficult to keep.

But tea and porridge—

these I promise to provide.

(CAO *speaks*) In that case, I will move over immediately. (WANG) Elder
   brother, if you are coming, I have one favor to ask you. The district

level examination for *xiucai* was just held a few days ago.[6] Having been busy with mundane tasks, I have not been able to read the examination papers yet. Could I trouble you to lend me your sharp eyes and read them? (CAO) Certainly, I am at your service!

> (CAO *sings*)
> Childhood bonds cannot be forgotten in old age,
> how much more so when we cross paths in other places.
> The years have slipped by as quickly as a steed galloping
>   past a crack in the wall,[7]
> We shared our surprise at how long each other's graying
>   locks have grown!

SCENE 5

<hr>

GUIDANCE FROM THE GODS

In the Mode of *Beixianlü: Dianjiangchun*
(Brushing Crimson Lips)

(SAKYAMUNI BUDDHA, *the young male lead, appears on stage sitting on a golden lotus seat in a five-colored-cloud carriage. He is accompanied by* MAÑJUŚRĪ, BODHISATTVA OF ULTIMATE KNOWLEDGE, *the older male role, riding a lion, and* SAMANTABHADRA, BODHISATTVA OF UNIVERSAL BENEVOLENCE, *the supporting male, riding an elephant.*)

(SAKYAMUNI *takes the lead to sing, with the others joining him in unison*)
A speck of radiance
like a bolt of lightning that, exploding,
fills the sky to the horizon.
The power of Buddha's dharma is beyond measure,
and its luminescence can never be exhausted.

(SAKYAMUNI *recites*) The Western Paradise is close at hand, not way up in heaven. / But why do mortals still insist on sinking into the abyss?

(MAÑJUŚRĪ) We extend a helping hand to humans, but alas, it is in vain. (SAMANTABHADRA) Who can find the way to the Buddha's ferry? (SAKYAMUNI) I am Sakyamuni Buddha. (MAÑJUŚRĪ) I am Mañjuśrī Bodhisattva. (SAMANTABHADRA) I am Samantabhadra Bodhisattva. (MAÑJUŚRĪ) When County Magistrate Fan was here, he converted his private villa into a temple. He spent hundreds and thousands in gold and jewels to fashion images of the three of us. How delightful that this place is unsoiled by mortal dust, and free of the din of the city. This is indeed a pure, serene place for conducting religious rites!

To the Tune of *Hunjianglong* (Dragon Churns Up the River)

(SAKYAMUNI *sings*)
A secluded sacred space,
concealed deep in the shade,
palms surround the garden and ivies creep over the fence.
This was originally the cottage
for playing chess of a scholar from East Mountain,[1]
but was turned into a place for performing Buddhist rites
from India in the West.
Luckily, Mr. Fan parted with his worldly possessions while
still alive,
bringing him great karmic merit—
how much better than hoarding them—
only to have everything fall into ruin after his passing.
I have seen enough of the forlorn remnants of the Wu
Palace
and the desolation of Chu Garden.
How could that compare to paving the temple sanctuary
with gold, and

inscribing on high the name of Anāthapindika,
all good deeds live on in eternity!²

(SAMANTABHADRA *speaks*) In my opinion, Magistrate Fan is morally
impeccable, with a heart filled with compassion and kindness. As an
official, his good deeds benefit the ordinary people; at home, his acts
of kindness benefit the many members of his extended clan. Such a
kind-hearted and trustworthy official, how is it that he has no heir?
How can Heaven be so ignorant!

To the Tune of *Youhulu* (A Gourd of Oil)

(SAKYAMUNI *sings*)
Though we may lament Heaven's error in allowing Bodao to
die with no heir,³
[I can see that] it still provides for all creatures.
Mortals don't realize that
there is a completely impartial court of justice in the
heavenly realm.

(SAKYAMUNI *speaks*) Although Magistrate Fan has no son, his adopted
heir Fan Shi is able to continue the family tradition of distinction in
scholarship, and will go far in life, his achievements boundless. Is
this not a reward for Mr. Fan's good deeds? (SAMANTABHADRA)
What you just said, Bhagawan, is absolutely right. The Way of
Heaven is impartial, and makes no distinctions between the "self"
and the "other." As long as the young Fan can continue the family's
traditions of hard work and skillfulness, how is an adopted son different from one's own flesh and blood? It is just as when our Buddhist dharma is transmitted from master to disciple, there is no
interruption to the "blood line." Indeed, what you have said is true.

(SAKYAMUNI *sings*)

The sage kings Yao and Yu[4] were impartial;

whether they passed the throne to a worthy person or to a
son,

they treated them all equally.

If they had insisted that only their own flesh and blood
counted as a son,

why would Yao have passed over his unworthy son
Danzhu,

or Yi Yin imprisoned Prince Taijia in Tong Palace?[5]

In that case, there would have been no need

to confer posthumous titles on these adopted heirs'
ancestors!

(YUHUA *enters with her* MAID *and recites*) Like duckweed floating on water, I temporarily sojourn by the Dharma King's side. / Who says this coincidence is not fate? / I shall take advantage of this and pray for love, / and not waste my youth on vulgar companions. Liuchun [*calling out to her* MAID], yesterday when we moved into the nunnery, we did not pay our respects to the Buddha. Today I have fasted and bathed, so let's go burn some incense in the main hall. (*Walking and arriving at the prayer room*) (YUHUA'S MAID) Look, Young Mistress, how dignified are those statues of the Buddhist three saints! (YUHUA *picks up incense and worships*) To the Three Treasures on high, your disciple Cao Yuhua takes refuge. With a kowtow and this offering of incense, I pray to you: my first wish is that my late mother soon reaches the heavenly realm; my second wish is that my father succeeds in his career; my third wish . . . (*looks at her* MAID *and stops*) (YUHUA'S MAID) Young Mistress, why did you break off suddenly, without finishing your prayers? Is it because you have a secret that you don't want me to overhear? Let me move back and allow you to finish your prayer. (*Someone acts as* CAO GECHEN *shouting sternly from behind stage*) Liuchun! There are many people coming and going in the Buddha hall. Come back with your young mistress right away! (YUHUA'S MAID *answers*) (YUHUA) Let's go back. I came here to pay respect to these Buddhist statues, and now I must go back to avoid other visitors. (*They exit stage together*) (MAÑJUŚRĪ) What a decorous young lady she is! She behaves quite differently from the frivolous young women of Yangzhou.

To the Tune of *Tianxiale* (The World Is Happy)

(SAKYAMUNI *sings*)
Look at her, gentle and serene are her manners, stately in
her demeanor.
In her fine garments and elegantly light makeup,
she surpasses Yangzhou style with her simple,
unpretentious ways.
Practicing a small act of devotion, she prays at the Buddhist
shrine,
confessing her secret desires to the merciful Buddha.
She cannot bring herself to utter a word about those deep
feelings troubling her perspicacious mind!

(MAÑJUŚRĪ *speaks*) I know what it is that this girl wanted to say but couldn't come out with words just now. It was none other than "pitying oneself in the mirror," fearing that she would be given to an undeserving mate. She wants to marry a husband who is both talented and handsome, so that she will not have lived her life in vain. (SAMANTABHADRA) This is the wish of all women; we should come to her aid.

To the Tune of *Nezhaling* (Nezha's Song)

(SAKYAMUNI *sings*)

Look at her, with such elegant dress and graceful
   disposition.

How could she be paired with a country bumpkin or a city
   hooligan?

With her brains and talent,

how could she marry a drunkard or a glutton?

She prays that we bless her with merciful guidance and a
   safe voyage,

and deliver her to a lover like Liu Chen or Ruan Zhao on
   the Heavenly Terrace.[6]

I fear only that a bad marriage has already been predetermined,

and rash matchmaking will not do.

We must not needlessly break off your bud of pure
   fragrance!

(SAKYAMUNI *speaks*)To my discerning eyes, this young lady and the
   local woman Cui Jianyun are both meant to join the family of Fan's
   adopted son. Ms. Cui has already become his bride, but this girl has
   yet to fulfill her proper destiny as his wife, and at present is lodged
   in this temple. Today Ms. Cui has come here to make her offerings,
   so we shouldn't allow them to miss this chance to meet. We need to
   conjure up an opportunity for Yuhua to join this couple in blissful
   matrimony. (SAKYAMUNI *sings*)

To the Tune of *Quetazhi* (Magpies Step on a Branch)

One is a bashful young maiden, afraid of strangers;

another is a stately bride who barely raises her head to look
   into others' eyes.

I fear only that events will follow their own course,
indifferent to the fragrance of blossoms;
in order to set her up for a romantic, devoted husband like
  Zhang Chang,[7]
we need a resourceful main wife who knows when to knit
  her brows to achieve her aim.

(SAMANTABHADRA *speaks*) Though our work is not yet done, lo and behold, our love messenger has come early. (THE LOVE MESSENGER, *the supporting young man role, enters holding a feather fan and recites*) I hold a red thread to secretly tie the knot; / I dissolve mortal hatreds to bring about good matches. / If marriages are not brought to fruition by the gods' helping hands, / then all the eligible young men and women's angry complaints will rise up to scorch the heavens. (THE LOVE MESSENGER *meets the* BUDDHA) (SAKYAMUNI) Is your mission here to make a match for the Cui and Cao girls? (THE LOVE MESSENGER) Indeed. (SAKYAMUNI) We can see that the gods and Buddha have the same agenda. It's just that while Ms. Cui has just arrived, Ms. Cao is about to leave. They are like the shrike and swallow who will soon take off in opposite directions:[8] How might you introduce them to each other? (THE LOVE MESSENGER) Ms. Cao's body emits a very special fragrance. When Ms. Cui comes in, I will flap my fan and make her detect it, so that she will take notice. If they fall in love at first sight, then the seed of their future love will have been successfully planted.

To the Tune of *Jishengcao* (Clinging Vine)

(SAKYAMUNI *sings*)
Though it's said that no jealousy exists between soul mates,
appreciation for talent might stem from another source.

I guarantee that a whiff of the orchid's scent brews a
    remarkable romance;
once one has answered the other in song,
their literary thoughts will mingle together unimpeded,
one sip of fine ale will intoxicate their souls with love.
This is indeed for tearing up the boundaries of love
and completely dismantling all of those old-fashioned fences,
so let us not disrupt this matrimonial match, the likes of
    which this world has never seen!

(THE LOVE MESSENGER *speaks*) Although these two women are destined to be together, there is one malevolent star in their fates. Therefore, after they meet, they will have to experience some suffering before Yuhua can become the young Fan's wife. (SAKYAMUNI) As long as this good affair ends well, a bit of obstruction will be harmless. (SAKYAMUNI *sings*)

To the Tune of *Yaopian* (Short Piece)

Although happiness is ensured by the Red Star of Love,[9]
interference from the White Tiger Star[10] is inescapable.
Even someone like me, the Buddha himself, can be
    challenged by a demon;
you, a Daoist immortal, also must hide from a once-in-a-
    millennium calamity.
Even powerful spirits cannot defy the will of Heaven!
I only hope that once the stars align for the Shepherd Boy
    and Weaver Girl
to finally meet one day;[11]
it will be worth having drowned a thousand times in the
    river on dark stormy nights.[12]

(MAÑJUŚRĪ) *speaks* In that case, when the two of them arrive, we should work together to help them. (*All stand up and move*)

To the Tune of *Zhuansha* (Deadly Deception)

(SAKYAMUNI *leads and the chorus joins to sing*)
Shadows of clouds stir devotional pennants,
forces of wind carry elephants and lions:
the golden Buddhist terrace is shaking up the lotus petals.
Do not say that my clay body is rigid and inflexible;
you should know that when I activate my spirit,
I can come and go without limit.
Do not say that I open my eyes in vain simply because I
never raise my head to look out;
you need to know that I often raise my fist to strike the head
of an unsuspecting meditator!
Sentient beings, if you want to test my extraordinary power
and exhaust my various transformations,
then try counting all of the sand grains in the Ganges
River, one by one!

SCENE 6

(JINGGUAN, *the older woman role, enters, and recites*) Sweeping the path, opening the window, and dusting the chair, / all for inviting a lady guest into the meditation chamber. / I came here to escape the suffering caused by worldly attachments; / yet I ended up having to run around playing host in this mountain temple. I am Jingguan, the nun. Miss Cao who moved in here recently gets along with me swimmingly. But now she's moving over to the school, and I have no idea why. As of today, Fan Jiefu and his bride have been married for a whole month, and I heard that she is coming here to burn incense; I shall sweep the path and wait for her.

Prelude in the Mode of *Shuangdiao: Xinshuiling* (A Song of New Water)

(JIANYUN *enters with her* MAID *and sings*)
How lucky I am to marry a lad so romantic that he has
    painted my brows;
moved by Buddha's beneficence in looking out for me,
I come here to kowtow to him in gratitude.

(JIANYUN'S MAID *sings*)

Accompanying her on this mission

ensures that next year my wishes will be fulfilled, too.

(*Sounds of bells and drums are heard from within.* JIANYUN *picks up incense and worships before she recites*) (*Huanxisha* [*Silk-Washing Stream*]): Like a ripe peach picked from the tree, I have found my home;[1] / indeed the spring breeze has not forsaken the bloom. / God of Spring,[2] please stay forever; / do not let him fly away! (JIANYUN'S MAID *prays*) The peaches and plums have all been picked clean and paired off; / why, Heaven, have you left an old plum tree alone untouched? / What a pity that over several seasons this plum tree has borne only private fruits / which were all buried, unconsumed, beneath moss.[3] (JIANYUN *and* JINGGUAN *see each other*) (JINGGUAN) Mrs. Fan, your husband is extremely talented, and now with someone as beautiful as you for his mate, this is truly a match made in Heaven. (JIANYUN) I am undeserving of your praise! (YUHUA *and her* MAID *enter, and they look on in secret*) (THE LOVE MESSENGER *stands behind* YUHUA *and fans her*) (YUHUA *to her* MAID) Liuchun, look! What a pretty lady. (YUHUA *sings*)

Passing Tune in the Mode of *Nanlü: Lanhuamei*
(Too Lazy to Paint My Brows)

Opening a window, I steal a glance at her sensuous visage;

when all is said and done the flowers of Yangzhou are the
most marvelous.

How could I not envy her lovely moth brows?

From whence has this heavenly breeze blown her here?

Could this temple visitor be surnamed Cui?[4]

(JIANYUN *inhales and says*) Master, may I ask, why is there a laywoman's fragrant scent in this nunnery? (JINGGUAN) What makes you say so? (JIANYUN) Just now, a waft of orchid musk passed over here; how can there be such a scent within these clerical precincts? (JIANYUN *sings*)

> (*To the same tune as before*)
> How surprising that the breeze travels through flowers;
> how is it that the scent carries with it a whiff of musk?

(JIANYUN'S MAID *points at the window and says*) Mistress, someone is looking at us from the window.

> (JIANYUN *sings*)
> Behind that green gauze screen at the window, someone is
>   peeping at us;
> clearly, I see a raven black cloud-shaped chignon.
> Could it be a girl who has just joined the nunnery, but has
>   yet to receive the tonsure?

(YUHUA *and her* MAID *exit*, THE LOVE MESSENGER *follows them*) (JINGGUAN *speaks*) She is Miss Cao from Zhejiang, staying here for the time being. She will be moving out very shortly. (JIANYUN) In that case, why don't you invite her over to meet us? (JINGGUAN *invites* CAO) (YUHUA *enters again with her* MAID *and recites*) Embarrassed by my plain dress, / I am not fit to meet someone so elegant and beautiful. (JINGGUAN) Miss, this is the wife of Mr. Fan, our benefactor. (JIANYUN *greets them*) I have troubled you to make your way over to see me, without first making a special trip to pay my respects to you. (YUHUA *recites*) Your arrival is so sudden; / forgive me for not venturing out to welcome you here. (JIANYUN) May I ask for your provenance and name?

To the Tune of *Xiangluodai* (Fragrant Silk Belt)

(YUHUA *sings*)
This kitty wren has an old nest, and
it is Cao E's place of origin.[5]
I am called Yuhua, a name unworthy of mentioning.
(JIANYUN *sings*)
Is your mother still with us?
(YUHUA *sings*)
An orphan, I have been long bereft of my mother's care,
and since a young age have gone to my father for care and
comfort.

(JIANYUN *speaks*) How old are you?

(YUHUA *sings*)
This year I will reach my fifteenth spring.

(JIANYUN *speaks*) Have you been betrothed to a good family?

(YUHUA *sings*)
Barely out of swaddling clothes, I am still subject to bouts
of childish silliness;
my freshly coiled cloud-buns are not yet ready for a lady's
hairpin.
May I have the young mistress's honorable first and last names,
and whether your mother is still with us?

(*To the same tune as before*)

(JIANYUN *sings*)
I am called Jianyun and Cui is my surname.

My father has already passed away;
my mother is alive and in good health.

(YUHUA *speaks*) I see that you are wearing a new dress; you must be
recently married?

> (JIANYUN *sings*)
> I feel ashamed that,
> having found a matrimonial home before reaching the
> proper age to write "Falling Plums,"[6]
> I have alas left my mother
> without proper support.
> I am still shy when meeting people in my wifely
> ornaments and hairpin.

(YUHUA *speaks*) A beauty like you, Mistress, must have married a talented scholar!

> (JIANYUN *sings*)
> I am ashamed that an ugly duckling like me has come upon a
> stroke of unusual fortune:
> the lad I married is not a complete idiot!

(JIANYUN *turns her back to* YUHUA *and says*) Look at her, she does not
wear makeup and has a natural charm; such an unmatched beauty!
To say nothing of men; as a woman, even I find myself attracted to
her! (CAO'S FAMILY SERVANT *enters*) The palanquin is here, Miss, it
is time to leave. (YUHUA) We have just barely met; how can we part
so soon? Please stay and chat for a moment longer. (JINGGUAN *talks
to* JIANYUN) I have long admired Mistress's poetic talent. Today we
have chanced to meet; may I ask you for a poem? (JIANYUN) Living
alone with nothing to do, I write to pass the time. How can I be

praised as a poet? (JINGGUAN) Please do not be overly modest, you must teach us a thing or two. (JIANYUN) What shall we take as our topic? (JINGGUAN) Just now Mistress smelled a woman's scent; let's use that as a topic. (JIANYUN) In that case, Miss, why don't you compose the first one? (YUHUA) I am barely literate, what do I know about writing poetry? (JIANYUN) Well in that case, Reverend Mother, you please go first. (JINGGUAN) I learned how to use a writing brush when I was little. But after taking holy vows, it has been ten years since I have written flowery verses. (JIANYUN) If that's the case, I'll embarrass myself then. Miss Cao and Reverend Mother, please do not laugh at me. (*She finishes writing and* JINGGUAN *reads*) "Warmth of the perfume seems to come from a scented hamper; / or is it from the cool breeze by the watery palace? / This thread-like wisp, so near, where indeed does it comes from? / Oh, from a loose gap in the beauty's crimson sashes." Marvelous! Marvelous! (YUHUA *receives the poem and reads it*) (YUHUA *then sings*)

To the Tune of *Xueshi jiecheng* (Scholars Sobering Up) (*Sanxueshi* [Three Scholars])

> Flourishing her brush for us, she wrote without even
> pausing to think,
> supremely self-confident, like a man leaning against his
> horse.[7]

(JINGGUAN *speaks*) Miss, if you are barely literate, how come you keep reading this poem over and over again? (YUHUA'S MAID) Although my young mistress does not know how to write poetry, she can read a little. (YUHUA) After carefully reading Mrs. Fan's poem, I can see that it is refreshing and elegant. This poem is on par with Li Bai's poems for Lady Yang.[8] You should be known as the female Li Bai. (JIANYUN) You are too kind. (JINGGUAN) It turns out that not only is Miss Cao literate, but she also understands poetry! (YUHUA'S MAID) My young mistress can also write a poem or two; but she is afraid they are no good.

(YUHUA *speaks*) Mrs. Fan's poem writes only of someone else's appearance, and not of her own. In my opinion, my perfumed rouge and powder are inferior to the fragrance of Mrs. Fan's ink.

> (YUHUA *sings*)
> It is difficult to smell your own fragrance; only when it
> penetrates the nostrils of others can it be known.

(JINGGUAN *speaks*) Since she does not want to write about herself, why don't you write a poem about her?

To the Tune of *Jiesancheng* (Thrice-Drunk but Sobering Up)

> (YUHUA *sings*)
> I am only afraid that with demons clinging to my wrist,[9] it
> is hard to write a decent poem;
> without flowers sprouting from my brush,[10]
> I cannot unfurl my imagination.
> It is hard to find my match in talent;
> truly, when songs are lofty, few can harmonize with them;[11]
> those who understand my deepest intentions are few and
> far between.

(JIANYUN *speaks*) Miss Cao not only understands poetry but is deeply versed in the art of poetry! Displaying my minor magic in front of a great wizard like her, how mortifying! Now you must teach me a thing or two. (YUHUA) Please do not heed my maid; I really cannot versify. (JINGGUAN *grinds ink;* JIANYUN *sticks a brush into* YUHUA's *hand*) What shall I do? I'll just have to try and scrawl out something. (YUHUA *finishes writing,* JIANYUN *reads*) "Musk and orchid perfumes are not the right guess, / as their fragrance pales beside a talent like Xie. / From behind the curtain I thought the scent came from plum blossoms, / but little did I know, it comes from poems about snow."[12] Marvelous! Marvelous! Free-spirited like Bao Zhao and refreshing like Yu Xin. You combine both talents![13] (JIANYUN *sings*)

> (*To the same tune as before*)
> Like a good merchant who hides his wealth, and conceals
>   his treasure,
> through disguise you appear like a beggar.
> Little did I know you are like Shi Chong who built a
>   walking screen of fine damask,
> leaving my Wang Kai's coral in the dust.[14]
> A poem like yours combines the purity of snow with the
>   winter bones of plum blossoms, full of rare rhymes and
>   subtle sweetness.
> In this dim light, I catch a waft of sweetness drifting about;
> but when I try to recognize it, how hard to separate
>   shadows from its essence!
> What a truly wonderful encounter this is!
> I daresay that she adores me,
> yet I am even more taken with her!

(CAO'S FAMILY SERVANT *speaks*) The old master has been waiting long, and he asks the young mistress to please hurry onto the palanquin. (YUHUA *gets angry*) Why must you prattle on! (JINGGUAN) I am going to copy both of your poems down on paper, so that I can preserve them as treasured relics for this temple.[15] (*She finishes copying the poems*)

To the Tune of *Jiejiegao* (Ascending, Notch by Notch)

(JINGGUAN *sings*)
Your talents are like the neighboring states of Lu and
    Wei,[16] equally matched.
If, together you "race saddle to saddle" in the world of
    poetry,
matching your wits, marching in lockstep, and
    coordinating your strategies,
you'll strike before even men have a chance to best you.
It has long been true that women warriors are at an
    advantage. (CAO'S FAMILY SERVANT *urges* YUHUA *to
    leave*)

(*They sing in unison*)
We only grieve that we have no strategy to hold onto
    spring,
and with each cry, the cuckoo urges us to hurry
    homeward.[17]

(JIANYUN *speaks*) Reverend Mother, may I borrow the poems you wrote down, so that I can make a copy? I will return them to you tomorrow. (*The old nun gives the poems to her*) (JIANYUN *holds the hand of* YUHUA) Miss, although I am slow of wit, my eyes are sharp. Not only am I dissatisfied with the recent poems written by my lady friends, I also find the collections of poetry published by these male poets at odds with my temperament. Today my ears have enjoyed the clear, pure sound of your poem; it accords perfectly with my own tastes. How might we regularly bring our inkstones together, to fuse this poetic bond of ours?

(*To the same tune as before*)
(JIANYUN *and* YUHUA *sing together*)
Who says we are the lucky ones?
Alas, soul mates are far and few between!
This morning, a chess player has finally met her match.
How can we make it so that we will live in the same place,
be married to the same man, and
lie on the same mat reciting poetry?
Exchanging adornments and garments as our vows,
we shall besot ourselves with fine nuptial ale.

(*They sing together as before*)

(JIANYUN *speaks*) After parting today, is it possible for us to meet again?
(YUHUA) Soon I shall follow my father to the capital. Although I still have several days to spend here, my father is very strict and I am afraid that it would be difficult to enjoy your presence again. (*Both cover their faces to wipe tears*) (JIANYUN *and* YUHUA *sing*).

To the Tune of *Dashengle* (The Joy of Great Victory)

Heaven never repeats a happy moment,
alas, how cruel is the setting Sun.
The discerning listener bursts into tears at the side of
 Boya's lute.[18]
Oh, my soul mate, woe is our parting,
and how vexing is this meeting, so late in the day!
We chanced to meet only to be pulled apart in haste.
When will we reunite again, like a pair of swords?

Alas, how scarce are soul mates in this world!

From now on, the smashed zither will make no sound,

I'll burn my brush and toss out my inkstone!

(JINGGUAN *speaks*) Since you two are so attached to each other, you should devise a way to meet again. Why act like a pair of Chu prisoners grieving over your common misery?[19] (JIANYUN *and* YUHUA), Reverend Mother, can you come up with a plan? (JINGGUAN) On the first day of the tenth month, I will hold a Buddhist prayer service. Miss Cao could say that you have paid for a Buddhist service for your mother. I bet that your father would not stop you from coming. You two could then meet here and have a good heart-to-heart talk. What could stop us from carrying this out? (JIANYUN *and* YUHUA *are both pleased*) Reverend Mother is greatly merciful! In that case, let's bid farewell for now. (JIANYUN *and* YUHUA *sing*)

(*To the same tune as before*)

Now that we have set a date,

let us interrupt this tête-à-tête,

and part for the time being.

We rely entirely on your merciful heart to shrink the gap

    between our two pining bosoms,

you save us from misery, and grant us your kind mercy.

If you, the host, have not seen enough of our talents,

we will happily write poetry again on another topic.

Our only worry is that this harmonious union will not last,

And foresee that our next parting will be in tears, just like

    today!

(YUHUA, YUHUA'S MAID, *and* CAO'S FAMILY SERVANT *exit;* YUHUA'S MAID *then reenters*) My young mistress wants me to tell Mrs. Fan to come early on the first day of the tenth month. Please do not break your promise. (JIANYUN) I will certainly not. (YUHUA'S MAID *exits again;* JIANYUN *and her* MAID *also exit stage, but* JIANYUN'S MAID *reenters*) Reverend Mother, Mrs. Fan is afraid that Mr. Cao will not allow Miss Cao to come; you must help to make it happen. (JINGGUAN) All right, I will. (YUHUA'S MAID *leaves;* JINGGUAN *smiles and says*) The two of them have come together like steel to magnets, fused by an inseparable bond. This goes to show that it is not only physical beauty that can bewitch people; literary talent can produce the same effect. This was why I forced myself to give up writing poetry at the start of my monastic life; I was afraid of precisely such attachments as this. Today's events have given me one more enlightening blow![20] (JINGGUAN *sings*)

Yuwen (Coda)

Beauty and talent are tied by the same thread;
from now on, I shan't even bring up the recitation of
Buddhist gathas.
Thanks to you, a pair of Bodhisattvas, for giving this old
nun a good lesson.

SCENE 7

~~~~~~~~~~~~

CONJUGAL HARMONY

To the Tune of *Huatangchun* (Spring in the
Painted Hall)

(FAN SHI *sings*)
Autumn wind brings chilliness everywhere
except the wedding-chamber, where spring happily lingers.
On this day last spring I was grieving the fall,
leaning on my study's railing all alone.
I wanted to ask the blue birds up in the clouds to
deliver my message to the Heavenly immortals:[1]
the realm of passionate love is where I wish to make my
mark;
I envy not the immortals' paradise on Yingzhou.[2]

(FAN SHI *speaks*) Ever since I married Miss Cui, we have composed
linked verses bosom to bosom, and discussed essays with our necks
entwined. Although husband and wife, we are more like friends in
the same literary club. (*Doesn't that make others envious!*)

(FAN SHI *sings*)
My thirst for romantic love fully quenched,

I covet nothing beyond what I have.

Even worldly success and fame, or longevity,

can come and go as they please;

I am beyond them.

Early this morning, she went to a nunnery to burn
incense.

Now it is dusk, but she has yet to return.

I can't stand this loneliness.

Passing Tune in the Mode of Xianlü: *Zuifugui* (Carried Home Drunk)

Could it be that she is praying on and on to the gods of
good tidings?

Could it be that she is playing a prank on me to make me
feel anxious?

Could it be that she has gone off with an old acquaintance?

Could it be that, like the Goddess of the Moon, she regrets
having stolen the elixir of immortality?[3]

Could it be that she is angry at me for not accompanying
her to the nunnery,

and is thus unwilling to return home at a decent hour?

(FAN SHI *speaks*) Why don't I take a nap by my desk? (FAN SHI *sleeps*)
(JIANYUN *enters with her* MAID *and recites*) Having just met my soul
mate, my happiness suddenly turns into lament. / Composing only
one piece of poetry together, we parted to opposite corners of the
world. / The "High-Mountain" does not make Zhong Ziqi stay; /
"Flowing Water" can only sob for Yu Boya in vain.[4] The poetic
exchange that I had today with Miss Cao in the Rain-Flower Nunnery will live on as a literary legend, a marvelous convergence in a
woman's fragrant boudoir! I was going to tell my husband about it,

and share these beautiful verses with him. But now that I have made a date to see her again, if my husband gets wind of it, he will definitely want to go with me and steal a glimpse of Miss Cao. If he did something frivolous and unceremonious, and her father heard about it, that would be a death knell for any future union between us! Therefore, today I will only show him Yuhua's poem and not tell him what her name is, allowing him to appreciate her poem only in anonymity. I will tell him the truth after my next meeting with Yuhua. If one wants to enjoy the "flower" for a bit longer, she must be wary of butterflies. / I shall wait till the honey grows sweet, then thank the bee.[5] (JIANYUN *and her* MAID *enter the house*) (JIANYUN'S MAID *says*) Oh, the young master is sleeping here! (JIANYUN) He is sound asleep; do not awaken him from his dream. (JIANYUN *sings*)

> (*To the same tune as before*)
> Do not interrupt him from dreaming of writing "pond-grass" poetry.[6]
> Fearing a draft, I close the window for him, so that
> chilly wind cannot shatter his "reverie of capturing his prey."[7]
> Poor thing, look how he has pillowed his head on a rock-hard book,
> and rested his body against some pointy, insubstantial flowers.

(JIANYUN *speaks*) Taking advantage of his sleeping soundly, why don't I place Yuhua's poem on his desk, and ask him:

> (JIANYUN *sings*)
> Is the "Pen-Flower" more charming than a "Talking-Flower?"[8]
> Let me use a "Paper-Cloud" to envelop him like a "Romantic Cloud."[9]

(FAN SHI *awakes*) (JIANYUN *speaks*) Dear, I bet you got impatient waiting for me. (FAN SHI) Don't even mention it! (FAN SHI *sings*)

To the Tune of *Zaoluopao* (Black Silk Robe)

> You left me sitting sad and alone in this empty study;
> I looked for you in the dream of Gaotang,[10] and
> there I found you, my lady!
> (FAN SHI *sees the poems*) Where did these come from?
> In my sleepiness I do not remember resting my head on
> these poems.
> How have I awakened to find these sheets of a manuscript
> by my side?

(FAN SHI *looks at the poems and mutters to himself*) How strange! These characters do not look like those written by a poet and the poem does not seem to be written by a calligrapher. (JIANYUN) Why do you think so? (FAN SHI *sings*)

> These poems are full of an ethereal flavor,
> like fairies, about to drift up toward Heaven;
> the calligraphy reveals a taste of Chan,
> like an ascetic, gaunt and wizened.
> But why do these delicately tinged sheets also carry an
> amorous aroma?

(FAN SHI *speaks*) My lady, where do these poems come from? (JIANYUN) I do not know what you are talking about! (*She picks up the poems and takes a look*) Oh, these are verses of "A Beauty's Fragrance." I have been using them as a bookmark. Who took them out and left them here? (FAN SHI *asks*) Who wrote the poems? (JIANYUN *answers*) They were written by some proper young ladies. The poems have been widely circulated, and I happened to receive a copy, too. (JIANYUN *sings*)

(*To the same tune as before*)
They are new verses by two damsels of the inner quarters;
because everyone is copying and passing them around,
I too have included them among the verses I recite when I
    have time for leisure.

(FAN SHI *speaks*) Do you know the names of the poets? (JIANYUN)
The names of the poets are unknown; I only know that they were
written about a belle with the last name Cao. (JIANYUN *sings*)

These marvelous pieces were penned for a maiden of the
    Cao family,
Although her name is unidentified, I hear that she is a
    first-class beauty.

(JIANYUN *speaks*) My lord, which one of the two poems do you think is
better? (FAN SHI) While the first one is uplifting and pure, the second one is elegant and unrestrained; they are both on par with one
another, and it is difficult to rank one over the other.

(JIANYUN *sings*)
You could say that they are like the royal sisters Ehuang and
    Nüying,[11]
who were a pair of pearls, both adorned in brocaded
    robes; or
the Lu brothers, Ji and Yun,
or the prodigiously talented Lu Ji and Pan Yue.[12]
Neither of them could be praised as the better of
    the pair!

(JIANYUN *speaks*) If an examiner read these two poems, he would have
to pick a winner among the two. He most certainly could not award
first place to both of them! (FAN SHI) If you want me to pick a

winner, you will need to invite both of them here. I will have to sit them down by my side, give them a face-to-face exam, and only then will I be able to pick a winner. Right now, I can only rule this a tie. (JIANYUN) If that's the case, can you compose a couple of response poems in matching rhymes? (FAN SHI *laughs at her*) You have not yet passed the civil service examination and earned the rank of "Elevated Scholar," yet you want to test the examiner? All right, I will write one. (*He takes a brush in hand and whispers to him-self*) Let me first visualize this beautiful girl, then sniff the air with my nose for her scent; only in this way can I produce a captivating piece. (*He makes a gesture of smelling*) (JIANYUN *looks at him and laughs*)

(*To the same tune as before*)
(FAN SHI *sings*)
My nose has caught a rare scent, barely detectable,
like a wisp of particles from ancient ink,
suffusing the hairs of my writing brush.

(FAN SHI *speaks*) Bah! How can I ignore the beautiful woman stand-ing before me and try to sniff out that imaginary one? All I have to do is to catch a whiff of the scent on my wife's body, then it won't be just two poems—I can come up with ten of them! (FAN SHI *sings*)

A beautiful mountain rises in front of me but does not invite me in,
where in the vast empty sky can a poet go to find inspiration?

(FAN SHI *leans towards his wife and sniffs, saying*) Here is the scent of her rouge-covered lips, here is the scent of her raven hair, here is the scent of her delicate fingers, and here is the scent of her tiny lotus feet. (FAN SHI *sings*)

The scent of her powder is sweet and pure,
the scent of her locks, luxuriantly lovely,
the scent of her fingers, pointily succulent,
and the scent of her feet, faintly alluring.

(FAN SHI *speaks*) There is another type of scent that I need to taste. As is said in one of the poems, "Oh, from the belle's crimson sashes it comes forth." I beg you to loosen your sashes, so that I can smell this particular scent. (*He tries to untie* JIANYUN'S *sashes*) (JIANYUN) You are not writing the poems, but pestering me with your mischievous intentions. (*She pushes him away*) (FAN SHI) Your adorable little fit of pique has spurred me to finish my poems: here they are! (*He writes down the poems.* JIANYUN *reads them out loud*) "The aroma is not borrowed from scenting hampers, / even Lily of the Valley pales in comparison. / Do not blame the poet for surrendering to its sweet intoxication, / he finds his "tender home" among the myriad flowers.[13] / Stop guessing, you common butterflies; / she speaks a special language of the flowers. / If like Xun Yu, she sits with me for three days,[14] / it's no wonder that I am captive to her scent." These are good answering verses; it's just that the last two lines are a bit frivolous. (JIANYUN *sings*)

> (*To the same tune as before*)
> Your poems are as good as the songs of "White Snow" and
>   "Spring Time,"[15]
> but they are overly amorous, and a bit overwrought.
> If I allow you to come into the presence of that talented
>   belle,
> I worry that you would devise some wicked scheme to
>   seduce her.

(FAN SHI *speaks*) I was just joking! How come you've turned jealous? My lady, let's talk this over. Now that I've written some answering poems, how can we find a way to send them to these beauties, so that my hard work will not have been in vain? (JIANYUN) Delivering the poems would not be too difficult; I am just afraid that after reading your verses (JIANYUN *sings*)

their lovely faces would burst with ire.
The paper on which your poems are written would meet
    disaster,
torn to pieces, and quickly thrown into a fire
or roiled up into a flood,
which will sweep away this silly infatuation that has
    consumed you this whole day!

(JIANYUN *sings*)
Talking of poetry with my beloved late into the night,
I enjoy his gentle teasing but pretend to be upset.

(FAN SHI *sings*)
Standing right beside the flower I failed to detect its
    fragrance;
only after writing about it, did I realize how rare is its
    sweetness.

SCENE 8

BRIBING FOR A RECOMMENDATION

(WANG ZHONGXIANG, *the assistant painted-face role, enters and recites*) One matter can be viewed from two perspectives; / the farmer likes rain while the traveler wants sun. / Toward the same prefectural examinations held every third year, / examiners feel gleeful while examinees live in dread. (WANG *speaks*) I am Wang Zhongxiang, and I am about to travel to the capital to take the metropolitan examinations. However, I also received official instructions authorizing me to undertake the grading of the exams of the lower-level local examinees. A teacher looks forward to this much as a farmer who eagerly awaits his harvest. What sense does it make to abandon this good harvest that lies in front of my eyes and go to till a fallow field of unknown potential? It would make sense to delay a bit, until I have collected the tuition fees from the new students, and then make haste for the capital. Now as there is not much time left to spare, I shall summon the clerk and errand boy to carry out my orders. Where are the clerk and the errand boy? (THE CLERK, *the older man role, and* THE ERRAND BOY, *the clown role, enter and recite*) The officials of this state school are long time vegetarians; / for two meals, we should buy one and a half kilos of bean curd. / Though the study is cold and empty for days on end, / the servants guarding the examination gates become gods [during test times].

The clerk and errand boy await your order. (WANG *says*) Since I first arrived here to take up this position, most of the *xiucai*[1] have not been over to see me. Now that it is time for the examinations, I reckon they have no way to hide or escape. You two go ask each and every one of them to come and see me. (WANG *sings*)

Passing Tune in the Mode of *Shuangdiao:*
Yubaodu (Jade Belt)[2]

You ought to wait on the street;
when you see the students, just drag them in to me.
Their tuition and interest for three years, together
amount to a gift of at least three taels of silver.

(WANG *speaks*) One more thing, ask the students not to write anything on their calling card. (WANG *sings*)

I only want no-name no-word empty cards,
so that I can resell the gifts and collect the proceeds.

(THE CLERK *and* THE ERRAND BOY) We want to ask your honor: Have you decided how many of the students are to be given "good-behavior" status and how many "bad-behavior" status? (WANG) "Good-behavior" is quite different from "bad-behavior." If one is recognized for his "good behavior," even if he places in the sixth [bottom] tier of exam takers, he can still retake it in the future. The sons of affluent families will come and seek my aid in attaining this status of their own accord. We shall limit the number of "bad-behavior" students to just one. I have heard of a certain Zhou Gongmeng, who has engaged in all sorts of depravities such as drunkenness, gambling, whoring, and inciting frivolous lawsuits. In addition, he has yet to pay me a single visit since I came. Let's give him "bad-behavior" status and be done with it. (THE CLERK *and* THE ERRAND BOY) Your honor only knows the old rules of giving "good-behavior" status but has not heard of the new trick of meting out "bad-behavior." You ought to put the squeeze on the sons of rich families, one by one. First give "bad-behavior" status to a few of them, and once they have "reformed," then give the "bad-behavior" to those who haven't. In this way, your honor will be able to collect all of the money you'll need for your travel expenses. (WANG *laughs loudly*) I did not know that the two of you were such loyal ministers, capable of "managing money to enrich the nation." I will follow your memorial to the letter. (WANG *sings*)

> (*To the same tune as before*)
> What a clever plot you have devised,
> such useful words
> should be inscribed on a screen for the emperor's perusal.
> To carry out this scheme, I rely entirely on your bag of
>   unctuous tricks learned at the office,
> and on your wiliness gained from long service guarding
>   the gate.

(WANG *speaks*) This opportunity only comes once every three years; you two should work hard to help me pull this off. If I make a big fortune, you'll be sure to make a decent one too.

> (WANG *sings*)
> A rich state's wealth trickles down to the family;
> A ten percent share would hardly be unprecedented.
>   (WANG *exits with* THE CLERK *and* THE ERRAND BOY)

(ZHOU GONGMENG *enters and recites*) Scholar is just another name for *xiucai* (budding talent), / but out of the ten Confucian classics, nine are terra incognita. / And when exam time comes around, / the whole city is filled with the sound of recitation. I am Zhou Gong-meng. Ever since I bought myself a *xiucai* title, thanks to my parents—who croaked one after the other—as a "filial" son I was able to apply for certificates of mourning twice and ducked those annoying annual exams for two years. From morning till night I sleep among flowers and get drunk by the willows, shooting craps and throwing dice. Such carefree joy! Now here comes a damned proctor, demanding that I sit for the annual exam. I can do what it takes to hold onto my rank, but there's no way I can sit for the annual exam. I originally thought I could induce someone in authority to vouch for my status in the third rank, but who knew that this proctor could be so tough, rejecting all such petitions! Now that I'm out of other options, I'm forced to try to review the Confucian Four Books. (ZHOU *spreads the books and starts to read*) I've barely made it through a single line, / but my eyes are already blurry; / though my name means the "dream of Duke Zhou," / it looks like I'm going to dream of the Zhou Duke.[3] (ZHOU *sings*)

To the Tune of *Yue shang haitang* (Moon Rising Over Crabapple)

Though I force my eyes to stay open,
Just one line and I'm already drowsy. (ZHOU *falls asleep;
suddenly he wakes with a start*)
Suddenly I remember the examination,
even while dreaming I start with fright! All right!
I boldly write this: I your student humbly express my
deferential respect.
Though I hardly expect a knife to be applied to my neck,
why is it that I tremble like a cow before the butcher,
imploring these books to save my life?

(THE CLERK *and* THE ERRAND BOY *enter and recite*) A *xiucai* is fearless as long as he is not subjected to a test, / and silver does not flow if its owner is not intimidated. (*They enter* ZHOU's *house and make a salute*) So Mr. Zhou, I see that you are cramming at the last minute. (ZHOU) I am not lying to you, there are a few annotations that I haven't mastered, and that is why I am reviewing them. (THE CLERK *and* THE ERRAND BOY) We want to report something to you. Please do not be angry, but you are to be given "bad-behavior" status this time. (ZHOU *is terrified*) How terrible! Has the document been sent out? (THE CLERK *and* THE ERRAND BOY) The document has already been printed, and we are waiting to deliver it in person to the provincial official when he arrives. (ZHOU) In that case, the matter is still mendable. I would not mind spending a few taels of silver to ask the proctor to give the bad status to someone else instead. Do you happen to have any clues about the desires of the proctor? (THE CLERK *and* THE ERRAND BOY) Do you still want to purchase a slot as a supernumerary student eligible for a stipend? (ZHOU) Who would do such an impractical thing? I just want to have smooth sailing and make sure I hold onto my current title. (THE CLERK *and* THE ERRAND BOY) In that case, you do not need to know anything special about the proctor. What you need to do is to ask the proctor to give you "good-behavior" status. With "good-behavior" status, even if you are ranked as number four, five, or six on the exam, you could still do better than the first-, second-, and third-ranked examinees. (ZHOU) Marvelous! This is indeed marvelous! Turning misfortune into good fortune, your scheme is indeed a life-saving turnaround! (ZHOU *sings*)

> (*To the same tune as before*)
> Thanks to your efforts,
> my scholar's robe and cap are secure;

your life-saving plan is simply remarkable, like a sutra that
 alleviates suffering.
If I chance to write a decent essay,
the high ladder of officialdom might be brought out for
 me to climb.
This is cause for major celebration!
Should I be saved from a calamitous fate this time,
 I can enjoy another three years of carefree profligacy.

(ZHOU *turns his back to* THE CLERK *and* THE ERRAND BOY *and says*) My
xiucai scholar status is a "money tree." As long as I have it, the money
will keep on spinning out. (*He turns to face* THE CLERK *and* THE
ERRAND BOY) Here is what I propose: I will give the proctor thirty
taels of silver and three taels to each of you. I shall have the silver
packed up separately and go to see the proctor with the two of you.

(THE CLERK *and* THE ERRAND BOY *sing*)
He had money but no plan—but his worries were for
 naught, thanks to our help in providing a clever
 strategy.

(ZHOU *sings*)
Knowing the consequences now, I see that a lantern can
 cause a fire.
With the right plot I can turn bad behavior—and bad
 luck—into good.

SCENE 9

FELT GATHERING

Prelude in the Mode of *Huangzhong: Xidijin*
(Westland Brocade)

(ZHANG ZHONGYOU *enters and sings*)
Elated that my *fu*[1] was recognized by discerning eyes,
I have placed at the top of my class.
Only because there is no "commander-in-chief" among
    the crowd,
    this "assistant general" occasionally takes the lead.

(ZHANG *speaks*) I am Zhang Sanyi and my sobriquet is Zhongyou.
Aspiring to join officialdom through the civil service examination,
I have buried my head in my books to prepare for the tests. Fan Shi
(*whose sobriquet is* JIEFU] and I are both listed as students at the
county school. Out of the ten examinations we took together, he
came in first nine times. Always ranked second or third, I have not
been able to surpass him. Recently, we were given another exam by
Mr. Wang, and Jiefu was absent because of his wedding. For this
reason I took first place. Although that was only a prequalifying
examination, I was still elated to be recognized. Today I have
brought a jug of wine and there is no harm in paying Mr. Wang a

friendly visit and reminiscing about the days when I benefited from his tutelage. When discussing literature, one ought to bring wine; / parsing each character is never done in vain! (ZHANG *exits*)

(WANG ZHONGXIANG *enters and sings*)
(*To the same tune as before*)
This petty official's ancient blue-felt cap cannot fend off
   the cold.
Giving lessons to young men, I while away my idle days.
Being frugal, my worries are multiplied when guests
   arrive;
   it looks like dipping into my savings cannot be avoided.

(WANG *speaks*) Ever since I was appointed to this poorly paid teaching position and "sat down on this hard, cold stool,"[2] I have been sub-sisting on thin gruel with bits of ginger and drops of vinegar mixed in. I can't even afford to buy a house and land, not to mention hav-ing more children with whom to share my already meager fare, or paying to entertain guests by plucking hairs out from my thin felt cap. Ever since Mr. Cao moved into the school, he became my neighbor but never once has he acted as a host. A few days ago, I had a conversation with some school staff and was told that Mr. Cao gave them a list of his daily needs, often asking for a half kilo of pork, a whole chicken, or a whole fish. If he keeps on squandering money like this, I am afraid that my modest salary cannot last long. We have to be patient for a few more days, and after receiving the "good-and bad-behavior" gift money from my students, there will be plenty of time to live it up. A few days ago, we held a preliminary examination and I asked for Mr. Cao's help with reading the exam papers. As a result, we ranked Zhang Zhongyou first. I predict that he will come to express his gratitude today. Let me ask the staff to prepare tea and wait for him. (THE SERVANT *enters with* ZHANG, *carrying two wine boxes*). (ZHANG *recites*) The teacher's wine and food should be amply provided, / so that the students can receive Confucius's teaching unhindered. (THE SERVANT *recites*) If for three months the teacher has not known the taste of meat, / I would not blame him for wanting a well-cooked pork dish. There is a clapper at the gate, let me knock on it to announce our arrival. (THE SERVANT *knocks on the clapper*) (WANG) The errand boy is busy with the sundry duties of the examination; I shall answer the door myself. Oh, it turns out to be Zhang Zhongyou. (ZHANG *and* WANG *salute to each other*) (ZHANG *recites*) Though poor in talent, and negligent in my studies, / you still deigned to recognize me. (WANG *recites*) Your essay demonstrated profound learning; / with my limited scholarship, I measured the sea with a gourd ladle. Have you just come back from a picnic? Why do you have food boxes with you? (ZHANG) I thought that Your Excellency might have some free time now and took the liberty to pay you a visit. (WANG) Thank you for thinking of me. (WANG *turns his back to* ZHANG) Just a moment ago, I was worrying about breaking the bank to entertain Mr. Cao. Why not invite him to share the meal? But if I let Mr. Cao know that the food and wine were brought by my student, I won't get the credit for being the host. I have an idea. (WANG *turns to face* ZHANG) Since you have brought such a rich repast, besides which it could get a little lonely with only the two of us, I suggest inviting my guest and fellow provincial classmate Mr. Cao to join us. What do you think? (ZHANG) Since Mr. Cao is your friend, it would be my honor. (WANG) That would be great. However, Mr. Cao is very proud and punctilious, and he never accepts any invitation for a meal without a good reason. If we tell him that you are the host, he will definitely not come. Or even if he came, he would not stay to the end. Only if I act as the host will he be unable to decline the invitation. I now call my servant: go to the western study and invite Mr. Cao over.

To the Tune of *Chuanyan Yunü qian*
(A Message to the Jade Maid)

(CAO GECHEN *enters and sings*)
My room is cold and my pockets are empty,
nothing goes smoothly and without a hitch.

(CAO, WANG, *and* ZHANG *salute to each other*) (WANG *speaks*) This is Mr. Zhang whom we ranked as the top candidate in the recent examination. Since you've gotten to know him through his examination essay, I've invited him to keep us company today. Mr. Zhang, because I was busy handling miscellaneous business related to the exams, I asked Mr. Cao to help with reading the examination essays. (ZHANG) In that case, Mr. Cao should be considered my mentor, as well. (ZHOU GONGMENG *enters with* THE CLERK *and* THE ERRAND BOY). Here is a big ingot of pure silver / on behalf of the top-ranked candidate for "best behavior." (THE CLERK *and* THE ERRAND BOY) Mr. Zhou, please wait here for a minute, let us go and have a word with the teacher first, and then we will invite you in. (*They enter and one of them whispers to* WANG, *who is ecstatic and says*) Come on in! Come on in! (ZHOU *comes in and greets* WANG *and his guests*) Ah, I see that my classmate Mr. Zhang is also here. May I have the honor to be introduced to this distinguished gentleman? (ZHANG) This is Mr. Wang's classmate and old friend, Mr. Cao. (CAO) May I ask the last name of this young man? (ZHANG) This is my friend Zhou Gongmeng. (*Everyone sits down*) (CAO) Mr. Zhang, I read your marvelous essay yesterday. It was spirited and thorough, and I predict that you will pass high in the examination and rise to eminence in no time at all.

To the Passing Tune: *Zhuomu'er* (Woodpecker)

(ZHANG *sings*)

Like a useless tree, dull and recalcitrant by nature,[3]
or a piece of rotting wood, I am deeply ashamed to be
    unfit for carving.[4]
Never expecting to be discovered by a mentor who
    recognized my worth—
a craftsman who rescued me from the fires of oblivion
lying amidst the ashes by the roadside—
I sigh for the one who heard my soul's cry,
and for the carpenter who placed his hopes in my timber.
Though I fear that when both ends of this piece of lumber
    are scorched,
    no good will come to the middle part.[5]

(WANG *speaks*) This Mr. Zhou is not only talented but also virtuous in his conduct. (CAO) Having virtue is rarer than having good essays. One needs to develop the self-cultivation of Confucius's disciples such as Yan Hui and Min Sun first, before he is able to have the achievements of Yi Yin and Lü Shang.[6] (ZHOU) I am flattered. (ZHOU *sings*)

> (*To the same tune as before*)
> Yan and Min, Lü and Yi, they all put me to shame.
> An insignificant nobody, I have yet to serve my country as
>   a loyal citizen should.

(CAO *speaks to* ZHOU) How come I did not see your work among the examination essays a few days ago? (ZHOU) That day was the anniversary of my father's passing. I was suddenly beset with grief over his parting and paid a visit to his grave. As a result, I missed the examination. (ZHOU *sings*)

> Although I am fond of writing and do so on a regular basis,
> I do observe filial mourning on the anniversaries of my
> parents' deaths.

(CAO *speaks*) You could make up the examination even though you missed it. (ZHOU) I wanted to make it up on the following day, but unfortunately my older brother got sick. I spent the whole day mixing medicines for him, so I was not able to attend the make-up examination. On the third day I planned on taking it, but a friend of mine suddenly passed away from a bout of illness, and I had to help with collecting donations and preparing for the burial service, so I missed my chance again. On the fourth day the results were already announced to the public. (ZHOU *sings*)

> I was encumbered by a series of trifling obligations;
> having missed the examination, I can only sigh in regret.

(CAO *smiles and says*) Mr. Zhou has fulfilled four of the five cardinal duties.[7] (ZHOU) Thank you, but about that fifth cardinal duty, I have yet to find a wife, a condition that causes me endless worry. (CAO *speaks to* WANG) My old classmate, today's banquet is far too extravagant, not at all what a humble schoolteacher can afford. (WANG's *face changes color; he says*) This . . . this was indeed prepared and paid for by me.

To the Tune of *Sanduanzi* (Three Suites)

(CAO *sings*)
Your salary is low, your school makes no profit,
    it is far from easy for you to come up with this kind of
    money.

Let's forego this formality.

Why indulge in needless extravagance?

(WANG *sings*)

Although this is humble fare prepared for close family
    friends,

with only a few plain vegetable dishes,

you may thank your hostess's cooking and my own efforts
    to put this together.

(CAO *speaks*) I will have to take my leave. (*Everyone gets up*)
    (CAO *turns to* ZHANG)

To the Tune of *Guichaohuan* (Happy to Be
Back at Court)

(CAO *speaks*) Mr. Zhang, (CAO *sings*)

Though lacking in talent, I

have found a precious new friend in you;

my only regret is that this meeting has come so late.

(ZHANG *sings*)

Sir, as your most grateful junior, it is my good fortune to
    be able to look up to your leadership.

How can I find ways to seek your instruction more often?
    (WANG *turns to* ZHOU) Mr. Zhou, for you,

I will send a letter of recommendation to the head
    examiner,

(ZHOU *responds, singing*) Teacher,

You have helped me twice, saving face for my brother
    and me.

(*In unison*) Two pairs of bosom friends, each playing a
  different tune.

(CAO *sings*) Drinking wine and discussing essays, without
  realizing it our faces flush crimson,

(WANG *sings*) Borrowing a flower to worship Buddha[8] I
  saved a lot of money.

(ZHANG *sings*) My essay occasionally ranks above all of my
  fellow scholars.

(ZHOU *sings*) My towering virtue exemplifies the four
  cardinal relationships.

SCENE 10

~~~~~~~~~~~~~~~~~~~~~~~~~~~~~~

A JOKING, BANTERING ALLIANCE

Prelude in the Mode of *Yuediao: Shuangtian xiaojiao*
(Reveille Under a Frosty Sky)

(JINGGUAN *enters and sings*)
I halted my sermon about the Surangama sutra
at the first ring of the prayer bell.
Since I made a date for the two misses to return here,
I shall arrange for their ritual tea and vegetarian repast to
be prepared.

(JINGGUAN *speaks*) Today is the first day of the tenth month. My nunnery is holding a Buddhist service on behalf of our patron, to pray for the souls of the dead. Disciples, it's time to set up the altar for the service. I will begin the observances after I've received Mrs. Fan and Miss Cao. (*Many people respond from the back of the stage, at the same time making noises of setting up the altar*)

Passing Tune in the Mode of *Nanlü: Yijiangfeng*
(Wind on the River)

(JIANYUN *enters with her* MAID *and sings*)
Looking over at the temple's altar,

like coiling snakes and dragons, the prayer flags flutter,
sounds of hymnals ring sharp and clear.

(JIANYUN'S MAID *speaks*) Mrs. Fan, we've arrived. I'm just afraid that
Miss Cao may not manage to get away and come over.

(JIANYUN *continues to sing*)
I pray that the Buddha looks after her
so that she can sneak out of her boudoir,
and hurry here to this "altar" of poetry.
I long for her faint aroma, which
stirred up by the wind, seems to linger on over there,
    still.
How come Wei Sheng did not
wait for me first by the bridge?[1] (JINGGUAN *meets* JIANYUN
    and her MAID)

(*To the same tune as before*)
(YUHUA *enters with her* MAID *and sings*)
I am going to the temple,
not to perform an exorcism to avert impending
    disaster,
nor to give thanks for my father's succor;
no, I lied to him, deceiving humans and gods alike,
to renew my poetic liaison.

(YUHUA'S MAID *speaks*) Miss, you've come so early. Mrs. Fan is a newlywed and she probably has yet to rise from her bed.

(YUHUA *sings*) You say that
she is enjoying conjugal bliss,

enjoying conjugal bliss,

slow to move her lotus feet off the bed. But I suspect that
she is tired of nuptial pleasures, and cannot wait for
the sun to rise from the east.

(YUHUA *sees* JIANYUN *and both are delighted*) (JINGGUAN *speaks*)
Mrs. Fan and Miss Cui, the two of you take your time to sit
down and chat. I shall go and host the prayer service. When I
have some spare time, I will come to keep you company. (JIANYUN
and YUHUA *speak in unison*) Please do so at your leisure, Reverend
Mother. (JINGGUAN *exits*) (JIANYUN) Miss Cao, when I returned
home after our last meeting, I showed our poems to my husband
Jiefu. He composed two poems using the same rhyme words.
(JIANYUN *hands the poems to* YUHUA. YUHUA *reads them and says*)
His poems are graceful and free-spirited. He fully lives up to his
reputation as a talented scholar. (YUHUA *returns the poems to*
JIANYUN *and says*) Mrs. Fan, after our single chance meeting the
other day, you and I have already become bosom friends. I want
us to swear an oath of "sisterhood." Would you be willing?
(JIANYUN) I was just thinking the same thing. It is just that our
pact should be different from those ordinary ones, for which the
couple swears to be together only for their present lifetimes. We
should pray to be sisters even in the next life, too. (YUHUA) In
that case, let's become sworn sisters in this life, and vow to be
blood sisters in the next one. (JIANYUN) That is no good. Doesn't
that mean that we would have to be women forever, lifetime after
lifetime? (YUHUA) Oh, in that case, why don't we swear to be sisters in this life, and bond together as brothers in the next one?
(JIANYUN) This is no good either. Many brothers don't get along.
Even the ones who do are not as intimate as husbands and wives
who don't get along. Why don't we become husband and wife in
the next life? (YUHUA *smiles*)

To the Tune of *Jinluosuo* (Golden Coiled Rope)

[*JINWUTONG* (GOLDEN PARASOL TREE)]

(JIANYUN *sings*)
Brothers and sisters are born of the same parents,
but although they share the natural bonds of blood
relations,
their affection doesn't plumb the depths.
[Like] a ruler sitting high up on his dais, separated from
his subjects.

[*DONG'OULING* (SONG OF DONG'OU)]

Even with one's parents, filial affection hardly compares to
the conjugal union of heart and belly;
only through the rapturous pleasures of a shared pillow
and mat can souls truly entwine.

[*ZHENXIANXIANG* (A BOX FOR NEEDLE AND THREAD)]

Never parting in life, paired together even in death.

[*JIESANCHENG* (THRICE-DRUNK BUT SOBERING UP)]

I am not telling lies.

[*LANHUAMEI* (TOO LAZY TO PAINT ONE'S BROWS)]

Have you not heard that Liang Shanbo and Zhu Yingtai
were former classmates?

[*JISHENGZI* (PARASITIC SEEDS)]

Even if in the next life they could not become a pair of
    phoenix lovers,
by turning into two inseparable butterflies in death,
they paid each other's love debts.[2]

(YUHUA *turns her back to* JIANYUN *and says*) Swearing oaths before the
gods is no laughing matter. It's one thing to pledge sisterhood;
but is it really all right to pledge to be husband and wife? (YUHUA
sings)

    (*To the same tune as before*)
    The temple with its gods is no mere stage or prop;
    slowly, I deliberate over her words in my mind:
    Have people ever tied a conjugal knot
    even before their bodies have taken shape?

(YUHUA *speaks*) But so be it. I do not know who will be male and who
will be female in our next lives. I might turn out to be the husband
and she, the wife?! (YUHUA *continues to sing*)

    Our gender assignment in the next life is still unclear;
    but I shan't worry if I am the female phoenix.
    It may not turn out that she is reborn as a lad, and I,
    a miss.

    (YUHUA *speaks*) Even if she ends up as a man in her
    next life, as long as she (he) possesses the same talent
    and looks, I would eagerly become her (his) wife.
    I only hope that in the next life (YUHUA *continues
    to sing*)

her romantic flair remains intact, so that
I would not mind being assigned to the lesser gender.

(YUHUA *turns to* JIANYUN *and sings*) Mrs. Fan,
you and I are bold and unrestrained,
just look at how the Maitreya Buddha laughs at our antics
    from his altar.
There is just one thing that worries me.

(JIANYUN *speaks*) What is that?

(YUHUA *speaks*) I only fear that (*and then sings*)

our effervescent bond cannot be forgotten
and will last beyond this lifetime, bubbling over into the
    next one, too.

(JIANYUN *says to her* MAID) Hualing, light the candles and let us swear our oaths. (JIANYUN'S MAID) The old saying goes: when one imitates a dragon, he ought to look like a dragon; when one pretends to be a tiger, he should act like a tiger. If the two of you want to pray to be husband and wife, then you should dress up as a couple to carry out the ceremony. (JIANYUN *and* YUHUA) How can we do that? (JIANYUN'S MAID) The left wing of this compound is Mr. Fan's study; we can find his caps and clothes there. One of you can wear his clothing for the ceremony. Once the Buddha sees you and bears witness, neither of you can break your promise in the next life. (JIANYUN *laughs and says*) Although this girl is joking, what she just said makes sense to me. Let's go and get the clothes. (YUHUA'S MAID *says*) In that case, we still need someone to officiate. (JIANYUN'S MAID) That is easy. My family has worked as wedding attendants for several generations, and I have been thoroughly familiar with these rituals since youth. There are men's caps and round-collar robes in Mr. Fan's study, all ready and waiting for you to have them brought over for you to put on. (*One of the maids gets the clothing*) (YUHUA'S MAID) My mistress should be the groom. (JIANYUN'S MAID) No, my mistress ought to be the husband. (*The two maids argue*) (JIANYUN'S MAID) Fine, since we cannot persuade each other, how about asking both mistresses to try on Mr. Fan's clothes, and the one for whom they fit best will take the role of groom. (YUHUA *tries on the clothes*) (JIANYUN'S MAID) The cap covers her brows and the robe touches the ground. They are too large for her. (JIANYUN *wears the clothes*) (JIANYUN'S MAID) Look, the cap is neither too large nor too small, and the robe is neither too long nor too short. She is perfect for the part. Let's now conduct the ceremony. (JIANYUN'S MAID *wears a scholar cap and carries out the rituals of the ceremony;* YUHUA'S MAID *helps* YUHUA *kowtow with* JIANYUN) (JINGGUAN *enters and laughs at the scene. She leaves to avoid embarrassing the young ladies.* JIANYUN *and* YUHUA *complete the ceremony and smile to each other*)

To the Tune of *Sanhuantou* (Three Variation)

> (JIANYUN *sings*)
> Holding hands and looking at each other,
> this marriage has opened an extraordinary new chapter in the history of love.
> A fake groom and a real bride,
> such innovation can only be found in the theater.

(JIANYUN *speaks*) Miss Cao, since I am a year older than you, I should be the husband.

> (JIANYUN *sings*)
> The husband should be older;
> do not blame me for prevailing over you.

(JIANYUN *speaks*) Although I am not a real man, dressed as one and seeing your sweet, delicate face, I cannot help but feel giddy.

> (JIANYUN *sings*)
> I love you to death, and
> My unquenchable passion is driving me to distraction.[3]

(JIANYUN *speaks*) Not only am I in a frenzy, young lady, your desires
have also been stirred. You now are like

> (JIANYUN *sings*)
> a sprig of apricot that reaches over the fence,
> your longing heart stripped of its defenses.

(YUHUA *turns her back to* JIANYUN *and says*) Dressed as a man, Mrs. Fan
is no less handsome than the legendary Pan An and Song Yu.[4]
Where can I find such a handsome man in the world? If only I were
able to marry a husband like her, I would gladly give my life. (YUHUA
sings)

> (*To the same tune as before*)
> Dressing up in a man's clothes,
> she suddenly turns into the ideal mate, a veritable Zhang
>   Chang![5]
> Even the handsome Pan An and Wei Jie[6] would be
>   outshone by her lovely looks.

> (YUHUA *turns to* JIANYUN *and sings*) Mrs. Fan,
> as my elder, you should take the role of groom, but not only
>   for that—
> I should also defer to you as an old hand in the pleasures
>   of the nuptial chamber.

How laughable that our romantic feeling is but
　　self-deceiving:
this is like that make-believe terrace of love,
　where a goddess won fame for her dalliance with the King
　　of Chu, though it was but a dream.[7]

(YUHUA *speaks*) In my opinion, anything can be treated as a joke except
　for the bond of husband and wife. A chaste woman only takes one
　husband. If I married you today and then married another man
　later, although I would not be considered unchaste, still it would
　look unbecoming. Besides, we are so attached to each other, how
　could we ever stand to part! We need to figure out a way to be
　together for the rest of our lives. (JIANYUN *responds*) I have a good
　strategy, but I feel embarrassed to say it out loud. (YUHUA) Given
　how close we are to each other, how could there still be anything
　that you cannot share with me? (JIANYUN) Even if I tell you, you
　may not be willing to go along with it. (YUHUA) The ancients say: "A
　gentleman [*shi*] would die for his soul mate."[8] If even death is not
　out of the question, what else is there that I won't agree to do?
　(JIANYUN) I am now married to Mr. Fan. If you are also willing to
　marry him, you and I would both be his wives, equal in status. In
　that way, we could write poems together every day and never part
　from each other. We would be even closer than husband and wife.
　What do you think of this idea? (JIANYUN *sings*)

To the Tune of *Dong'ouling* (Song of Dong'ou)

　　Sharing dreams at night, donning makeup together at dawn,
　　we are a pair of flowers reflected in the mirror, rising from
　　　the same stem.
　　Writing poetry in lockstep in the inner chamber,
　　we should be just like any other couple.

(JIANYUN *speaks*) If you agree to marry Mr. Fan, I am even willing to defer to you as the principal wife.

> (JIANYUN *sings*)
> I defer to your superior virtue and sagacity,
> surely you shall receive our husband's full attention.

(YUHUA *turns her back to* JIANYUN *and speaks*) Even if it is as she says, I am still hesitant.

> (YUHUA *sings*)
> (*To the same tune as before*)
> Do not be rash, let's discuss this further;
> wanting to marry a mock groom, I am offered a different paramour.

(YUHUA *speaks*) I can see that Mr. Fan's literary talents are comparable to ours. However, I wonder what he looks like? I imagine that he was rather careful when he selected his mate. (YUHUA *signs*) Oh, heavens! Since I've already met my soul mate, I should not hold back. (YUHUA *turns to* JIANYUN) Elder lady, I expect that (YUHUA *sings*)

> you, my lady, will treat me like an equal consort;
> being your soul mate, I can see into your heart.
> My only wish is for the two of us not to be separated like
> Orion from Antares,
> Even if I am made a concubine, this will be fine by me!

(JIANYUN *speaks*) Even if you agree to this, I am afraid that your father would object. (YUHUA) If I am to be made his concubine, my father certainly would object. We could simply tell him that

you are willing to be the secondary wife and make me the principal wife. Once I have entered the Fan household, I would yield the
status of principal wife to you. (JIANYUN) If this is what you want
to do, let's now swear an oath to Buddha. (YUHUA) To the Three
Treasures on high: I, Yuhua, deeply attracted to Jianyun, swear an
oath to marry Mr. Fan. If I break this promise, may I live not a
day past sixteen. (JIANYUN) If Yuhua indeed marries Mr. Fan and I
treat her as a secondary wife, may I live not a day past eighteen.

To the Tune of *Liu Po mao* (Liu Po's Hat)

(JIANYUN *and* YUHUA *sing together*)
Deities are numinous and cannot be cheated,
those who betray others shall meet with disaster.
We wish only to be together in many lives ahead,
taking turns to be man and woman, sharing quilt and bed.

(*Someone from the back of the stage calls out and says*) Mrs. Fan and Miss
Cao, please come to burn incense in the meditation hall.

(YUHUA *sings*)
Like neighboring vines intertwined,
a king's mock enfeoffment must be honored.[9]

(JIANYUN *sings*)
Women can break rules to appreciate talents,
Rabid jealousy has always belonged mostly to men.

(THE MAIDS OF YUHUA *and* JIANYUN *stay on stage to close this act*)[10]
(JIANYUN'S MAID *says to* YUHUA'S MAID) Since our mistresses have
become man and wife, we should do the same. And since we still
have Mr. Fan's clothes here, why don't we get married too! (YUHUA'S

MAID) In that case, I will play the groom. (JIANYUN'S MAID) Since ancient times, people say that "a beautiful wife often sleeps with an ugly husband." You have good looks, and I don't. The prettier one should be the wife and the unattractive one should be the husband. (YUHUA'S MAID) All right, it would be beneficial to have ugly offspring; good looks bring big problems. (*The two of them conduct the ceremony and sing*).

(*To the same tune as before*)

These romantics act out a romance,
undoing their undergarments, a waft of plum fragrance
   bursts forth from each one.
How come not a single twig of plum is at hand?[11]
These bare tree crotches, rubbing against each another,
only make their flower buds itchier.
(*Embracing, they exit the stage*)

SCENE 11

ASKING FOR ENFEOFFMENT

To the Tune of *Bei fendieer*
(Northern Powdery Butterfly)

(THE KING OF THE RYUKYU ISLANDS, *the painted-face role,*
enters leading a group, and he sings)
Vast seas and boundless sky,
limitless waters and lands have I conquered,
expanding my writ across the wide world.
Eastern immortal isles at my fingertips,
shadowed by vermilion clouds,
enshrouded in auspicious mist,
a rising sun shines over all.
Galloping across the southern seas to the very edge of the
    Milky Way,
all of this lies within earshot of my sonorous bellow!

(THE KING *recites*) Having established a kingdom in the Eastern
Sea, / on an island near the dragon's palace I make my capital. / I
wonder who is now ruling China? / The seas are calm and blustery
winds scarce. I am the king of the Ryukyu Islands, Shang Bazhi.[1]
(THE KING *speaks*) My kingdom lies on the opposite shore of the
Eastern Sea, adjacent to Japan. My ancestors were heroic, and my

family is skilled in the ways of warfare. We were neither conquered by the Sui army, nor induced to surrender by the Yuan envoy. Truly, I am the overlord of the seas, with few rivals. Our islands used to be divided into three states. Since my ancestor Cha Du, we have lived for generations in the Central Mountains [Zhongshan]. Since I ascended the throne, our country has been strong and prosperous, our settlements are flourishing, and we have brought both the Northern and the Southern Mountains into our realm. Although I am far from having unified all under heaven as the First Emperor of Qin did,[2] I have managed to end the tripartite division that befell the Han.[3] Now in this propitious time when the people are at peace and well provided for, I am going with the Prime Minister and the Minister of Defense to the Pescadores Islands to survey the region. Soldiers, please summon the Prime Minister and Minister of Defense here! (*Soldiers pass the order*) (THE PRIME MINISTER *and* THE MINISTER OF DEFENSE *enter*) (PRIME MINISTER *recites*) Our country can be compared to China, / and our people resemble the ancients. (MINISTER OF DEFENSE *recites*) When rebels and bandits overran the land during the Spring and Autumn period, / the eastern and northern barbarians produced capable rulers and ministers. (PRIME MINISTER) I am the Prime Minister of the Ryukyu Islands. (MINISTER OF DEFENSE) I am the Minister of Defense of the Ryukyu Islands. (*They both salute* THE KING) Your Majesty summoned us; what is your command? (THE KING) I am going to pay a visit to the Pescadores Islands and I want you two to accompany me. (BOTH MINISTERS) Yes, we will accompany you. (*They all walk on stage*) (BOTH MINISTERS *sing*)

In the Mode of *Nanzhonglü: Qi Yan Hui*
(Crying for Yan Hui)

The flowers may be jealous of my crimson red robe,
but how could they perfume the sky on a spring dawn?

The east wind is buttery sweet,
    exquisite birds make clucking sounds with their tongues;
soft and moist is the grassy shore,
    indeed, the enchanting Pescadores Islands
are no less beautiful than the paradise of Penglai.
Jade green peaks reach up to the sky,
    the boundless sea extends far beyond the crashing breakers.

(BOTH MINISTERS *climb to a high place . They look into the distance and say to* THE KING: Your Majesty, look at the sea so vast, the mountains on our archipelago coil around it like a woman's chignon. Looking down from up here, what majestic mountains and rivers we have!

To the Tune of *Bei shiliuhua*
(Northern Pomegranate Blossom)

(*The* KING *sings*)
One after another, specks of "nautilus shells"[4] rise and fall,
    as if playing in the spring tide,
it must be like riding over the sea to seek the divine turtle.
How joyful that the water is peaceful, flat as a palm,
like the mermaid spreading out her silk shawl.
Clouds pull out ribbon-like colors from the dawning sun,
to tie around the mountain's waist.
I am afraid that our brash, noisy laughter will awaken the
    horned dragon from his lair.
With its multiple, impenetrable layers,
his palace holds him back.
The deep, deep blue ancient Cangzhou[5]
permits no Red Dust[6] to enter;
only I am allowed to halt my horse and salute the wind
    and waves.

(*A minor role actor playing a dragon appears*) (PRIME MINISTER *speaks*)
Over there appears a divine dragon! I am sure that it comes to pay
its respects to you, my lord. (PRIME MINISTER *sings*)

To the Tune of *Nan Qi Yan Hui*
(Southern Crying for Yan Hui)

The divine animal appears in the waves,
lo and behold, it bares its fangs and brandishes its claws.
The dragon comes and goes with us,
as if it is of a mind to be tamed.
With its golden scales aglow,
its dragon skin illuminated;
iridescent colors flow.
This is because your kingly benevolence subdues birds
　　and fishes,
and your thunderous might can tame tigers and
　　dragons.

(MINISTER OF DEFENSE *says*) There is a bank of clouds or perhaps fog
hovering over the water; could it be a mirage? (*From the back of the
stage someone makes smoke to create mist*)

To the Tune of *Bei pudeng'e fan* (Northern Moth
to the Flame, Redux)

(THE KING *sings*)
Rising steamily like a woman's chignon over the sea,
darkly, like fog spreading out to cover the whole sky—
in a sudden flash, the heavens open up in brilliant colors.
Billowing, as the wind blows through, the sea turns a
　　sparkling emerald green.

(A group of minor performers playing horses, men, and women, holding different jewels, appear on the stage, but disappear immediately) (MINISTER OF DEFENSE *speaks*) The Mirage has appeared! How marvelous, how magnificent!

> (THE KING *sings*)
> Towers reflected on water like layered brocades;
> houses next to the rainbow bridge arranged in densely
>   packed rows.
> A tangle of people and horses run amok;
> no painter's brush could ever capture the riotous splendor
>   of this scene.

(MINISTER OF DEFENSE *speaks*) Ever since we unified the south with the north, the winds are calm, the waves are at peace, and no tidal waves buffet our shores. Today the appearance of a mirage is an auspicious sign, and the divine dragon offers us good fortune. This is all because my lord's benevolence brings these divinities into your service. I have heard that to the west is the Central Plain, and it is a prosperous place. Why don't we take some troops, ride the waves, and go loot its treasures? This will extend your power and prestige tens of thousands of miles. (MINISTER OF DEFENSE *sings*)

To the Tune of *Nan shangxiaolou fan* (Southern Ascending the Small Tower, Redux)

> Taking advantage of our troops' high spirits,
> valiantly we ride over the rolling seas.
> Let us rob their gold, loot their jewels, and snatch their
>   lassies.

This shall then demonstrate our peerless bravery to friend
  and foe,
and spread respect for us, the ferocious Zhongshan lads
  that we are, both near and far.
My lord, I request a tiger-shaped tally[7] from you to
  authorize the mobilization of our troops!

(THE KING *speaks*) Raising an army for looting is unbefitting of a benevolent ruler. (*Speaking to the* PRIME MINISTER) What do you think about this, Prime Minister? (PRIME MINISTER) Based on my reading of the stars and the ethers, I can see that there is a sagely ruler reigning in China. We can only pledge our allegiance to them; how could we possibly violate their sovereignty? (THE KING) What do you mean by allegiance? (PRIME MINISTER) Japan and other neighbors all recognize the rightful sovereignty of China, and observe its customs. Now that we have unified the south with the north, our neighboring states are all on the look-out for any small opening from which to pounce on us. In my humble opinion, it would be better for us to send an envoy to China and propose to pay tribute to China's imperial court, so that China will send its emissary to confer a title upon you, my lord. When the neighboring countries hear this, they will not only not dare to wage war against us, but will even elevate my lord as head of a new alliance. (MINISTER OF DEFENSE) We have not yet sent our troops to China; this already lets them off the hook. How could we go and seek their recognition of our legitimacy? Wouldn't this be boosting another's morale and dampening our own? (PRIME MINISTER) Those who recognize the needs of their times and conform to them are hailed as true heroes. I hope Your Majesty will think this over carefully. (THE KING) What the Prime Minister just said makes sense to me. (THE KING *sings*)

To the Tune of *Bei diezier fan* (Northern Doubled Words, Redux)

A stately title, conferred by the Middle Kingdom,
will ensure the obeisance of all of our neighbors.
And what's more:
with glittering golden cap and gorgeous dragon robe, my
    visage will gleam ever more splendidly,
enhancing my royal aura.
On my waist will hang alabaster white Lantian jades,[8]
I will hold court smartly in pearl-encrusted shoes;
a purple canopy billowing over the imperial carriage.
My palace's inner quarters will brim with winsome smiles.
We have brought tranquility to our neighbors in every
    direction,
the beacon-fires of war have all burned out.

(THE KING *speaks*) Now that we are going to ask for recognition of our royal authority, who can be sent as an envoy? (MINISTER OF DEFENSE) If leading troops into battle, I can certainly be in the vanguard. But for a dispiriting mission like this one, I will not go, certainly not I! (PRIME MINISTER) I will be at my lord's service, and I shall work hard to bring this to fruition. (THE KING) In that case, I shall make haste and write a missive to China's emperor; prepare some gifts, then pick an auspicious day to set off on your journey.

To the Tune of *Nanwei* (Southern Ending)

(PRIME MINISTER, MINISTER OF DEFENSE, *and* THE
    KING *sing in unison*)
Humbly requesting China's recognition of our royal
    authority,

we pray for the envoy's speedy return.

Bringing with him a royal decree,

He shall have seen his share of that great nation's faunal
and floral delights.

SCENE 12

ECSTASY

Prelude in the Mode of *Shangdiao: Fengma'er*
(Wind Horse)

(FAN SHI *and* JIANYUN *enter together*)
(FAN SHI *sings*)
Clear skies, gentle breeze, cool shadows under the Sun,
look how the chrysanthemums perfume the paths of our
    secluded garden.
(JIANYUN *sings*)
Only when in full bloom are flowers worthy of being
    admired,
Let's pretend it's still the Double Ninth[1] Festival,
And bring out some wine to celebrate, tête-à-tête.

[*Changxiangsi* (*Everlasting Longing*)] (FAN SHI *recites*) Look at all these
flowers, / some of them stand out proudly; / and I've found a single
white jade flower; / her celestial beauty is peerless. (JIANYUN) Speaking of flowers, / my looks pale in comparison; / I have found
another lovelier than I, / your lucky star of love will be doubled.
(FAN SHI *speaks*) My dear, although now it is already the beginning of the tenth month, chrysanthemums are in even fuller bloom

than back during the Double Ninth Festival. Although one should not idle away the spring, it's even worse to allow autumnal colors to pass without savoring their beauty. The floral season concludes with chrysanthemums, the finale to the year's fragrant blooms. I have prepared a pair of crab claws to have with wine.[2] Let's enjoy these together. Hualing, bring us some wine. (JIANYUN'S MAID *brings wine*)

To the Passing Tune: *Erlangshen* (Erlang the God)

(FAN SHI *sings*)
In early wintertime,
clear skies and refreshing air are most rare,
I'm happy that golden flowers have not held back their
  glory.
Blooming with feelings despite their gauntness,
leaning against bamboos and climbing on trellises,
    spreading their restrained, delicate fragrance. Safe and
    sound even after a bitter frost,
they resemble hermits proudly and vigorously residing in
    the mountains.
We lovers of autumnal brilliance
rely on them completely to harvest the whole year's
    fragrance.

(*To the same tune as before, variation*)
(JIANYUN *sings*)
Now that the sun is out, the wind has subsided, and rain
    stopped,
nature protects all flowers.
I clutch on to these frosted branches,
pretending my heart is still under the autumnal sun,

although now it is already winter.

(JIANYUN *holds a cup and toasts*) My dear, why don't you

hold a wine cup in your right hand, and a crab claw in
    your left, and

wash away all worldly thoughts.

Changing my getup,

I will transform from a white-robed friend, into a maiden
    of "colorful and floating sleeves."

(FAN SHI *speaks*) My lady, I reread the two poems composed by the young ladies a few days ago, and the more I think about them, the more intrigued I become. I did not expect women to possess this level of talent. If they could live here with you, you could compose poems together day and night, and print a collection of all of your poetry. Wouldn't that be an elegant and stylish thing to do? (JIANYUN) I have met these two young ladies. They are not only tremendously talented, but also supremely beautiful. One of them actually resembles me, while the other one is practically the reincarnation of legendary beauties such as Xi Shi and Yang Yuhuan.[3] In front of her pearly radiance, even I feel ashamed of my ungainly appearance. (FAN SHI) She is even prettier than you? I don't believe it! (FAN SHI *sings*)

To the Tune of *Jixianbin* (Gathering Worthy Guests)

You praise others and deprecate yourself,
    such humility!

When did the two ladies of Emperor Wu ever come
    together and meet?

It is only because each feared that her beauty would be
    eclipsed by the other.[4]

It seems that you have too fanciful an imagination,

and conjured up the image of a ravishing enchantress.

Don't fool yourself.

How could anyone compare to your beauty?

(JIANYUN *speaks*) My dear, if these two female poets were not married yet, and you were in a position to choose between them, which one would you pick? (FAN SHI) My lady, you and I are a perfect match in every way, as inseparable as fish and water. I've already sworn not to love anyone else for the rest of my life. Why would you say something so inauspicious? (JIANYUN) I am only making a joke, there is no harm in that. (FAN SHI) In that case, let me think. (*He mutters to himself*) If I married one, I would not be able to stop thinking about the other one, and vice versa. I guess I would have no other choice but to marry both of them. (JIANYUN) Since you want to marry both, you need to decide who would be the principal wife, and who would be the secondary one. So, who would be the principal one? (FAN SHI *mutters again*) If I made one my principal wife, I would be doing an injustice to the other; and vice versa. I have no choice but to treat them equally as sisters. (JIANYUN) Which one would be the older sister? And which the younger? (FAN SHI) This would have to be decided based on their ages. (JIANYUN) If that is how you think, then you have some good sense in you. What if I asked them both to marry you for real? (FAN SHI) You are joking again. (JIANYUN) To tell you the truth, the first poem was composed by me. (FAN SHI) I did suspect that it was written by you, but the handwriting was different. Then what about the other one? (JIANYUN) If you ask about this young lady, she is (JIANYUN *sings*):

> (*To the same tune as before*)
> a Xi Shi reborn who left her hometown on a light skiff,
> passing through Yangzhou,
> she is staying temporarily at the Rain-Flower Nunnery
> while visiting friends.

Before meeting her face-to-face I detected her unique
  fragrance,
and composed a verse to compliment her, which elicited
  her marvelous response.
We shared our deep appreciation for each other,
  unable to exhaust in words the depth of our affection.

(FAN SHI *is surprised to hear this and says*) I see ... Who is her father? Where are they from? And where are they going? Please tell me all about them. (JIANYUN) Her father, Cao Gechen, is a scholar with the title of *xiaolian*[5] from Zhejiang Province, who is about to set off for the capital to take the metropolitan examination. (FAN SHI) I see, so she and you hit it off after composing poems together. What happened after that? Please tell me everything. (JIANYUN) She and I are like soul-mates who, upon meeting each other, are loathe to part. Therefore, we made plans to meet again in the tenth month at the nunnery. At our second meeting we felt even more intimate, and swore vows of sisterhood before the Buddha. (FAN SHI *is delighted and says*) In that case, now she is a younger sister to me as well. (JIANYUN) She said that although we have become sisters, eventually we will have to separate. Hence, she asked me to figure out a long-term plan. I jokingly said to her that she will not be able to stay with me for the rest of her life unless she marries into the Fan household. Who would have known that she took my suggestion for real and agreed to it? (FAN SHI) But there are no other brothers or nephews in my house. Whom can she marry? (JIANYUN) None other than you! (FAN SHI *appears to be taken by surprise*) What? Would ... would ... would she marry me? Why would she want to marry me? (JIANYUN) She would become your secondary wife. (FAN SHI *laughs*) Pooh, don't make fun of me! All this time I have been listening to you earnestly. I thought that you were being serious, but it turned out that you were joking the whole time. (FAN SHI *sings*)

To the Tune of *Huangying'er* (Yellow Oriole)

> This story is simply too ridiculous,
> made up out of whole cloth,
> one long dream,
> mostly a pack of lies coated in a mystery.

(FAN SHI *speaks*) Her father is a *xiaolian* [a provincial graduate] and there are no limits to the wealth and status he will attain in the future. How could he be willing to give his precious daughter to someone as a secondary wife? (FAN SHI *sings*)

> Who has seen the two daughters of the Qiao clan,[6]
> willing to become concubines?
> Merely talking about this leaves me tongue-tied!

(FAN SHI *SPEAKS*) One cannot be overly greedy. With your looks and talent, you're the cream of the crop of our times. I have no intention of overextending myself and going beyond the conquest I've already made of you. Even if she might be willing, I am not. (FAN SHI *sings*)

> I have no such thoughts,
> marrying one beauty is already more than enough.
> Who would expect to wed a pair of them?

(JIANYUN *speaks*) I also told her that there's no such thing in this world. But she said that "a gentleman [*shi*] would die for his soul mate." Death notwithstanding, is anything else impossible? (JIANYUN *sings*)

> (*To the same tune as before*)
> She volunteers to marry a talented and handsome lad;[7]

we will be sisters through marriage.

Although she will be the newcomer, place her above me!

(FAN SHI *speaks*) All right, let's suppose that even if she is willing, I bet her father will not give his approval. In addition, where can we find a matchmaker bold enough to deliver this proposal? (JIANYUN) I have already discussed this with her. If we offer her the secondary position, her father will certainly not agree; we ought to say that I am willing to be the secondary wife, and she will be made the principal wife. After she enters our household, she will then yield to me. For now, we could just say (JIANYUN *sings*):

The imperial favorite, with her virtue slackening, and her beauty in decline,

willingly resigns from her post as head of the harem.

(FAN SHI *speaks*) Let's say that we carry out your plan, what if her father still withholds his consent? (JIANYUN) She swore in front of Buddha that if her father persists in refusing, she will take her own life. (JIANYUN *sings*)

Her promise is as pure as ice;

if her father disapproves of the marriage,

she would rather die than marry someone else.

(FAN SHI *turns his back to* JIANYUN *and says*) Having heard what she has said, this may very well be true. I would not have imagined that someone as impractical and crazy as I would have such crazy good fortune! I only worry about one thing: the whims of a woman's heart. Although for now they are willing to go through thick and thin together, there is no guarantee that in the long term they will not fall into bitter rivalry for my affections. The base of a wall needs to be solidly built. For now, I should pretend to be firmly against this marriage, and only relent after they refuse to take no for an answer. Only in this way will there be no future reversals. (FAN SHI *turns to* JIANYUN) My lady, we shouldn't go ahead with this deal. As the old saying goes, "he who wants domestic disharmony takes a second wife." Right now, you only think of the joy of intimate sisterhood, and have not considered the misery of sleeping alone. If by any chance, after the wedding, warm hearts turn into cold stone and a pair of bosom friends become bitter enemies, [what could you do then?] Ordinary concubines who don't fit in to the household can be married off to others, but she is the daughter of a gentry family, and there is no way that we could send her away to remarry elsewhere. Wouldn't that ruin her life for good? (FAN SHI *sings*)

To the Tune of *Maoerzhui* (The Cat's Fall)

Reading through every single manual of medicine,
one can scarcely find an effective prescription for jealousy.
You, my lady, have never tasted the flavor of envy
once you've tasted it, you shall have second thoughts.
I hope you will not regret this, as for now you are like
Xiang Yu and Liu Bang who drew up a boundary and
    declared a truce;
I'm afraid that you will end up in total defeat.[8]

(JIANYUN *speaks*) I think that as long as you put your heart in the right place, what rivalry can there be? (FAN SHI) Although at present you may have no worries, my concern is for the distant future. If you insist on going ahead with this, I need you to write a letter guaranteeing that you will not become jealous. (JIANYUN *turns her back to* FAN SHI) Look at him, it's clear that underneath his pious refusal, he's already chomping at the bit. Let me scare him a little. (*She turns to* FAN SHI) You absolutely disapprove of this marriage? (FAN SHI)

Absolutely! (JIANYUN) My dear, since you are so determined, I cannot force you into it. Let me write a letter of refusal, asking her to marry into another good family so that she won't waste her youth. Hualing, bring my writing brush and ink-stone. (FAN SHI *panics*) My dear lady, let's discuss this a little further. (JIANYUN) There's nothing left to talk about. (JIANYUN's MAID *brings the brush and ink-stone,* JIANYUN *writes*) (FAN SHI *pulls on her sleeve and says*) But since that young lady has a mind to do this, how can we let her down! Let me find a matchmaker to deliver a proposal to her.

(*To the same tune as before*)
(JIANYUN *sings*)
Gingerly I throw a goddess to this rash young lad.
He even tries to push me to write a letter of guarantee,
　　driving me half-mad!
Don't be regretful,
although you made a false objection,
I will treat it as a true rejection.

(FAN SHI *speaks*) My lady, I want to discuss whom to entrust as our matchmaker. (JIANYUN) I have heard that a few days ago her father helped Mr. Wang grade examination essays. They ranked my cousin Mr. Zhang Number One in the examination; why not ask Cousin Zhang to be the go-between? (FAN SHI) If you say so, I will go to make this request of him tomorrow.

Weisheng (Closing Tune)

(*They sing in unison*)
A marriage proposal will be delivered first thing in the
　　morning;
We hope good news arrives shortly, so that
a stick of incense can be lit to thank Heaven above!

SCENE 13

FAWNING SMILES

(YUHUA'S MAID *enters and recites*) A belle longs for a belle, / a genius yearns for a genius. / Although they have not shared a bed, / they understand the pain of lovesickness. (YUHUA'S MAID *speaks*) It's funny that ever since the mistress came back from meeting Mrs. Fan, she has lost all interest in eating and drinking, and appears to be asleep upon waking, and awake when sleeping. Even though their conjugal bond is only for pretend, her lovesickness is very real. Today is the fifteenth day of the tenth month; I have to persuade her to go upstairs, where she can watch the incense-burning ceremony[1] conducted by the county magistrate, and take her mind off her misery. Opening the window, we cast out our sorrows, / sweeping the path, we await the marriage broker. (YUHUA'S MAID *exits the stage*) (ZHOU GONGMENG *enters and recites*) If a young scholar does not make an alliance with officials, / he will be in a real pickle, drowning in bitterness.[2] / One shouldn't complain how tough it is to find an "in;" / the harder the wall, the harder you need to drill! I, Zhou Gongmeng, have been able to lead a frivolous and dissolute lifestyle as a *xiucai*, all thanks to making friends in high places. The costs for my gambling and whoring have all been paid out thanks to my possession of an official title. However, the newcomer county magistrate is a young *jinshi*[3] who assumes an air of self-importance and doesn't want to befriend scholars. I have left my calling card with him on several occasions, but never once have I been invited in for tea. This time I've asked Mr. Wang to recommend me as a master of ceremonies in the Confucian temple. By using the Confucian temple as a stepping stone, it's only a matter of time before I become a regular guest at the reception hall of government officials. Today is the day of the incense-burning ceremony, and I am waiting to provide my services. (WANG ZHONGXIANG *enters, wearing official attire and recites*) My round-collar robe is crimson like logwood; / my gauze hat has the color of eaglewood. / If I do not accompany officials to worship Confucius, / this attire will be forever folded and locked up at the bottom of my clothes basket. (ZHOU *greets* WANG *and says*) When we meet the county magistrate in a few moments, I hope that you will introduce me to him. (WANG) I certainly can do that.

Prelude in the Mode of *Zhonglü: Xingxiangzi* (Offering Incense)

(*A group of people acting as yamen runners*[4] *enter, playing drums, gongs, and horns. They are followed by a county official,* THE MAGISTRATE *sings*)
Leaving my books behind, and taking up the duties of my
    post to manage local affairs,
governing this busy entrepot is exhausting!
Its customs are extravagant,
retaining the florid conventions of the Sui,
I lament how difficult it is to
pacify its administration,
transform its local mores,
or reform its local customs.

(ZHOU GONGMENG *conducts the ritual ceremony and* THE MAGISTRATE *pays homage to the Confucius memorial tablet*) (WANG *and* THE MAGISTRATE *greet each other*) (ZHOU *acts very humble toward him*) (THE

MAGISTRATE *speaks*) How come there is only one master of ceremonies? (WANG) To be honest with you, chief, the local *xiucai* do not
read unless there is an examination. Now that the announcement of
the annual examination has been issued, everyone rushes to grab
hold of the Buddha's feet to pray for divine intervention in their
hour of need. This is the only one of them who is not afraid of the
examination, and that is why he came to provide this service. (THE
MAGISTRATE *smiles and sings*)

To the Passing Tune: *Zhuyunfei*
(Halting a Flying Cloud)

Who has ever seen an eligible girl, awaiting marriage,
procrastinate till her very wedding day to prepare her gown?
Even if she smears on some makeup to disguise her haste,
she will lack natural beauty.

(THE MAGISTRATE *speaks*) I will supervise the seasonal examination
in a few days. Those who are ranked at the top will receive a stipend
for lamp oil. (THE MAGISTRATE *sings*)

Huh! The carefree young maiden need not worry about
going hungry, only that she isn't ready.[5]
If he is both talented and virtuous,
Upright but in dire straits,
I would deliver his meals myself, and provide him with a
change of new clothes, too.

(THE MAGISTRATE *speaks to* WANG) Now that the metropolitan
examination is approaching, when are you going to the capital to
take it? (WANG) I am ashamed to mention this. My home is cold, my
salary insufficient to meet my needs for heating or cooking, and I

haven't been able to come up with the money for this long trip. This is why I have not left for the capital. (WANG *sings*)

> (*To the same tune as before*)
> Full of aspirations but with an empty belly,
> My heart desires to climb high into the sky but my feet
>   cannot find the ladder up.
> I am like Sima Xiangru exchanging his fur coat for wine,[6]
> and Su Qin still wearing his beat-up sable jacket.[7]

(WANG *speaks to* THE MAGISTRATE) I hope you, honorable magistrate, might provide me with some support. (WANG *sings*)

> Huh! Don't wait too long to flood the river,
> for the fish in its parched channel is desperate.
> If my thirst can be quenched by a few drops of your
>   beneficent showers,
> enabling me to ascend the clouds and ride them to the
>   palace exam;
> then at the celebratory banquet I will certainly remember
>   your thunderous cheers of support.

(THE MAGISTRATE *speaks*) I have one thing to ask for your opinion. (WANG) It has not yet been a month since your honor assumed your post here, but your virtuous influence has spread all across the surrounding areas. Everywhere people praise you, calling you the reincarnation of benevolent officials such as Zhao Xinchen from the Western Han dynasty and Du Shi from the Eastern Han dynasty.[8] (WANG *sings*)

> (*To the same tune as before*)
> Only when the rains are timely,

will children play happily;

locusts flee into neighboring states, and

in villages blooming with flowers, dogs do not snarl or howl.

(WANG *speaks*) I've composed a few eulogies praising your virtuous governance; I'd like to print copies and have them posted in the streets. I will also invite some friends and villagers to report your honest and excellent governance to your superiors. (WANG *sings*)

Huh! Since our ten thousand words of praise cannot all fit onto one stele,

we can only record your most outstanding achievements.

Knocking on palace doors and delivering eulogies,

we will request that you be given a top promotion.

(THE MAGISTRATE *speaks*) Since I've just barely arrived here, I've neglected many administrative tasks, and I'm not familiar with local customs and sentiments. What achievements do I have that are worthy of reporting? No need to do that! I shall now take my leave. (THE MAGISTRATE *sings*)

Stealing a moment's leisure from reading reports,

I sit casually on a school mat as if visiting a mountain retreat.

(WANG *sings*)

When a coldly indifferent official bids farewell to a warm-hearted, enthusiastic one,

as with ice and burning coals, they are totally incompatible.

(ZHOU *concludes this act,*[9] *bowing to* THE MAGISTRATE *and seeing him off*) (YUHUA *and her* MAID *are looking at them from the top of a tower*) (YUHUA'S MAID) Mistress, look! That *xiucai* is so good at bowing and scraping! (ZHOU *lifts his head and sees them, surprised*) (YUHUA) Liuchun, there is someone looking at us from downstairs. Let's go. (*They leave together*) (ZHOU) Marvelous, indeed marvelous! Isn't that the Moon Goddess or an angel from heaven? I would have missed her had I not overheard her sweet murmurs. (ZHOU *sings*)

> (*To the same tune as before*)
> One glance at her, and my soul has flown skyward,
> I've caught a glimpse of the Moon Goddess herself!
> Her melodic voice enchants my ears,
> her sweet scent bewitches my senses.

(ZHOU *speaks*)

If I weren't wearing my scholar's attire, how could she have known that I am a *xiucai*? In addition, I was bowing to the magistrate when she saw me, how honorable was that? (ZHOU *sings*)

> Huh! My scholar's cap makes a good matchmaker,
> my literati garb makes me a desirable husband.

(ZHOU *speaks*) I have heard that Cao Gechen has a daughter who has not been engaged to anyone yet. I was just about to send a marriage proposal to them, but I knew nothing of her appearance. Who would have known that she is a peerless beauty? This is indeed (ZHOU *sings again*)

> the Qiao daughter locked away in the Bronze Sparrow tower,
> whom would you marry other than Mr. Zhou?[10]

(ZHOU *speaks*) The only thing is, whom can I ask to be my go-between? (*He mutters to himself*) Oh, I have an idea. Mr. Cao graded Zhang Zhongyou as number one in the recent examination. He would be perfect, so I'll go to make my request immediately. An unparalleled beauty is difficult to find; / and a felicitous event cannot be delayed. (ZHOU *exits*)

SCENE 14

~~~~~~~~~~~~~~~~~~~~~~~~~~~~~~~~

A REQUEST FOR MATCHMAKING

Passing Tune in the Mode of *Zhonglü: Lülüjin*
(Strand After Strand of Gold)

(ZHANG ZHONGYOU *enters and sings*)
Residing in a villa,
shirking mundane duties;
having just bought wine,
I am enjoying it over "Encountering Sorrow."[1]
With no one to dissect the disputed passages with me,
I long for a likeminded friend. (*Someone makes dog barking
sounds from off stage*)

Now a dog is barking its greeting in the direction of the
wooded grove;
It must be that a guest has arrived, and indeed,
Someone has come for a visit.

(ZHANG *speaks*) I am Zhang Zhongyou. In order to escape the din of
the city, I sit alone at this villa beside the Sui dike. Just now I heard
barking from outside. I wonder who is paying me a visit?

(*To the same tune as before*)

(FAN SHI *enters and sings*)

The destiny of a scholar is far too lofty.

Having just tasted a delicious fish,

I am again offered bear's paw.[2]

Having tasted all of the wines of romance,

now I only worry about overindulgence.

Since my star of love rises again and will not let me

escape,

I am forced to find a matchmaker,

a matchmaker I must find.

(FAN SHI *greets* ZHANG) (ZHANG *speaks*) Cousin-in-law, you are full of smiles, why are you in such a good mood? (FAN SHI) I have come to ask for your help with some felicitous business, and I have no time for small talk. I need to tell you about it right away. (*Barking is heard again off stage*)

(*To the same tune as before*)

(ZHOU GONGMENG *enters in a hurry and sings*)

Destined for love,

a dazzling beauty crossed my path.

My amorous desires are awakened,

my spirits sky high.

Hastily taking off my scholar's cap,

changing out of my plain blue robe

with no time to remove my black boots,

I fly off to see the matchmaker; indeed,

a matchmaker I must see.

(ZHOU *greets* FAN SHI *and* ZHANG) (ZHOU *says*) Ah, my good friend Fan is here already. (ZHANG) My cousin-in-law was just about to tell me about some good tidings. I am all ears. (FAN SHI) It's rather like the first half of a new play; the second half is waiting for my cousin-in-law to complete. (ZHOU) Please tell us immediately! Even if I'm not qualified to play the male or female lead in this play, I could still help out in the role of a villain or a clown.

To the Tune of *Zhumating* (Stop the Horse and Listen)

(FAN SHI *sings*)
This may sound laughable, but
I'll tell you a tale about a beautiful girl from the Cao family.
She recently left her old home,
going far away aboard a small watercraft.
At Rain-Flower Nunnery, she and my wife met by chance, and
discovered that they are kindred spirits who share similar literary interests.
Unwilling to be apart in life or in death,
they want to form a lifelong alliance.

(ZHOU *turns his back to* FAN SHI *and* ZHANG) (ZHOU *speaks*) This sounds like it might just fit in with my own plans. (ZHANG) Are you talking about the daughter of Mr. Cao Gechen? (FAN SHI) Yes, that is she. (ZHOU *turns away from the other two*) Wonderful! Now I can enlist an additional matchmaker. (FAN SHI) When Miss Cao first arrived, she resided at the Rain-Flower Nunnery. When my wife went to the temple to worship the Buddha, she suddenly noticed a waft of fragrance. She asked the old nun Jingguan how a young lady's perfumed aroma had entered these clerical precincts. Jingguan replied: "There is a Miss Cao here." She then asked Miss Cao to come out and meet my wife. The two of them immediately hit it off. That busybody Jingguan then proposed that the two ladies compose poems using "The Scent of Beauty" as their topic. (ZHANG) It is indeed a novel theme. My cousin is certainly capable of composing poems in front of guests, but Miss Cao might not be able to improvise something on the spot. (FAN SHI) You'd never guess! With Miss Cao, although your cousin was not exactly like "a small magician in the presence of a great one,"[3] nevertheless in her she met a formidable opponent. (FAN SHI *takes out the poems*) Look here! The first one was written by your cousin, the middle one is that of Miss Cao, and the last two are my matching verses. (ZHANG *reads the poems and comments*) Indeed, these two poems are equally good. Mr. Cao's daughter is certainly very talented. (ZHOU *reads the poems, nods his head, and loudly praises*) What prodigious talent! (ZHANG) I'm guessing that they enjoyed writing poems together so much that they decided to form a lifelong friendship. (FAN SHI) That's not all! Just after they completed the poems, Miss Cao was forced to move out from the nunnery. No sooner had they happily met than sadly they had to part ways, and both burst into tears. Fortunately, again Jingguan came up with an idea and arranged for the two of them to meet again in the tenth month. If on the first time they were still well-behaved, at their second meeting they engaged in quite a bit of naughtiness. (ZHOU) What sort of naughtiness? (FAN SHI) They wanted to form a lifelong alliance. (ZHOU) Alliances are perfectly acceptable. (FAN SHI) Their alliance is not like the usual one that we men form. We only pledge an alliance for this lifetime, but they wanted to be together in the next life; we only want to become brothers, but they wanted to be bound together as husband and wife. (ZHOU) Even if they wanted to be a couple, they would have to wait for the next life anyway. (FAN SHI) How could they bear to wait that long?! They went into my study and took out my cap and robe. My wife dressed as the groom, and Miss Cao took the role of the bride. One of the naughty maids acted as the master of ceremonies, and the two of them went so far as to recite wedding vows! (ZHANG *and* ZHOU *laugh loudly*) That is indeed quite naughty!

> (*To the same tune as before*)
> (FAN SHI *sings*)
> Turning a trickle of a joke into a tidal wave,
> telling this story makes my spirits surge.
> It is indeed a play acted out by young ladies,
> bizarre tales from overseas, like
> Wang Wei's painting of plantains in snow.[4]

(ZHOU *speaks*) Mr. Fan,

> (ZHOU *sings*)
> although the two of them are similarly enchanting,
> It is your wife who has the advantage.

(ZHOU *speaks*) It is fortunate that Miss Cao has not been engaged yet. Otherwise, her man would be jealous of your wife. (ZHOU *sings*)

> Although their idea for this sprang out of their boredom,
> It is as if they were composing a romantic tale on their own
> "[Rain-] flower [Cloud-]paper."

(ZHOU *speaks*) Mr. Fan, is your play over? (FAN SHI) Not yet. (ZHOU) Please hurry up! I want to get up on the stage with them, too. (FAN SHI) In the beginning they were just pretending, but later on they wanted to make it all come true. Miss Cao said to my wife, "A chaste woman would never marry a second time; I have recited my wedding vows with you today, so how could I exchange the nuptial goblet with anyone else?" My wife joked, "Why don't you also marry my husband? Although nominally you and I will be ranked as first and second wives, in actuality we will be sisters. In fact, although you and I are sisters in name, we will be de facto 'husband and wife.' How about that?" Who could have expected that Miss Cao took this suggestion seriously and happily accepted it? (ZHOU *is startled*) What? She accepted it?! (ZHANG) This is just a joke between two young ladies. Cousin-in-law said it was a "play" and we should treat it as such. How come you're taking it seriously? (ZHOU laughs) All right, that sounds sensible to me. (FAN SHI) My dear cousin-in-law: (FAN SHI *sings*)

> (*To the same tune as before*)
> You shouldn't treat this as an exaggerated gest,
> the most amazing stories often verge on the absurd.

(FAN SHI *speaks*) My wife also said that this was a joke and could not be taken at face value. Miss Cao then swore a solemn oath in front of the Buddha, and urged my wife to hurry up and find someone to entrust with this marriage proposal. She is (FAN SHI *sings*)

> like a fish that awaits water,
> a horse that needs a saddle, or
> the Weaver Girl who waits for magpies to build a bridge.[5]

(FAN SHI *speaks*) Miss Cao also worried that if we told her father that she would be a concubine, he would definitely disapprove. Therefore, she suggested that we tell the matchmaker that (FAN SHI *sings*)

> firewood added to the fire later will end up on top,
> and freshly deposited sand doesn't envy the grains that
> washed ashore before it.

Let's fool her father into permitting them to tie the knot,
then the late-coming small star will move into a minor
    constellation.

(ZHOU *turns his back to the other two men and says*) What Mr. Fan just said
jeopardizes my plan. Let me see whom he will ask to be the matchmaker? (FAN SHI) My wife said that cousin-in-law and Mr. Cao are
literary friends; this is why I came to ask you to be our matchmaker.
(ZHOU) In that case, Mr. Zhang is obliged to accept!

> (*To the same tune as before*)
> (ZHANG *sings*)
> You have recommended me for this position in vain.
> How could I possibly sail against the current?

(ZHANG *speaks*) This marriage proposal departs completely from the
norm; how could I possibly approach Mr. Cao about it? (ZHANG
sings)

> How can I come up with the opening lines of an essay
>   topic like this one?
> I'll need to reinvent the usual conventions,
> It's going to be hard to copy from my previous
>   examination essays.

(FAN SHI *speaks*) You just tell it like I told you, and I am sure that
Mr. Cao will give his approval.

> (ZHANG *sings*)
> Although you have devised a most clever plan,
> I fear that Mr. Cao will not step into this trap.

(FAN SHI) This has all been devised by your cousin; it has nothing to do with me. If you do not accept our request, you ought to talk to her yourself. It's time for me to go. (ZHANG) This is a request that I cannot refuse. It's just that if Mr. Cao does not approve, don't blame me for not being a skillful matchmaker. (FAN SHI) I will then wait to hear the good news from you.

> (ZHANG *sings*)
> There's no guarantee that good things can be brought to fruition,
> Don't blame the messenger if the message is delayed.
> For this matchmaking, finding the right words is a tall order.
> I worry that such an unconventional proposal will arouse suspicion.

> (FAN SHI *sings*)
> I had no intention to seek such a fortuitous union,
> but luck has been thrust onto me when I least expected it.

(ZHOU *concludes this act, saying*) What is happening? Today I came to seek out Mr. Zhang to be my matchmaker. Who would have thought that I would run straight into this highway robber?! The two of them are close relatives and good friends. How can there be any way that Zhang Zhongyou would decline Fan Shi and act as a go-between for me instead? It is best that I not tell them of my plans. But how will I be able to overcome my indignation? (ZHOU *contemplates*) I have an idea: Early tomorrow I will pay a visit to Cao Gechen and casually drop some remarks that will negatively predispose him toward Fan, so that he rejects their proposal. I then will ask Mr. Wang to be my matchmaker, and I bet it will work like a charm. (ZHOU *sings*)

Excellent plan! Excellent plan!

(*To the same tune as before*)
(ZHOU *sings again*)
Old Fan, I laugh at you for overreaching:
Just like Cao Cao who vainly desired the two Qiao sisters,[6]
I'm afraid that your love-stars are misaligned,
Your horoscopes are in conflict, and
Your ships will be burned up at Red Cliff, all for naught.
I'll make sure that your romantic adventure turns to disaster,
    and
Your love is disrupted, without your even knowing why.
At that time you will see me leisurely row up,
Sailing smoothly with a gust of east wind at my back,
Quickly wrapping up my victory,[7]
And winning the lady without losing even a single soldier!

SCENE 15

A BRUSH WITH INDIGNATION

Prelude in the Mode of *Shuangdiao: Yejinmen*
(Paying a Visit to Golden Gate)

(CAO GECHEN *enters with his servant and sings*)
A parent's "debt" to his children weighs me down
    wherever I go.
How is it that even a thousand miles from home,
I'm still carrying this heavy load of worry?

(CAO *speaks*) I am Cao Gechen, now a guest at Yangzhou, waiting for Mr. Wang to join me to travel up north together. Who would have known that he has been delayed by his responsibility to supervise the examination and cannot leave right away? Because I brought my daughter along on this trip, I cannot leave even half a step from her side. I now sit cooped up in this desolate abode, with nothing to pass the time. Yesterday, Zhang Zhongyou gave me a couple of his essays to read. Why don't I write some comments on them for him? (CAO *reads the essays*) Excellent writing! Excellent writing! The refined expressions are too many to count; I only regret that I didn't find these remarkable pieces earlier! (CAO *circles the expressions he considers especially good*)

To the Tune of *Hudaolian* (Song of the Washerwoman)

(ZHOU GONGMENG *enters with an extra and sings*)
With my name card I visit these desolate quarters,
my tongue razor-sharp like Su Qin and Zhang Yi.[1]
In order to succeed I must first destroy my competitor;
one stone kills two birds,
one man's fortune is another's disaster.

(CAO'S SERVANT *reports* ZHOU'S *arrival*) (CAO GECHEN *meets* ZHOU)
(ZHOU *speaks*) I have been preoccupied by sundry duties recently;
please forgive my delay in calling. (CAO GECHEN) I have not paid a
visit to you yet, and now I trouble you to come to see me first.
(ZHOU) Sir, what is that book on your desk that you are reading?
And why have you drawn so many red circles on it?[2] (CAO) These are
Zhang Zhongyou's recent writings. (ZHOU) You have a good eye for
literary talent. His writings are indeed noteworthy. (CAO) He is both
talented and learned. I predict that it won't be long till he passes the
examinations with high marks.

To the Passing Tune: *Suonanzhi* (Locking South Bough)

(ZHOU *sings*)
Learned and talented he certainly is, and deserving of
being ranked at the very top,
if it's essays we're speaking about.

(ZHOU *speaks*) He would have passed the highest level of the civil-
service examination a long time ago, if only he hadn't been somewhat negligent in regulating his conduct. I'm afraid he may have
to wait somewhat longer. (ZHOU *sings*)

He lacks virtuous deeds,
and still awaits the nod from red-robed officials.[3]

(CAO *speaks*) Oh, so it turns out that Zhang Zhongyou has plenty of talent but is short on virtuous conduct. In that case, could you give me a few examples of his misdeeds?

(ZHOU *sings*)
Although one should avoid revealing a friend's shortcomings,
How could I cover up for him, in the face of an upright
    man like you?

(ZHOU *speaks*) Since Zhang Zhongyou sent you his recent writings, I will only talk about his recent deeds. He has a friend named Fan Jiefu who studies at the Rain-Flower Nunnery. A few days ago, a young lady went to the nunnery to burn incense and while there, composed a poem that she chanted out loud. Fan just happened to hear it from behind a curtain and composed a poem using the same rhyme words, intending to flirt with the young mistress. That young lady seems to have ignored his flirtation, but being rather dissolute, Fan Jiefu took her silence as an invitation to something further. He went to discuss the matter with Zhang Zhongyou, to hatch a plan to commit some ungodly act. If Zhang Zhongyou were an upright person, he should have admonished his friend to refrain from this kind of behavior. But to the contrary, Zhang actually helped a tyrant to victimize his subjects!![4] (CAO *asks*) What do you mean by that? (ZHOU *responds*) Zhang gladly volunteered to act as a go-between, pretending to propose to the young lady that she marry Fan Jiefu as his principal wife, but in reality bringing her in as his concubine. Sir, just judging from this one instance, would you say that this is the behavior of someone with upright intentions? (CAO *is startled and asks*) What is the surname of the young lady? (ZHOU *responds*) He only bragged to me about this, and did not tell me the name of the young lady. (CAO *asks*) Do you remember the poems that were chanted? (ZHOU) I only remember two lines from each of the poems. The young lady's lines are: "From behind the curtain I thought the scent comes from plum blossoms, / But little did I know, it comes from poems about snow." And Fan Jiefu's two lines are: "If like Xun Yu, she sits with me for three days, / It's no wonder that my feelings are captive to her scent." (CAO *recites the lines silently and then speaks*) Zhang turns out to be such a contemptible fellow! If you hadn't told me, I would have been deceived by his beguiling writing. (ZHOU) Since you asked me, sir, as your junior I could only tell you the truth. However, when Zhang comes to see you, please don't tell him that I have spoken of his faults. I take my leave now. (ZHOU *gets up and recites to the audience*) An intentional remark disguised as a slip of the tongue; / A few words of slander can amount to a thousand-word indictment. (ZHOU *exits with the extra*). (CAO *speaks*) If the matter is already on one's mind, words then enter one's ears easily. What he just said is very suspicious. Does he mean that my daughter did something immoral in the Rain-Flower Nunnery? (CAO *mutters to himself*) I imagine that many female worshipers come and go at the nunnery, and my daughter certainly was not the only woman burning incense there. I need not be overly concerned. Thankfully I took precautions and moved out of the nunnery! If we had stayed there, in proximity to that beastly Fan Jiefu, what good could have come out of it? Let me now finish writing my comments on Zhang Zhongyou's essays, then ponder this matter further. (CAO *reads* ZHANG'S *essay and says*) How strange! It is the same essay, yet how come every word in the first half was noteworthy, but the second half doesn't contain even a single line to praise?! (CAO *sings*)

> (*To the same tune as before*)
> A fine steed at first glimpse,
> a worthless nag upon careful inspection,
> such a stark difference, how perplexing!

(CAO *speaks*) Ah, it seems that I had no preconceptions about the writer before and was able to judge the essays objectively, and hence was able to find its merits. But now that the writer's reputation has been ruined and I am no longer impartial, I have allowed his beauty to turn into unsightliness. A Confucian gentleman should not judge words according to who has uttered them. I ought to evaluate these essays objectively and add more marks. (CAO *sings*)

> In punctuating the essay, my hands are lazy,
> in circling words for emphasis, my brush grows heavy.

(CAO *speaks*) Thinking this over, it's hard to believe that Zhou Gongmeng spoke the whole truth. How do I know that he isn't motivated by jealousy or rancor? (CAO *sings*)

> If Zhou indeed opens his mouth to slander, and plots
> revenge, then
> I would be someone who credulously listens to one
> palace lady,
> badmouthing another.

To the Tune of *Hudaolian* (Song of the Washerwoman)

(ZHANG ZHONGYOU, *dressed formally, enters with his
servant who holds a red card and sings*)

> At my cousin's behest,
> I carry out this difficult task.
> How will I tie these two hills together in a conjugal
> knot?
> Even if the dragon is drowsy,
> stealing the pearl from his embrace will not be easy![5]

(CAO'S SERVANT *gestures for* ZHANG *to come in*) (CAO *sees the red card and speaks to the audience*) Why suddenly a red-card visit?[6] There must be a reason for this. (CAO *greets* ZHANG) Mr. Zhang, today you are all dressed up and carrying a red card. Could you be bringing news of something to celebrate? (ZHANG) Today I make this special visit for ... (CAO *interrupts*) Since we know each other well, why not tell me directly what is on your mind instead of fumbling around searching for the right words? (ZHANG *responds*) I have come to propose a match for your daughter. (CAO *is startled*) Oh, I see. What family is the young man from? (ZHANG) Please let me explain: (ZHANG *sings*)

To the Tune of *Suonanzhi* (Locking South Bough)

> A descendant of Fan Zhongyan,[7]
> this suitor comes from a family of noblemen;
> with the sobriquet Jiefu, he is a talented scholar in this town.

(CAO *turns his back to* ZHANG *and says*) This is the same person Zhou just mentioned. (CAO *turns to* ZHANG) How old is the young gentleman?

> (ZHANG *sings*)
> Distinguished at twenty like Ruan Xiaoxu,[8]
> he is as handsome as Wei Jie.[9]

(CAO *asks*) If he is from a gentry family, why has he not thought about marriage until now, when he is already twenty years old? (ZHANG *responds*) He has already married once. It is just that (ZHANG *sings*)

> his lady is obtuse and lacks domestic talents, and for this
> reason,
> he has reserved the position of principal wife, to await a
> wiser candidate.

(CAO *becomes angry and says*) Although I am not considered talented and successful, I am still a *juren* who has passed the provincial level examination. Do you think that I would agree to make my daughter someone's concubine? (ZHANG) How could we dare to make her a *concubine*? Mr. Fan married my cousin in his first marriage. Now my cousin is willing to be the secondary wife and asks your daughter to take charge of the household. (CAO) This is absurd! Demoting a first wife to the status of concubine without a good reason, Mr. Fan is lacking in moral rectitude; tolerating Fan's behavior and making your cousin a concubine, you are guilty of betraying your conscience as well. Now I see that the two of you are not far apart in your degeneracy! (ZHANG) There is a reason behind this. (CAO) What reason? (ZHANG) Your daughter . . . (CAO *panics*) What about my daughter? (ZHANG) Your daughter met my cousin at the Rain-Flower Nunnery and became her dear friend through an exchange of poems. They started by swearing an oath of sisterhood, and then talked about joining together through a marriage. This is the reason why I have dared to approach you about this. (CAO *becomes furious and stands up*) Nonsense! This is obviously a devious scheme of yours, intended to turn a daughter of a good family into Fan's concubine! He'll have to try this plot on someone else. How dare he try to deceive me like this! (CAO *sings*)

> (*To the same tune as before*)
> Your words are ridiculous,
> your intentions are devious;
> your heart is not in the right place, and
> it is a pity that you're talented for naught.

(CAO *speaks*) You think that I am an old *juren* with no future? (CAO *sings*)

Even if I am

getting on in years,

my ambitions are a lot bigger than yours!

(ZHANG *speaks*) How could I dare to disrespect you! (CAO) On account of your good writing I treat you with courtesy, but you've taken advantage of me to act with total disregard for everyone! I refuse to see you ever again! (ZHANG) Gentlemen do not use abusive words when they end friendships. Why such outrage? (CAO) Get out of here, you little beast! (CAO *sings*)

You are a wolf in sheep's clothing,

we belong to different species of men! I call to my servant,

throw out this crazy lad, and

shut the door behind him!

(CAO'S SERVANT *speaks*) Mr. Zhang, please leave! (ZHANG) I will go on my own. Do you think I want to stay here any longer, after this? (ZHANG *leaves*) (CAO'S SERVANT *drives away* ZHANG'S SERVANT) (ZHANG) What is this? As the saying goes, "A family with an unwed daughter receives hundreds of marriage proposals." It is my right to deliver a marriage proposal, just as it is your right to accept or reject it. What's the need for such hostility, such condescension? (ZHANG'S SERVANT) It's not just you, master, even I felt angry. Standing outside his door, we should return his insults in kind before we leave for home. (ZHANG) Now that I think it over, I've realized that it's really my fault, after all. If we have it out with Mr. Cao and engage in a serious altercation, people will say that we are in the wrong. Let's swallow this insult and go back. Matchmaking has always been a difficult job; not to mention that this kind of match is of unprecedented difficulty. (ZHANG'S SERVANT *follows* ZHANG *as he exits*) (CAO) Judging from what just happened, it seems that what Mr. Zhou told me is all true. My daughter must have done something unseemly. I will have to interrogate her maid Liuchun. (CAO *starts to call* JIANYUN'S MAID *but stops*) I'd better think carefully before I act, so I'll stop here for now. Once I begin the inquiry, I'm going to have to get to the bottom of it. As a guest here, I must do things differently from back at home. If Mr. Wang hears about this, even a rumor can turn into a fact; then, what good would come out of this? Thinking back on what has happened, when we first stayed at the nunnery, I was with my daughter most of the time. Although she went back there alone once after we had moved out, she returned not long after in the same sedan. In ruminating over the words in her poem, such as "penetrating the curtain" and "perhaps welcomes," it seems that even if the intention was there, it wasn't carried out in action. Now I'd better pretend not to know anything and take my leave at the earliest convenience. It's just that I can't bear to let Fan Jiefu, that little beast, off so easily. (CAO *thinks a while*) All right, I have an idea. Now that it's time for the annual examination at the school, I could ask Mr. Wang to rank him as someone of "bad behavior," strip him of his scholar's rank and ruin his future. There's nothing wrong with venting my anger this way. (CAO *sings*)

> Out of water, a dragon is humiliated;
> a bee can exact some small revenge with its sting.
> Although this may not be how a gentleman normally acts,
> it should be expected of a hero with mettle.

SCENE 16

DOLEFUL EXPECTATIONS

Passing Tune in the Mode of *Shuangdiao: Shanpoyang*
(Sheep on the Slope)

(JIANYUN *enters and sings*)
Throughout this endless night
plunged into inauspicious dreams;
in the morning the din of a flock of magpies disturbs my
languor, but
no news of victory reaches my expectant ears, and
no battle pennants appear before my anxiously searching
eyes.

(JIANYUN *speaks*) Yesterday I asked my cousin to send a marriage proposal to the Caos, but I have yet to hear back. This morning I sent
my husband to inquire about it from my cousin, but he also has not
returned. This quite worries me! Let me go downstairs to take a
brief stroll. (JIANYUN *sings*)

Trying to relieve my solitude,
I pace back and forth, waiting for news,
Trampling directly over the wet moss,
without bothering to seek a drier path.

(JIANYUN *speaks*) Not a living soul in sight! (JIANYUN *sings*)

> There are only shadows of bamboo and spirits of flowers,
> all replying to me with deceptions.
> Unquenchable is this lovesick heart, burnt to a crisp;
> and hard to hail is
> the bearer of good news, still so far from here!

> (*To the same tune as before*)
> (FAN SHI *enters and sings*)
> Hot and sweaty,
> I make haste without a moment's rest;
> cold and lonely,
> I'm still waiting for good news to come my way.
> Rambling on and on,
> the old man's sap never runs dry.
> Languorous and lethargic,
> the matchmaker makes no effort to understand our
>   feelings.

(FAN SHI *meets* JIANYUN) (JIANYUN *speaks*) You are back, my dear.
How did the proposal go? How come you were gone for such a long
time? (FAN SHI) Your cousin went out to deliver the marriage
proposal but has yet to return. I happened to pass by a fortune-
teller's house, and asked him to divine the future of this marriage.
That is why I am late. (JIANYUN) What did the divination predict
for this marriage?

> (FAN SHI *sings*)
> The marriage is auspicious, but
> its success is riddled with setbacks;
> a dark villain will interfere,

but in the end the red-thread tightly binds us together.[1]
Rereading and pondering this prognostication, it's still
   unclear where we will encounter this villain;
but set your mind at ease, please,
it won't be long till good tidings arrive.

To the Tune of *Bushilu* (Not the Way)

(ZHANG ZHONGYOU *enters in haste and sings*)
I've run into my nemesis, a man so vile that
he sought to provoke my ire for no good reason.

(JIANYUN, *seeing* ZHANG, *is elated and says*) Cousin is back!

   (ZHANG *greets her by clasping his hands together and sings*)
   All thanks to you, cousin,
     arguing on your behalf has brought me no end of trouble.

(JIANYUN *speaks*) So, esteemed matchmaker, how did it go? (ZHANG *sits
tongue-tied, refusing to answer*) (FAN SHI) He seems a little drunk;
I reckon that the marriage is all settled.

   (ZHANG *sings*) Stop your banter!
   I am so white with rage,
     that ice has covered me, an "iceman," from head to toe;[2]
   This matchmaker was sent on a fishing expedition, all for
     nothing!

(FAN SHI *and* JIANYUN *speak*) Regardless of whether or not they
accept the marriage proposal, they should explain the reasons for
their decision. Why were they so hard on you? (ZHANG *sings
again*)

> Please don't be annoyed, but
>
> if you want to hear good news,
>
> I am afraid that you are going to be utterly disappointed.

(ZHANG *speaks*) Turning down the proposal is one thing; but there was no reason for Mr. Cao to humiliate me so. (FAN SHI *and* JIANYUN *are both startled*) What happened? (ZHANG) If I tell you all of the details, both of you will be infuriated, so I will just give you a summary. I do not know why, but it seems that Mr. Cao knew everything already. As soon as I mentioned his daughter, he suddenly reddened. Just as the name "Fan Jiefu" left my mouth, his face quickly darkened. And when I said that my cousin was willing to be a concubine and cede the title of principal wife to his daughter, he became visibly agitated, saying that I had conspired with Fan Shi to trick his daughter into becoming a concubine. At first, we were still sitting and conversing normally, but as time went on, we stood up and locked horns. At first Mr. Cao only mocked me indirectly, but he eventually subjected me to a harsh scolding. First, he was like the Emperor Gaozu of Han who only cursed scholars, but then he turned into the First Emperor of Qin who threw his guests out of the palace.[3] Can you imagine the humiliation I went through? (JIANYUN *sits down, dejected*) (FAN SHI *turns his back to her and* ZHANG) Does this mean that this fine marriage proposal will turn into a pipe dream? I will have to ask my lady to come up with another plan. I have an idea: provoking someone into action often works better than asking nicely. Let me try some reverse psychology on her, and maybe that will inspire her to hatch a good idea. (FAN SHI *turns to* JIANYUN) My dear, I told you before that this would not work out. But you felt so confident that this marriage was in the bag and were determined to send out a matchmaker. Now look at what such good matchmaking and such a good proposal have brought us! I have yet to smell even a tiny bit of Miss Cao's scent, but my matchmaker has already bagged a belly full of resentment. (FAN SHI *sings*)

To the Tune of *Zaojiaoer* (Little Black Table)[4]

> I left you, a standout among womenfolk, alone to work
> your talents,
> but in the end, you came up short, just as this man—I—
> fully expected.
> Now that the sun has risen high above our heads,
> I chide you for still not awakening from your "Dream of
> the Southern Bough".[5]
> Don't even think about
> composing new poems,
> rekindling old friendships,
> becoming a married couple,
> addressing each other as sisters, or
> staying together till your hair turns gray.
> (FAN SHI *points to* ZHANG)
> You'd best stop trying to fill in names on the roster of
> marital destiny;
> (FAN *then points to* JIANYUN)
> and you should scratch out the debts listed in your love accounts;
> from now on, I will keep my mouth shut tight like a
> corked bottle, to avoid incurring the ridicule of others!

(ZHANG *speaks*) Now that I think about it, could it be that Miss Cao regretted her rashness, and told her father that she worried you would come and pester her until she married you? Perhaps she and her father conspired to fabricate this situation. If not, then why was

he already awaiting my arrival with such an angry mien? (ZHANG
sings)

> (*To the same tune as before*)
>
> Even if an emperor jokes around while knighting his
>   subject,
>
> he should still follow through by honoring him as a pillar
>   of state.[6]
>
> It's not like I knocked over a goblet that released an angry
>   deluge,[7]
>
> It looks more like Mr. Cao laid a trap, holding onto his
>   territory regardless of what was promised!
>
> What a waste of my time and energy to:
>
> put on my best suit,
>
> carry a fancy red card;
>
> deliver polite words,
>
> bow down deeply, and
>
> exhaust my efforts in humble toil.
>
> (ZHANG, *pointing to* JIANYUN)
>
> This is the mandate you produced to engage in
>   matchmaking,
>
> (*Pointing to* FAN SHI) this is the admonition given by your
>   instructor, Mr. Cao.
>
> (*Pointing to himself*)
>
> And this is all thanks to an unlucky star that just happened
>   to cross my path!

> (*To the same tune as before*)
>
> (JIANYUN *sings*)
>
> Our plan stymied—
>
> how hard it is to overcome this sorrow! a sworn promise
>   betrayed—

How can scorn be avoided?

I must find a fool-proof way of staying together,

I refuse to believe that our ties are either ephemeral or
tenuous.

(JIANYUN *speaks to* FAN SHI) According to you, we should just give up
the whole thing, right? (FAN SHI) I'm afraid we have no choice.
(JIANYUN) I cannot accept: (JIANYUN *sings*)

breaking the promise cast in stone,

going back on our solemn pledge, as deep as the sea,

separating couples meant to stay together for life,

parting a pair of lovebirds one from the other,

saying goodbye, for real.

(JIANYUN *speaks*) Although Miss Cao's father is stubborn, I am certain
that she will not break her promise. Unless both she and I die, we
will find a way to be together.

(JIANYUN *sings, pointing to* ZHANG)

Don't be frustrated, you—the matchmaker;

(*Pointing to* FAN SHI)

don't be anxious, you—the future groom;

as long as she and I, two strings of the same lute, remain
alive,

one day or another, we will come back together in blissful
harmony.

(ZHANG *speaks to* JIANYUN) I am also quite angry at that old curmud-
geon Cao. If you can find a way to turn his daughter into your husband's concubine, I will have had my revenge. I am just afraid that
you may not be capable of such tricks. (FAN SHI *speaks to* JIANYUN)

The prognostication says "misfortune followed by auspiciousness." I will wait and see what you do next. (JIANYUN) Let me write a letter to Miss Cao and ask Jingguan the nun to deliver it. We will figure out another way to deal with this. (ZHANG *sings*)

Weisheng (Closing Tune)

I am afraid that carving a mark on a drifting boat to locate
  a sword dropped overboard—this is a recipe for
  failure.[8]

(FAN SHI *sings*)

The pearls lying on this seafloor depend on you to bring
  them up.

(JIANYUN *sings*)

Mark my words—the day will come when
both sword and pearls are restored!

SCENE 17

<hr>

LEAVING IN A HURRY

(THE BOATMAN, *played by the clown, enters and sings*) Out of ten boatmen nine are married; baby boys and girls cry everywhere on deck.
The boatman's wife never gives him a day off; working together they
create a picture of a hundred sons.[1] I am the captain of the boat
heading toward the capital. Yesterday, a Mr. Cao hired my boat to
take him to the capital for the examination, dropping his family off
in Shandong on the way. I now see a sedan chair coming from afar;
I shall prepare the ramp for them. (CAO GECHEN *enters with his* SER-
VANT, *his daughter* YUHUA, *and* YUHUA'S MAID)

To the Tune of *Yexingchuan* (Sailing by Night)

(CAO *sings*)
Carrying newfound worries,
I travel again to a new place.
Although it's for only "half a son," the mere daughter that
  she is,
I move our abode three times, as Mencius' mother
  once did.[2]
(YUHUA *sings*)
A sudden downpour has destroyed the flowers,

and a fierce wind scatters catkins.
I have no way to reverse Heaven's will.

(*They embark onto the boat*) [*Langtaosha* (*Waves Washing the Sand*)] (CAO
recites) With a thousand miles to go, thrice changing boats, / the
capital is still a long way off. / With my purse growing lighter, / we'll
have to stick to the bare essentials on this leg of our journey. (YUHUA
turns her back to CAO) Poplars and willows crowd along the Sui dike; /
but who breaks off a branch to bid me farewell?³ / I secretly shed
my tears into the waters of Yangzhou; / although my heart remains
at the Four and Twenty Bridge, it is not for a mere friendship.⁴ (THE
BOATMAN) Mister, let's set sail. (CAO) Just a moment. I want to
wait for Mr. Wang to come over from the school to say goodbye.

To the Tune of *Xiaoshunge* (A Filial Song)

(WANG ZHONGXIANG *enters and sings*)
You promised me
we would travel together.
How can you leave without me?

(CAO'S SERVANT *announces* WANG'S *arrival*) (YUHUA *and* YUHUA'S
MAID *exit*) (WANG *gets on the boat and greets* CAO)
(WANG *speaks*) Brother Cao, you agreed to travel to the capital with me,
so why are you hurrying off now? (CAO) Since the local examinations here have just begun, it may be difficult for you to predict
when you can get away. I want to spend a few days with my brother-
in-law at his official residence in Shandong; therefore, I will be
waiting for you there. (WANG) That is fine. I have come to see you
off, but I also want to propose a marriage for your daughter. I am
glad that you have not departed yet. (WANG *sings*)

Not only did I come to bid you farewell on your long journey,

> I also come to facilitate a heaven-made match. How
> fortuitous!

(CAO *speaks*) I am in a hurry to leave; this is not the time to talk about marriage! (WANG) I only ask for a nod of approval. We can settle the wedding date another time. (CAO) Who is the one proposing? (WANG) It is my student Zhou Gongmeng. (CAO) Judging from the way this young man speaks, he seems to be a sincere gentleman. What about his literary talent? (WANG) His writing skills are also excellent. (WANG *sings*)

> His virtues are on par with Yan Yuan,[5]
> His literary talent can compare to Cao Zhi.[6]
> The two of you are pure and untainted, like jade and ice;
> I predict that you will appreciate each other very much!

(CAO *speaks*) I only have one daughter, and I will not marry her to a man without official status. If this young man aspires to rise to office, let's wait until he passes the higher level of the examinations; then I will consider his proposal. How about that? (WANG) All right, I will comply with your wish. (CAO) Now that the emperor's edict regarding civil affairs has been issued, there are certain to be both promotions and demotions. Have you decided on the rankings for behavior of the students under your supervision? (WANG) The "best behaved" candidate is Zhou Gongmeng. I have not chosen anyone to be the "worst behaved" yet. (CAO) In that case, I have found one for you. (CAO *sings*)

> (*To the same tune as before*)
> Sounding the zither,

taking up the instrument,
I have heard that one should attack the immoral by
playing the drums.[7]

(WANG *speaks*) What is the name of this scholar? (CAO) His style name
is Fan Jiefu. (WANG) Oh, this person has not called on me yet, which
I find a bit offensive. It's just that I haven't seen any proof of his evil-
doing. For what reason should I mark him down? (CAO) You need
only write "whoring and drinking" and "repeatedly appearing in
courts of law." That will be enough. (CAO *sings*)

No need to praise or criticize at length;
if you model your words on the style of the "Spring and
Autumn Annals,"[8]
right and wrong will be clear as day.

(CAO *speaks*) If you do not believe me, just ask Zhou Gongmeng
about him.

(CAO *sings again*) If you light a rhinoceros-horn flare,
it will illuminate all sorts of things hidden in deep, dark
recesses;[9]
chase out the monsters down there, and you will
drain the swamp as you rise up the ranks.

(WANG *speaks*) What you have heard about Fan Jiefu must be true.
There is no need for further investigation; I will go ahead and
demote him to the "worst behaved." I now say goodbye to you. I see
my guest off, on unsteady feet, from the western suburbs; I sing for
him at Yang Pass, in vain, not having brought any wine.[10] (CAO)
Please do not resent my leaving you behind halfway through our
journey; These migrating geese will eventually line up again further

along their way. (WANG *exits*) (YUHUA *and her* YUHUA'S MAID *enter*)
(CAO) Let's set sail! (THE BOATMAN *orders the sails unfurled.* JING-
GUAN *calls out to them loudly from behind the stage and enters*)
Mr. Cao, please do not depart yet. Someone is coming to say good-
bye. (JINGGUAN *sings*)

> (*To the same tune as before*)
> Make haste and shout,
> stop the boat!
> I am running over to deliver a message.

(JINGGUAN *speaks*) Please hurry and transmit this message: the nun
from the Rain-Flower Nunnery has come to see Miss Cao off.
(MR. CAO'S SERVANT *delivers the message*) (CAO *angrily responds*)
Tell her not to bother. (THE SERVANT *repeats* MR. CAO'S *words to*
JINGGUAN) (JINGGUAN *looks agitated*) Mrs. Fan has a letter for
Miss Cao, but her father does not allow me to see her. What can I
do about this? (*Spotting* JINGGUAN, YUHUA *appears worried and
anxious*) Look! I can see Miss Cao sighing and frowning at the
window. To have words to convey yet no way to deliver them, how
painful this is! (JINGGUAN *sings*)

> The sparrow's boat has locked up a lovely maiden, a gauze
>   screen separating her lovely face from mine.
> We sadly sigh in vain.
> Her hand gestures spell resentment, her brows are knitted
>   in sorrow,
> a helpless servant without a plan,
> I can only look on with pity at the sight of her misery.

(JINGGUAN *speaks*) Let me show her the letter, maybe she will ask someone to bring it to her. (*She shows the letter to* YUHUA *and waves at*

her) (YUHUA *says to her father*) Dad, when we lived at the nunnery, Jingguan was very hospitable and treated me well. Please allow her onto the boat, so that I can thank her properly before we leave. (CAO *does not respond*) (YUHUA'S MAID *says to* JINGGUAN) Please come on board, Reverend Mother. (JINGGUAN *steps on the boat;* CAO *becomes furious*) Little wench, do you want a good beating? I have not given you any instructions. Who allowed you to convey this invitation? Call the male servant to tell the nun to go back, and don't allow her into the cabin! (CAO'S SERVANT *and* THE BOATMAN *push the old nun back onto the shore*) (JINGGUAN) Miss, oh Miss, now that you are locked up behind the gates of your princely estate, do not blame me for turning round to the other shore, never looking back. (JINGGUAN *leaves*) (THE BOATMAN) Pah! If while setting off on a journey through a layman's gate one encounters a monk or a nun, everything will go wrong. That old nun was really obstinate! I worked up a bona fide official sweat pushing her out. (CAO) An "official sweat,"[11] now that's an auspicious sign! Let's set sail! (THE BOATMAN *starts to sail*) (CAO) Daughter, nuns like these are the least helpful people in all the world. You should not get too close to them. (CAO *sings*)

> (*To the same tune as before*)
> Since ancient times it has been said that,
> Among all the vermin that burrow into the women's
>   chambers,
> Including the three matrons and the six hags, nuns top
>   them all.[12]

(CAO *speaks*) Even the most decent among them ask for a donation as soon as they've opened their mouths. (CAO *sings*)

> She gushes out golden lotuses when preaching the
>   Dharma, and

sprays flowery mists while explaining Buddhist sutras;
but all she's really doing is extending her offertory tray.

(CAO *speaks again*) And if you run into some of the dishonest ones,
once they start to frequent your home, there is no end to the bad
luck they bring. (CAO *sings*)

> She may be standing in front of the bright mirror
>   demonstrating her enlightenment,
> fingering a string of rosary beads and leaning on a bodhi
>   tree, and looking very pious indeed,
> all while using thorns to pierce your maiden's walls of
>   defense.

(CAO *speaks*)

I am going to rest in the rear cabin. Liuchun, take good care of your
mistress. You two do some needle work, but do not open the window or engage in idle banter. Indeed, you should not worry your old
man any further, and allow me to have a sound sleep to rest my tired
body. (CAO *exits the stage.* YUHUA *stomps her feet, cries, and sings*)

To the Tune of *Wugongyang fan* (Five Ways of Providing for Parents, Redux)

> My resentment is piling up, sky high,
>   my filial affection has turned into loathing and enmity.
> Although I should resign myself to adversity,
> I cannot help but lower my gaze in anger.
> I hate this window screen separating me from the letter.
> From now on, we will be oceans apart.
> Who will deliver my sad missives?
> Teardrops ruin my makeup
>   and course down my face like strings of pearls!

(*To the same tune as before*)

(YUHUA'S MAID *sings*)

I urge my young mistress to seek ways to comfort yourself:
the whole affair is doomed;
you are only torturing yourself.

Please do not sacrifice your real life for this fake marriage;
heaven above does not intervene in tragic affairs among
human beings.

Even if you cry your heart out,
who will take notice?

What a pity, half of your handkerchief's color has bled out
in the flood of your tears.

To the Tune of *Jiang'ershui* (River Water)

(YUHUA *sings*)

Delicate strings drag me forward,
but silken cords of longing are pulling me back from
behind.[13]

How can I make it so that this fairy's boat runs aground at
Penglai, the island paradise,[14]
or martial conflagrations suddenly block our route ahead,
or a fierce headwind forces us to turn the ship around?

Then, I can fulfill my secret desire.

Facing the horizon, I send these words: at this juncture,
my breast is wracked with sorrow!

(*To the same tune as before*)

(YUHUA'S MAID *sings*) Mistress,

You should not think idle thoughts; otherwise,
you will waste your few good years.

Even if this fairy-boat is stranded at Penglai Island,

or battles break out in the waterway ahead, or
our ship is turned back by a headwind,
what can you do when your father refuses to go along?!
Whether you and Mistress Fan are inches apart, or at
    opposite ends of the horizon,
you will still suffer from a broken heart.

(YUHUA'S MAID *speaks*) It is late, time to go to bed, Miss.

Weisheng (Closing Tune)

(YUHUA *sings*)
Farther and farther I sail away from her;
our longing will be shared in equal parts.
(YUHUA'S MAID *sings*)
I can only arrange this "no-worry" pillow for her,[15] and urge
    her to bed.

SCENE 18

STARTLED BY A TYPHOON

Prelude in the Mode of *Nanlü: Linjiangxian*
(Immortal by the River)

(YANG YUGONG, *the secondary young male role, enters with a
group of people and sings*)
With a petty office job, but still living within view of
grand illusions,
I am ever more disenchanted with ethereal dreams of
wealth and status.
Far from my birthplace,
I cannot hear my native tongue.
Loved ones constantly appear in my dreams,
kith and kin are hard to find.

(YANG *speaks*) I am Yang Yugong, Inspector of Dengzhou and Laizhou.
I began my career in Zhejiang Province, and I am now posted at
Shandong. I hold the keys to the nation's northern gates, responsible for strengthening the Middle Kingdom's borders. I am fortunate to live in an era when the land is peaceful and the people are
industrious, so that civil officials can manage affairs even from a

sickbed. I have a brother-in-law named Cao Gechen who is also my dearest friend. He wrote me not long ago that he would bring my niece here, and then go on to the capital to sit for the examination. Now that the exam period is approaching, I expect them to be here at any moment. (CAO GECHEN *and* YUHUA *enter with her maid and* CAO'S SERVANT)

Passing Tune in the Mode of *Huangzhong:* *Chuduizi* (Breaking Ranks)

(CAO *sings*)
At an age when my hair is already streaked with gray,
I am still struggling to find a path to wealth and fame.
Wind and frost in a distant land are doubly hard to bear,
a relative encountered at the ends of the earth is
　　exceptionally dear.
Let's stop the boat, and
settle down for the night at this wayside house.

(CAO'S SERVANT *speaks*) Doorman, please report to your master that his relative Mr. Cao is here with his daughter. (*Several voices report this news*) (YANG) Open the middle gates and welcome them in! (CAO *and* YUHUA *enter the gate*) (CAO'S SERVANT *exits first*) (YANG) It's been so long, but you are frequently in my thoughts. (CAO) I have heard about your achievements from afar, which bring me much joy. (YUHUA *greets her uncle*) (YANG) In just a few years, my niece has grown into a young lady. But why do you look so sad? Are you tired from traveling? Why don't you go to the inner chambers to see your aunt? (YUHUA *and her maid exit*) (YANG) Please prepare a feast to give my bother-in-law a proper welcome. (*Many voices respond*) (*A yamen runner enters*) Master, a foreign boat has just moored at the shore. The captain says they came from the Ryukyu Islands to request the conferral of the royal title for their king. He is now getting the horses ready and will be here to see you momentarily. (YANG) Since he is a foreign envoy, we should treat him with courtesy. Everyone, please prepare another table of food and drink for the envoy. (*Many voices reply*) (THE ENVOY *leads a group of people entering the stage and sings*)

(*To the same tune as before*)
A sudden typhoon
completely disoriented us;
looking out over the sea, nowhere could we discover a
route to a safe harbor.
So, we lowered the sails and anchored at this shore;
with our calling card we seek refuge here,
hoping that the local magistrate will not be angry with us.

(*Many voices report* THE ENVOY's *arrival from the Ryukyu Islands*) (CAO *exits temporarily,* YANG *and* THE ENVOY *greet each other*). (YANG) Your ship arrived so unexpectedly; please forgive me for not coming out to welcome you. (THE ENVOY) Turbulent waves have brought us to cross your borders, for which we are deeply mortified. (YANG) What is the purpose of your sailing to China? (THE ENVOY) My country is located in a far distant corner of the sea, and we have not come bearing tribute to China for a long time. Now we have heard that a sage emperor is on the throne, and our monarch sent me here asking for an investiture, so that we could help China to strengthen its maritime borders. (YANG) Your country is close to the Eight Min,[1] why did you not anchor there? (THE ENVOY) Speaking of that, we originally planned to land at Haicheng; but midway in our journey we ran into a typhoon and were almost shipwrecked. The turbulent currents did not allow us to unfurl our sails, and thus we could only drift along with the wind, which carried us to your district. (YANG) It sounds like you had quite a frightening experience. Let me prepare some food and wine to help you get over the shock. I have a close relative who happens to have just arrived, too, so would you mind if I invited him to join us? (THE ENVOY) What have I done to deserve such hospitality? (YANG) Please invite Mr. Cao! (*Many voices calling* MR. CAO) (CAO *enters and greets* THE ENVOY, *and* YANG *takes both men to the banquet*)

To the Tune of *Jianghuanglong* (The Yellow Dragon Descends)

(THE ENVOY *sings*)
The host is hospitable,
and though having only just met, we have troubled him to
     prepare a jug of wine,
a variety of seafood delicacies,
repeated rounds of fancy wines,
mixed with rare wild game.
I hesitate to go forth, for
our host is dressed most tastefully, while
my shamefully crude attire only invites derision.
(*They sing in unison*)
But let us set aside these social conventions:
China and its neighbors are one, and
who is host and who, guest?

(*To the same tune as before*)
(CAO *and* YANG *sing together*)
Such toil! You plowed through the sea on your whale-like
     vessel,
climbed over the waves,

and trudged through fjords, all
to pay tribute in this distant place.
The god of the wind intentionally pulled your ship into
my vicinity.
How delightful! From now on
our friendship, as strong as gold and beautiful as orchids,[2]
    will expand far and wide
beyond the seas where, as good comrades, we will enjoy
    each other's company. (*Choral repetition of the lines just
    sung by* CAO *and* YANG)

(YANG *speaks*) Braving a typhoon while sailing on the sea must be a
    frightening experience. Your ship made it through safely; truly,
    the gods looked upon you with favor. (CAO GECHEN) Could you
    describe for us what it was like going through that tempestuous
    storm?

To the Tune of *Huanglonggun*
(The Yellow Dragon's Robe)

(THE ENVOY *sings*)
We only saw dark clouds enveloped by thick fog,
raging waves loud as thunder.
A mere floating leaf,
our skiff was tossed up and down aimlessly,
and we were almost swallowed up into the bellies of
    fishes, where our bones would have been ground
    into bits.
And thus, borne along by the churning tide,
and trusting our fate to the fierce gale winds,
we have taken refuge at your famed district.

(CAO *speaks*) I didn't know that storms in the outer seas could be as terrifying as that! (CAO *sings*)

> (*To the same tune as before*)
> Simply gazing at the ocean can frighten you out of your
>   wits,
> truly, out of your wits!
> Not to mention being stranded out in the middle of its
>   vast expanse.
> And once you've caught a breeze that blows you across the
>   waters,
> it's not at all like the steadiness you feel climbing a mountain.
> Having heard this story, my aspiration to ride the wind and
>   cut through the waves has diminished.
> I now truly believe that a wise man
> always avoids danger,
> stays away from hazardous situations, and
> appreciates what life has offered him.

(THE ENVOY *speaks*) Now I will take my leave.

Weisheng (Closing Tune)

(*All characters sing in unison*)
Washing away the Red Dust
frightens those with frosted temples.
(CAO *sings*)
Hearing this tale of wind and waves, my spirits darken.
(YANG *sing*)
But you should know that the seas one navigates during an
    official career are even rougher.

Guests have come from beyond the heavens by boat,
Taking off their swords, together they drink a toast
  with us.
No matter whether we're close neighbors or from far
  distant lands,
our paths fortuitously cross while moored together along
  this eastern seacoast.

SCENE 19

Prelude in the Mode of *Nanlü: Shengzhazi*
(Fresh Hawthorne)

(WANG ZHONGXIANG *enters in official attire and sings*)
The best and worst are all reported together,
their extraordinary stories fill up the page.
Laugh not at this petty officer:
even the richest may lose to me in the end.

(WANG *speaks*) I am Wang Zhongxiang. Yesterday, having finished grading this season's exams, I personally delivered the report of "the best- and worst-behaved scholars" for this year. Today, I have come to stand at the head of all of the registered scholars, to await the announcement of the results. The gate of the government office is not open yet; I will wait in the left corridor.

(*To the same tune as before*)
(FAN SHI *enters, wearing scholar's attire, and sings*)
I let my guard down.
From where has this disaster fallen down into my lap?

I must salvage my reputation after these slanderous
> remarks,
words that are totally at odds with the truth.

(FAN SHI *speaks*) I, Fan Jiefu, have acted as a proper *xiucai* at the school, just as a virgin does inside the women's quarters: careful and conscientious, I am constantly cultivating my integrity and self-restraint. I do not know who it was that slandered me to Mr. Wang, but he unexpectedly reported me as the "worst-behaved" scholar under his supervision. This matter not only affects my future, but also could potentially ruin my good name. I therefore wrote a letter of appeal and have come to defend my case. The magistrate has not opened the gate yet; I will wait in the righthand corridor.

To the Tune of *Puxian'ge* (Samantabhadra's Song)

(ZHOU GONGMENG *enters wearing scholar's attire and sings*)
Reeling, swaggering, and smirking, I am
a "best-behaved" scholar making my way.
What's the point of studying, if
a teacher can do anything to me?
My scholar's cap is made of steel, and it won't break even
> if I stumble!

(ZHOU *greets* FAN SHI *and says*) My good brother Fan, how come you look so unhappy? (FAN SHI) Please don't get me started. While some receive unexpected praises, I on the other hand am just trying hard to protect my reputation from slander. For reasons unknown, Mr. Wang reported me as "the worst-behaved scholar." (ZHOU) Oh, then what do you plan to do now? (FAN SHI) I will have to see Mr. Wang and defend myself. (ZHOU) Could you let me see your letter of appeal? (ZHOU *reads the letter*) (WANG *looks at the men and murmurs to himself)* The young man talking to Zhou Gongmeng is Fan Jiefu, whom I made "the worst-behaved scholar." Now he is holding a written complaint. Does he really want to sue me? I will ask Zhou Gongmeng. (WANG *beckons to* ZHOU) (ZHOU *says to* FAN SHI) This letter of appeal is brilliant; it does not offend Mr. Wang's feelings, but also clearly explains your case. After reading it, Mr. Wang will definitely clear your name. I will say goodbye for now. (ZHOU *turns his back to* FAN SHI) What now? He just said that "some receive unexpected praise; I on the other hand am just trying hard to protect my reputation against slander." The "unexpected praise" obviously refers to my receiving the "best-behaved scholar" title. How dare he ridicule me to my face! I shall start some trouble and make things even worse for him. (ZHOU *greets* WANG) (WANG) What is Fan Jiefu holding in his hand? (ZHOU) It is a written complaint against you, teacher. (WANG) What is he complaining about me? (ZHOU) He complains that you have taken bribes, resulting in distortions of fact, wrongfully ranking the best-behaved as worst- and the worst-behaved as best. He also included a list with the amount of money that you extorted from the *xiucai* scholars, along with evidence for each and every case. (WANG *panics*) What can I do? (ZHOU) If you ask my advice, I say "preemptively strike to gain the initiative." (WANG) How could I strike him? (ZHOU) Let me talk to him first; then you come interrupt us to scold him. If he talks back, then you could accuse him of disrespect toward his teacher. After that, even if he takes out his written complaint, it would be judged as an act of insubordination, and hence will not be accepted in court. (WANG) There needs to be evidence of offending his teacher. (ZHOU) Leave that to me, sir. (WANG) This plan is excellent! (ZHOU *goes over to see* FAN SHI *and pretends to be angry*) Terrible! It is simply terrible! I went over to explain your case to Mr. Wang, but he accused me of being your co-conspirator. The ancients say that "the fox is saddened by the death of a hare." This is totally outrageous! (FAN SHI) That old fool! (WANG *comes over and hears this comment*) What? How dare you call your teacher names? (FAN SHI) Can you tell me why I was chosen to be "the worst-behaved scholar?" (WANG) You go whoring and drinking—and go in and out of court. (FAN SHI) Which whore did I visit? When did I get drunk? And which court did I go in and out of? Provide me with the evidence for each of your allegations!

To the Tune of *Dayagu* (The Great Welcome Drum)

> (WANG *sings*)
> Young lad, don't scold me!
> Although your tongue is sharp as a spear, and
> your mouth resembles a raging river,
> I am afraid that as a teacher I will always outrank my
> students,
> and besides, your scholar's cap is far inferior to mine.
> Even if I have done you a slight wrong,
> what can you do about it?

> (*To the same tune as before*)
> (FAN SHI *sings*) I laugh at you that your hair has turned gray
> for nothing,
> you have converted fiction into fact,
> and misjudged good and bad behavior.
> Manipulating school regulations to fatten your wallet, you
> kidnap the living and switch their places with the dead,
> then falsify your reports to Yama himself.
> You're just another little demon lictor who's on the take.
> Could it be true that I have no way of getting back at you?

(WANG *speaks*) What a sharp tongue! (WANG *moves to hit* FAN SHI) (ZHOU *stops him*) Teacher, please use your mouth, not your hand.

(WANG *shouts out*) This student is hitting his teacher! (*A voice is heard from behind the stage*) Who is arguing outside? Patrol officer, bring him in. (THE PATROL OFFICER, *the clown role, enters wearing official attire*) It doesn't matter whether you are in or out of favor, when the magistrate superior is here, you will have to submit to arrest. Who is shouting outside? (WANG) This student is hitting his teacher. (FAN SHI) This teacher is hitting his student. (THE PATROL OFFICER) It doesn't matter whether you are a scholar or an official, you will not go unpunished. It is my superior who issued the arrest order; it has nothing to do with me.

To the Tune of *Buchan'gong* (Pacing the Lunar Frog's Palace)

(THE MAGISTRATE *for the county, the older man role, enters with his entourage and sings*)
Wearing my judge's cap over a steely, impartial face,
my fame spreads far and wide;
overseeing local academic affairs,
I am favored with the emperor's kind regard.
It is the recent literary achievements of the Yangzhou
scholars
that I am curious to see:
truly how flowery can their writing brushes be?[1]

(THE MAGISTRATE *speaks*) Summon the patrol officer to bring in the suspects who made all that racket just now. (THE PATROL OFFICER *brings in* WANG *and* FAN SHI) (THE MAGISTRATE) Who are you? And why were you having an altercation in front of the county government office? (WANG) I am the teacher and supervisor of the Jiangdu School. This *xiucai* is named Fan Shi. Because he habitually visits prostitutes and abuses alcohol, and repeatedly appears in court, I reported his misconduct to you, magistrate. For this, he bears me a grudge. When he and I met outside the office just now, not only did he not treat me as his teacher, but also cursed me and struck me with his fist. I am sorry that the commotion disturbed Your Honor. (WANG *sings*)

To the Tune of *Pudeng'e* (Moth to the Flame)

His life has been one of serial misconduct,
his disrepute spreads all over his hometown.
His misdeeds are too numerous to inscribe onto bamboo
slips.[2]
He resents that instead of ganging up with him,
I revealed his misdeeds.
He did not respect me as his teacher,
but treated me as an enemy in war.
He must have thought that there is nothing wrong with
imitating Fengmeng,
the traitor who killed his teacher, Yi.[3]

(THE MAGISTRATE *speaks*) *Xiucai*, tell me the truth! (FAN SHI) I have been scrupulously abiding by the school regulations and have not committed a single act of misconduct. It is only because I am poor and cannot provide the teacher with money and gifts that he reported me as "the worst-behaved scholar" in this district. When we met just now, he intentionally tried to provoke me into criticizing him, and then turned around and accused me of denigrating a teacher. (FAN SHI *sings*)

(*To the same tune as before*)
He had a mind to stir up angry waves,
and subjected me, for no valid reason, to a cascading series
of disasters.

I tried to explain myself,
but only fed the flames of his hysterical rage, leading
me to suffer this severe setback.
He gored me with his spear but then claimed that
he was the one to be attacked;
this false accusation against me is no small matter,
no less grievous than his mishandling of the good- and
bad-behavior students!

(THE MAGISTRATE *speaks*) Since when are these educational officials
fair! To them, those with money are made the "best behaved" and
those without are punished as the "worst behaved." How can I
believe them? I only ask you why you were arguing in front of
the county government office? (FAN SHI) Because he was hitting me.
(THE MAGISTRATE) Do you have an eyewitness? (FAN SHI) I have
Mr. Zhou as a witness. (THE MAGISTRATE) Call him in. (THE PATROL
OFFICER *calls* ZHOU GONGMENG *and admits him*) (THE MAGISTRATE)
Did the teacher hit the *xiucai*? (ZHOU) Oh, I swear to Heaven and
my conscience, the teacher did not hit the student. (THE MAGIS-
TRATE) In that case, it was the student who hit the teacher? (ZHOU)
No, the truth is that he only cursed the teacher a couple of times.
(ZHOU *sings*)

(*To the same tune as before*)
I only heard them cursing each other,
But did not witness any physical violence.

(THE MAGISTRATE *speaks*) You must tell me the truth.

(ZHOU *sings*)
Standing humbly before Your Honor,
How dare I not speak the truth, and cover up for a classmate?

(THE MAGISTRATE *speaks*) How did Fan Shi curse Mr. Wang?

> (ZHOU *sings*)
> He said: Mr. Wang should hurry up and kick the bucket,
> his hair has gone gray without any corresponding gain in
>   wisdom;
> he's a mediocrity who can only sully the professorial chair
>   he occupies
> better to be reassigned to work as a demon in the
>   underworld.

(FAN SHI *looks shocked and says*) Why is he suddenly switching sides?
(THE MAGISTRATE) Mr. Zhou, your own eyewitness, says that you
indeed committed an offense against Mr. Wang. What else is there
to add? Judging from how presumptuous you are in front of me, one
can imagine how you must misbehave in ordinary circumstances.
(FAN SHI) This is only one side of the story! I have another side to
tell you, Your Honor. Please allow me to present my complaint.
(FAN SHI *presents the complaint to* THE MAGISTRATE, *who throws it
down on the floor, sings*)

> (*To the same tune as before*)
> Your crimes truly are innumerable,
> I am now convinced of your bad reputation.
> Even in front of me, the county magistrate,
> you dare to act like a parricidal monster,
> spitting in the face of a gentle mentor;
> your brutishness behind my back must be unimaginable.
> I'll spare you the rod, but take off your scholar's jacket this
>   instant,
> a vile weed like you shouldn't stand among fair flowers!

(THE MAGISTRATE *speaks*) Guards! Come to take off his scholar's robe and drive him out of here! (*A group of yamen runners take off* FAN SHI'S *scholar's robe and cap, driving him out*) (THE MAGISTRATE) Dismiss the yamen runners, let the office calm down with music and the cries of cranes; retreat for a meal, it's time to enjoy some leisure after work.

Weisheng (Closing Tune)

(WANG *sings*)

Now do you recognize the authority of a government
   bureaucrat?

(ZHOU *sings*)

Please don't blame me, as I had no choice!

(FAN SHI *sings*)

Alas! Now I know how sinister the human heart can be!

SCENE 20

DEBATING A MOVE

Prelude in the Mode of *Nanlü: Guazhen'er*
(Genuine Attachment)

(JINGGUAN *enters and sings*)
My good intentions fell on empty ears, and
humiliated,
I've trudged about with nothing to show for it.
Like fish cowering in a storm,
or a carrier pigeon blocked by a typhoon,
I come to deliver Mrs. Fan's message back to her,
    unanswered.

(JINGGUAN *speaks*) This poor nun went to deliver a letter from Mrs. Fan, but not only did Mr. Cao refuse it, he turned around and humiliated me. I will have to return the letter unopened to Mrs. Fan. I've taken a roundabout path, but now I've finally arrived at the Fans.

(*To the same tune as before*)
(JIANYUN *enters and sings*)
My eyebrows are creased by chagrin,
disappointment
never comes singly.

Turning bad luck into a blessing,

replacing annoyance with happiness,

I listen intently to the birds singing tunes of blissful

reparteee beneath the eaves.

(JIANYUN, *meeting* JINGGUAN, *speaks*) The Reverend Mother is here! (JINGGUAN) I just ran into Mr. Fan angrily rushing out. Where was he going? (JIANYUN) Mr. Wang, the head of the school, ranked him as "the worst-behaved scholar." He was on his way there to deliver a complaint. (JINGGUAN) Oh, is that so? (JIANYUN) May I ask if you brought back a reply from Miss Cao? (JINGGUAN) I hate to tell you this, but Miss Cao has already left for Shandong. (JIANYUN *is shocked*) What? She has left already! In that case, you should have chased after her. (JINGGUAN) I indeed ran after her, but her father told his servants to do whatever it took to prevent me from seeing her. He wouldn't allow us to meet, and there was nothing I could do about it. (JINGGUAN *sings*)

To the Passing Tune: *Shengruhua*
(Better than Flowers)

I flew along clutching my staff, trying to stay on her trail,

fully intending to give her a proper send-off.

I tried my best to be discreet,

but how could I get past her father's fierce mien, let alone

his snarling, beastly gatekeepers?

We were separated by the window screen,

her knitted brows spoke of her suffering,

her mouth sealed shut, her eyes bloodshot from her tears,

she fully bared her lovesick heart, bringing pain to this

old lady's compassionate soul, too.

But we could only stare at each other, unable to pass a

single word of news!

(JINGGUAN *speaks*) I now return the letter to you. (JINGGUAN *takes out the letter and gives it to* JIANYUN) (JIANYUN *cries and sings*)

(*To the same tune as before*)
You bring a message
all too ominous, and frightening too, I daresay.
If it's true that she has flown away in a flash, then
both of our lives will be ruined.
How to stop my tears from gushing out in torrential
    waves?
This is not a divine letter exempting my boat from sinking,
but none other than a curse ordering the devil to snatch my
    soul from atop the deck!
Even if her boat catches a good tailwind
and sails vigorously ahead,
I will chase after her as a ghost incarnate.
I will surely be the one to go first down into the
    Yellow Springs[1]—
yes, my life will end before hers!

To the Tune of *Bushilu* (Not the Way)

(FAN SHI *enters without wearing a hat and sings*)
Returning home in haste,
after suffering humiliation, I am outraged!

(FAN SHI *speaks*) In such state as I am now, how could I return home
to face my wife?
    (FAN SHI *sings again*)
    I worry that her ridicule
    may be even more scathing than Su Qin's wife's when he
        returned home penniless.[2]

(FAN SHI *arrives at home and sits down angrily*) (JIANYUN *is shocked and says*) Why, where are your scholar's robe and cap? (JIANYUN *sings*)

> How strange, for what reason do
> you sit bareheaded under the pine?
> Was your cap blown off by a sudden gust of wind?
> (FAN SHI *sings*)
> How unsettling,
> you inquire about this apparent interruption of my studies,
> and that makes me truly ashamed.
> An unforeseen calamity has struck,
> an unforeseen calamity has struck!

(FAN SHI *speaks*) I ran into that old scoundrel Mr. Wang in front of the government office. He laid a trap for me, and then he called the magistrate and reported that I had insulted him, my teacher. The magistrate made no distinction between right and wrong and stripped off my scholar's attire. (JIANYUN) How did this happen? Hualing, quick, bring another scholar's cap for the young master. (JIANYUN's MAID *brings the cap and* JIANYUN *puts it on* FAN SHI's *head*)

> (*To the same tune as before*)
> (ZHANG ZHONGYOU *enters hurriedly and sings*)
> In an attempt to remove the obstacles in his path,
> I hurry over to rescue my friend and smooth his tousled
>   locks.
> But with nowhere to lodge my complaint, and
> consumed by anger, my own hair stands on end.

(ZHANG *greets* FAN SHI *and says*) Cousin-in-law, I am so sorry for what happened.

(JIANYUN *sings*)

I ask of you, my cousin,

how come you closed your doors and did nothing, and

only now shuffle over here to show us some sympathy

when the situation has reached the point of calamity?

(ZHANG *speaks*) I was at home when I heard about what happened to him, and hurried to gather several friends to rush over to the yamen to act as his guarantors. But by the time we arrived, he had already been stripped of his scholar's attire. (FAN SHI) Zhou Gongmeng acted as the mole; the situation was hopeless from the start. (ZHANG) This is outrageous! Tomorrow, we will have to take this case to court. If the magistrate does not hear this case, I will also take off my scholar's attire to see justice done. (ZHANG *sings*)

I am not bluffing.

If we can't go through thick and thin together,

then what's the use of being kith and kin, or bosom friends?

(FAN SHI *speaks*) Thank you for being so supportive. But as the old saying goes: "A good horse will never return to an old pasture." Even if I am given back my robe and cap, I still won't be able to wash away the humiliation. I will just have to earn another scholar's title. Now what about Miss Cao's reply? (JIANYUN *takes* JINGGUAN's *sleeve and sings to her privately*)

To the Tune of *Zhonglü: Qi Yan Hui*
(Crying for Yan Hui)

Reverend Mother, please break it to him gently, and

don't agitate him even further.

Having just lost a feather-topped trophy, he

can hardly withstand another shock,

this time the flight of his well-plumed female companion.

(FAN SHI *sings*)

Look at them gazing at each other and murmuring in low
tones,

I imagine the old nightmare is coming back to haunt me.

After all, it is not at all unusual for disasters to come in pairs,
and for misfortune to reach extremes.

(FAN SHI *speaks*) Judging from their expressions, my hunch must be right. You do not have to hide anything, please tell me the truth. (JINGGUAN) I won't keep it from you: she is already on her way to Shandong. (JIANYUN *covers her teary face with a handkerchief*). (FAN SHI *sighs and says*) What a pity that I cannot share my life with such a beauty! There, there, do not cry, my lady. From now on you and I will restrain our desires, and never again entertain such fanciful ideas. (FAN SHI *sings*)

(*To the same tune as before*)

Tumbleweed,

do not blame the east wind for blowing you about.

Even rare flowers do not bloom together in pairs on the
same stem.

In the end, it turns into an illusion;

only one can remain there to bloom.

Cherish what we possess,

don't cause this tender sprig any more damage.

(JIANYUN *sings*)

This clump of delicate flowers,

how can you replant her at the ends of the earth?

If two flowering plants with entwined branches take root,
they will have a hard time flourishing apart from each other.

(ZHANG *speaks*) Cousin-in-law, do you know why Mr. Wang reported
you as "the worst-behaved scholar?" (FAN SHI) How could I know?
(ZHANG) At first, I did not know either. But I asked a handyman at
the school, and he told me that it was Cao Gechen who asked
Mr. Wang to do so. (ZHANG *sings*)

> (*To the same tune as before*)
> It was Mr. Cao who took up arms on behalf of his
>   daughter;
> now he has sailed to the west, but
> left a disaster in the east.
> Such an elderly, worthless pedant;
> I thought he would be fair and square.

(FAN SHI *speaks*) It is more or less understandable that Mr. Cao would
find fault with me for proposing to his daughter. But what wrong
did I do to Zhou Gongmeng to cause him to turn his sights on me?
(ZHANG) You do not know this yet: the trouble with Mr. Wang
started with Mr. Cao; the trouble with Mr. Cao started with Zhou
Gongmeng. (FAN SHI) How so? (ZHANG) He asked Mr. Wang to be
his matchmaker for Miss Cao's hand in marriage. He heard that I
was planning on serving as a matchmaker for you, so he went there
ahead of me, spreading rumors to create trouble. When I showed up
afterward at the Cao's, I fell right into his trap. (ZHANG *sings*)

> Hiding in the dark, he made us into his puppets and
>   played us for fools;
> all of our joys and sorrows were manipulated by his hands.

(JIANYUN *speaks*) He asked Mr. Wang to make him a match? Did the Caos accept his proposal? (ZHANG) Although Cao did not agree to it, he did not reject Zhou, either. Mr. Cao said that he would approve the marriage if Zhou Gongmeng passed the higher level of examination. (FAN SHI) This means that Zhou Gongmeng is now my genuine rival. I swear, I will not live under the same sky as this scoundrel! (JINGGUAN) This person harms others to benefit himself, and his conscience is depraved. He does not need you, Mr. Fan, to take revenge on him. Heaven will deal him his just deserts. (JING-GUAN *sings*)

> (*To the same tune as before*)
> Stay calm,
> sinners will bring calamity on themselves.
> Zhou may hide in the dark, but the
> Buddha has double-pupiled eyes.
> Let's cast a cold eye,
> and watch this clownish crab splay out his claws all he
> wants.

(JINGGUAN *speaks*) I'm sure that Miss Cao will never marry him, and he will certainly never pass the highest level of examination. (JING-GUAN *sings*)

> It's no doubt that he will have little to show for his labor,
> let him daydream all he likes.
> Mr. Cao may have blurred vision,
> but the examiners are no fools.

(FAN SHI *speaks*) After today's terrible humiliation, how can I show my face again in public? My ancestral home is in Jiaxing, and my original last name was Shi. It would be better if I returned there and changed my name back to Shi. I will use a different identity to pass the examination there, and then I shall take my revenge on Zhou Gongmeng. (FAN SHI *sings*)

In the Mode of *Zhenggong: Cuipai*
(Pressing for the Beat)

We may have lost the battle in the east, but
with time, we will prevail in the west.
Setbacks create heroes,
let's break the cauldron and sink the boat,[3] and
turn defeat into victory.
In a few years,
my career will be soaring.
(*All sing in unison*)
Let the past be gone with the wind,
one day good and evil are bound to meet again.

(*To the same tune as before*)
(ZHANG *sings*) I see that
you are not at all worn down by the rough and bumpy
    road,
hardship and danger only make you stronger.
I bet you will succeed, you will indeed;
casting away your brush to accomplish great deeds,
your eminence and glory will have no rival.
You will follow in Sima Xiangru's magnificent footsteps,
Setting your sights on achieving great things and refusing
    to settle for anything less![4] (*All repeat this song once more
    in unison*)

(*To the same tune as before*)
(JIANYUN *sings*)
The lightning has already struck,
a lucky streak is on its way.
If your career takes off, it will soar,
and good things might not be just a fantasy.
That jade-like beauty may still be found in the pages you
    seek.[5]

(*All repeat this song once more in unison*)

(*To the same tune as before*)
(JINGGUAN *sings*)
A dragon once lay in wait in the lotus pond,
a steed can still be tied to the poplar tree.
Hurriedly we say goodbye, and goodbye we say;
when you return in the future,
even a four-horse carriage won't be enough to hold your
    retinue,
and the beautiful verses you penned before your rise to fame
will be lovingly preserved behind silk drapes. (*All repeat
    this song once more in unison*)

(FAN SHI *speaks*) As we shall leave early tomorrow morning, we will
not come by to bid you farewell. (FAN SHI *then sings*)

To the Tune of *Yicuozhao* (A Clutch of Oars)

Waving goodbye, rowing forward,
we will not complain about the hardships along the way.
(ZHANG *sings*)

At parting, a hero's tears will not be shed.

(JINGGUAN *sings*)

My guests are leaving; I will be lonely at the nunnery.

(JIANYUN *sings*)

One day in the future, our house's reputation shall be
     restored;

(*All sing in unison*)

Today we part for now,

tomorrow we will come again to bid farewell.

At the border pass,

we go our separate ways.

(ZHANG *sings*)

A good piece of timber comes from a tree with twisted
     roots and gnarly branches;

(FAN SHI *sings*)

grafted onto a different branch, it reaches up toward
     the sky.

(JINGGUAN *sings*)

Since ancient times there are countless high-quality
     timbers that

(JIANYUN *sings*)

persevered bravely through frost and snow.

SCENE 21

SEALING A SORROWFUL LETTER

Prelude in the Mode of *Nanlü: Buchan'gong*
(Pacing the Lunar Frog's Palace)

(CAO GECHEN, *dressed in official attire, enters with a group of people and sings*)
After ten attempts I finally passed the palace examination,
truly, for first-rate talents, success can never come too late.
Once a crotchety old loser, I have now ascended to
   Yingzhou,[1] the Daoist paradise.
I am curious, how will those mean-spirited youths handle
   news of this?

(CAO *speaks*) I am Cao Gechen. I came here to the capital for the palace examination, which I was fortunate enough to pass with flying colors. Thanks to the emperor's magnanimous decision to break with past convention and select candidates based on their scholarly stature instead of age and appearance, I was given a post in the Hanlin Academy. Thinking back to last year in Yangzhou, a couple of frivolous young fellows, thinking that I was an old geezer with no future prospects, tried to trick me into giving away my daughter as a concubine. If only they had known I would one day be so successful. I have dispatched an officer to fetch my daughter from Shandong, but how come she has not yet arrived? (*The clown playing* THE COURIER *enters dressed in official attire*) Arriving at one post I hurry on to the next; now back in the capital, I hereby report that I have completed the assignment. Master, the young lady has arrived.

To the Tune of *Yizhihua* (A Flowery Bough)

> (YUHUA, *looking ill, is riding in a carriage.* YUHUA'S MAID
>   *and* THE SERVANT *of the Yangs follow her on stage*)
> (YUHUA *sings*)

The boat and carriage have brought a wooden puppet,
the mules and horses bear a casket holding a living,
    breathing corpse.
My vitality sapped completely,
how can I last long?
(YUHUA'S MAID *sings*)
The mistress' illness has entered her vitals, and is beyond hope,
rest and relaxation will not save her.
She neither eats nor drinks;
on an empty stomach
how could she endure the travails of travel?

(YUHUA *is helped out of the carriage*) (CAO *is shocked to see her and says*)
Alas! My daughter, why are you so ill?! I am shocked beyond belief to see you like this! (*He sheds tears*) Tell me what it is that has made you so sick.

To the Passing Tune: *Hongnaao* (A Ragged Red Jacket)

> (YUHUA *sings*)
> Although I am touched by your inquiry about the cause of
>   my illness, Father,

please forgive your daughter for turning into a mute,
unable to open her mouth.

(CAO *speaks*) When did you fall ill?

(YUHUA *sings*)
Although the symptoms worsened in late spring, the
tumescence began to form last October.

(CAO *speaks*) Was it caused by the cold weather, or an improper diet?

(YUHUA *sings*)
It had nothing to do with catching a cold draft at the door,
and
you needn't suspect that something I ate caused the damage,
either.

(CAO *speaks*) Then could you have been violated by some evil spirit?

(YUHUA *sings*)
If my vitality has been stealthily sapped by lunar spirits or
flower demons,
why haven't they materialized in their true form to
scare me?

(CAO *speaks*) Then, why don't you tell me about your symptoms, so that
I can find a doctor to treat you?

(*To the same tune as before*)
(YUHUA *sings*)
It is neither an upset stomach
nor a cough that strains my breathing.

(CAO *speaks*) Do you feel feverish or chilly?

> (YUHUA *sings*)
> I am neither so hot as to desire winter frost,
> nor am I cold enough to long for a fur coat.

(CAO GECHEN) Is there anything you feel like eating or drinking?

> (YUHUA *sings*)
> No matter what sort of delectable seafood dish you might
> prepare,
> I will only become nauseous from the fishy odor.

(CAO GECHEN) It doesn't sound like you're terminally ill. But why have you lost so much weight?

> (YUHUA *sings*)
> It's just that my visage is deathly pale and, haunted by
> demons,
> the result is that my flesh is being eaten away under cover
> of darkness.

(CAO *meets* THE SERVANT) Are you the Yangs' steward, the one who brought my daughter here? (THE SERVANT) Yes, I am. (CAO GECHEN) Thank you for your trouble. (THE SERVANT) I will return to Shaoxing soon. Would you like me to take a letter to your relations back home, sir? (CAO) We do not have any relatives there; therefore, I have no letter to send. (CAO *speaks to* YUHUA) My daughter, you have a good rest, and I will ask a doctor from the imperial medical bureau to call on you. (CAO *sighs*) Poverty has barely left my house, and now sickness plagues our family. (CAO *exits*) (YUHUA *cries out*) Papa, you may be a learned scholar, who has earned a *jinshi* title and joined the

Hanlin Academy, but have you no common sense? You're the one who's wrecked my life, and yet you still ask me what's causing my illness? (YUHUA *sings*)

To the Tune of *Xiutaiping* (Embroidered Tranquility)

[XIUDAI'ER (EMBROIDERED BELT)]

> It is you, a living devil,
>> who have put me in chains to drag me down into
>>> hell; but
>> even now you pretend to be deaf and dumb,
>> and ask me why I'm headed straight for an untimely
>>> death.

(YUHUA *speaks*) Oh, I am wrong to say this. As the saying goes, "there are no misguided parents under heaven." I cannot complain about my father. (YUHUA *sings*)

[ZUITAIPING] (DRUNKEN TRANQUILITY)

> No hard feelings;
> I cannot hate the parent who gave me life.
> I should suffer willingly, crying out, "I can take it!"

(YUHUA *speaks*) As has been said since ancient times, one's life and body are all given by one's parents. If now I die by the order of my father, I am only giving back what was once his. (YUHUA *sings again*)

> Although this bag made of skin stinks,[2]
>> its original seal has not been broken, and can be sent back
>>> in perfect condition.

(YUHUA'S MAID *speaks*) Young Mistress, there are many love-stricken people in the world, but your brand of lovesickness is indeed rare. Longing comes from romantic feelings. If you are longing for a man, then as the saying goes, "after dying beneath a peony, even as a ghost you can still be romantic." But you have not even seen the face of a man, and Mistress Fan is a woman. What she has, you have too; and what you do not have, she doesn't have, either. There isn't any genuine romance here, so what do you desire of her that is worth dying for? This must be the result of some evil karmic debt left over from your former lives.

To the Tune of *Yichunle* (Pleasures Suited to Spring)

[*YICHUNLING* (SONG SUITED TO SPRING)]

(YUHUA *sings*)
You may say that this karmic bond comes out of nowhere,
that I don't owe anyone a debt of desire, and that
this lovesickness resembles nothing but a useless
excrescence.

(YUHUA *speaks*) You stupid girl, you only know that longing comes from romantic feelings, but you do not know the difference between physical and emotional love. What comes from the bottom of the heart is called emotional love; what comes from the bedroom is called physical desire. If one is lovesick because of physical desire, then even if one dies of longing, one can only be called a lecherous ghost, instead of a casualty of lovesickness. Throughout history only Du Liniang[3] can be said to have died for love. (YUHUA *sings*)

Don't you see that Miss Du fell in love, after
having only seen her lover in a dream?

(YUHUA *speaks again*) If I die and Mistress Fan finds out, she would certainly do what Liu Mengmei did for Du Liniang! (YUHUA *sings*)

> The soul of lovestruck Liniang may not return, but
> the female Mengmei would surely come to find my casket.

(YUHUA *speaks*) If I die, she will not live on alone. She and I are fated to be a couple in our next lives; we eagerly look forward to getting this life over with. (YUHUA *sings again*)

> [DASHENGLE] (THE JOY OF GREAT VICTORY)

> If we cannot be together for long in this life,
> we shall fulfill our heartfelt vows to each other
> in the next lifetime!

(YUHUA'S MAID *speaks*) Although Du Liniang did not see her man in real life, at least she had a romantic dream with him in it. But miss, you didn't even have a dream! How does that work? (YUHUA) If you talk about dreams, I actually did better than Du Liniang. After I parted with Mrs. Fan, was there ever a single night when I did not dream of her? In my dreams, she wears a scholar's cap and a man's robe, exactly like that day when we had our wedding ceremony at the nunnery. (YUHUA *sings*)

To the Tune of *Taishiyin* (The Grand Tutor's Introduction)

> She and I roved around in my dream, holding hands;
> handsome in the scholar's cap, when did she ever take
>   it off?
> We love each other just like any couple.

She is more romantic than any man.

Liniang's beautiful dream may be one of a kind,

but how can she compete with our tender caresses, night
after glorious night?

(YUHUA *speaks*) It's not just at night, but even during the daytime, I
sometimes go into a trance and see her standing in front of me.
(YUHUA *sings*)

Whether to my front or at my back, her spirit follows me
like a shadow;

no dream is needed

to summon her to my bosom!

(YUHUA'S MAID *speaks*) Young Mistress, the steward of Uncle Yang
said that he is returning to Shaoxing soon. He will pass through
Yangzhou on his way. Why don't you write a letter to Mrs. Fan and
ask him to take it to her?

(YUHUA *speaks*) That is a good idea. Please bring me my brush and ink.
(YUHUA'S MAID *brings both*. YUHUA *writes the letter and sings*)

To the Tune of *Dongouling* (Song of Dong'ou)

Caressing the flowery paper,

wielding my writing brush,

with tears flowing I finish this letter.

My feelings are deep but my supply of stationery is
limited, and I must leave much unsaid.

Although feelings are easy to pour out,

how can a broken heart still labor on?

Most likely we will meet again on barren hillocks,

recognizing each other as powdery skeletons.

(YUHUA *signs her name and says*) This letter is now done. But I do not know if I can wait for a reply.

To the Tune of *Liu Po mao* (Liu Po's Hat)

(YUHUA *sings to her* MAID)
If I die before she sends her reply
I ask you to burn it in front of my grave.
You should know that to wait for this letter,
in my grave I will raise up my head, and stand on my toes.
Don't make me curse the messenger goose.[4]
(YUHUA *hands over the letter to her* MAID *and sings*)

Weisheng (Closing Tune)

Tell the steward to place this letter into a delicate hand,
comfort my longing heart with an early reply;
by no means let this message bob atop the waters, never to
    arrive.

SCENE 22

A LETTER NOT DELIVERED

(THE YOUNG NUN, *the clown role, enters and says*) The mother superior of the nunnery has gone traveling, leaving this young nun on her own, unsupervised. The wooden gate is unlocked during the night; I leave it open for monks to come in under the moonlight. I am a disciple of Reverend Mother Jingguan at the Rain-Flower Nunnery. My mentor went to visit temples in the South Seas and left me to look after the nunnery. Today is sunny and cloudless, so I suspect there will be visitors to the nunnery. Although I am too lazy to recite sutras, I should make a show of beating the wooden fish and ringing the temple bell, to fool these visitors and keep their donations flowing in. (*She beats the ceremonial instruments*) (*The old man role playing* YANG YUGONG'S STEWARD *enters*) There are three thousand *li*[1] between here and the capital; I bear a letter for someone across great distances. Don't say that even if this place is on the way, I won't tarry; I still have to take the time to rest my oars and stay put for a bit. I am the steward of Yang Yugong, and I am delivering a letter from Miss Cao to Mrs. Fan. Miss Cao told me to find Jingguan at the Rain-Flower Nunnery and ask her to take me to the Fans. Here it is, and I am now entering the gate. (THE STEWARD *enters the nunnery*) Is the honorable Reverend Jingguan in?

(THE YOUNG NUN) Our teacher has gone to Putuo. Where are you coming from? (THE STEWARD) I am from the capital. The daughter of Mr. Cao from the Hanlin Academy has written a letter addressed to a certain Mrs. Fan. As I do not know the Fans, may I entrust you to deliver the letter to her? (THE YOUNG NUN) Although Mrs. Fan was a benefactress of our nunnery, she and her husband moved away last year. (THE YOUNG NUN *sings*)

Passing Tune in the Mode of *Shangdiao: Huangying'er* (Yellow Oriole)

Like Fan Li whisking away Xi Shi,[2]
the couple has taken off by boat to drift around the
region,
leaving their former residence long vacant.

(THE STEWARD *speaks*) Have they left anyone to look after the house?

(THE YOUNG NUN *sings*)
Neither dog nor chicken are left,
Only swallows guard their old nest.

(THE STEWARD *speaks*) In that case, I will leave this letter in your care. After your teacher returns, please ask her to arrange for the letter to be sent to Mrs. Fan. Would that be all right? (THE YOUNG NUN) Yes, that is fine. (THE STEWARD *gives the letter to her and* THE YOUNG NUN *sings*)

I now take the letter, and
we will soon find some wings
to have it flown to her, without delay!

(THE STEWARD *turns his back to* THE YOUNG NUN *and speaks*) One should think carefully before one acts. Miss Cao repeatedly told me that I should give the letter to Mrs. Fan in person and ask for a reply to bring back. Now not only have I not seen Mrs. Fan, I haven't even seen Jingguan. How can I leave the letter with this nun? I do not know what is written on the letter. If by chance it fell into the wrong hands and rumors spread, it might ruin both Mr. Cao's career and his daughter's reputation. (THE STEWARD *sings*)

> (*To the same tune as before*)
> I need to be discreet and not invite trouble,
> I can't just hand off this private letter so carelessly.
> I must guard against the danger of it falling into the
>   wrong hands.

(THE STEWARD *speaks to* THE YOUNG NUN) Miss Cao repeatedly urged me to hand this letter to Mrs. Fan in person. If there is a mistake, I will be blamed. I think it would be better to take this letter back to Miss Cao. (THE YOUNG NUN) That is fine too. (*She returns the letter to him and* THE STEWARD *sings*)

> Upon careful consideration,
> it's best to take back the letter, and
> return it, contents undivulged, to the sender.

(THE STEWARD *speaks*) Alas! Miss Cao is eagerly waiting for me to bring back a reply from Mistress Fan. Who would have known that we missed our chance? (THE STEWARD *sings*)

> I hate to add to Miss Cao's distress,
> and make her dark, limpid pupils gaze out languidly,
> scanning the waterways for word, but all in vain.

(THE STEWARD *speaks*) I bid goodbye. (THE STEWARD *sings again*)

> I sent a plum blossom by a messenger,
> but it did not reach the recipient.
> Why is it that between the north and south of the Yangzi
>   River
> the spring season differs so?

SCENE 23

ACCOMPANYING A HUSBAND TO THE CAPITAL

Prelude in the Mode of *Xianlü: Queqiaoxian*
(The Immortal of Magpie Bridge)

(JIANYUN *enters with her maid and sings*)
Three autumns have passed, yet each day has seemed an
  eternity,
my thoughts have drifted over a thousand *li*,
and now it is once again exam season.
Waiting for my handsome husband to climb up the ladder
  of clouds,[1]
I ask for news from the Moon Goddess.[2]

(JIANYUN *speaks*) After parting from Miss Cao, I came to Jiaxing with
my husband. Since then, for three years, my husband locked himself
inside the house and studied very diligently, never even glancing out
at the garden. This is the year of the metropolitan examination. He
changed his name from Fan Shi to Shi Jian and went off to take
the exam in the provincial capital. Given his talent, I cannot imagine
him not passing. But as for my conjugal alliance with Miss Cao, I do
not know whether anything will come of it. Though I do miss her,
I still have an affectionate husband by my side to provide me with
relief. But when she longs for me, she has no one but her strict

father, who can only add to her distress. She does not even have a caring and understanding mother to heal her broken heart. Alas! I don't even know if she has been able to last till now! (JIANYUN *sings*)

To the Passing Tune: *Guizhixiang*
(Cassia Boughs' Fragrance)

Delicate tendrils and tender buds
cannot bear the rigors of disappointment,
laden with snow and burned by frost,
no gentle breeze or clear skies relieve them.
Sorrow coils around my breast, endlessly!
I fear that like fragile crystal or brittle coral, I will shatter
    easily.
Miss Cao, if the worst happens to you,
send a raven to report it to me soon, so that
I may follow you to the netherworld post haste!

(THE MESSENGER, *a minor role, enters the stage while banging a gong*)
Hark! Hark! Mr. Shi has come in first in the Zhejiang provincial examination. (JIANYUN) Are you not mistaken? (THE MESSENGER) No, it is true. I have the report here, take a look! (JIANYUN *reads and then speaks to her maid*) Indeed, it is true. Hualing, give him a tip now and ask him to come back another day for a bigger reward. (THE MESSENGER *thanks* JIANYUN) Having reported the good news of the one and only man who placed first, I shall proceed to the house of the second-place winner. (THE MESSENGER *exits*) (JIANYUN) Thank goodness! My husband, you have passed the examination! (JIANYUN *sings*)

    (*To the same tune as before*)
    First, this wipes away our family's disgrace,
    second, it also makes me look good;

third, when Miss Cao hears of this, she will finally believe
 that
not only can a "three-sided" marriage endure,
there is no shame in wedding a worthy young fellow
 like him.
This makes me rejoice, indeed rejoice!
The wedding candles will certainly be lit again;
as she and I are both cursed by misfortune and our ties to
 each other are shallow,
we rely entirely on your
high literary achievements, which are matched by your
 good fortune.

To the Tune of *Queqiaoxian*
(Immortal of Magpie Bridge)

(SHI JIAN, *played by the young male lead, enters. He is dressed
 in a round-collar official robe with a red sash and wears a
 scholar's hat decorated with flowers. He is accompanied by
 an entourage playing music and carrying colorful banners.*
 (SHI JIAN *sings*)

Riding on the back of the Giant Turtle
inside the Moon Palace,
this first test of my learning was a success.
The Moon Goddess presented me a cassia branch with
 her own hands;[3]
its scent reminds me of a certain someone!

(SHI JIAN *meets* JIANYUN) (JIANYUN *speaks*) Congratulations, my lord!
 You have won the first battle, the provincial examination, which is
 a good sign for the metropolitan examination next spring. As your
 humble and plain wife, I too bask in your glory. (SHI JIAN) It is all

because of your virtue and talent at managing our affairs both inside and outside the home, that I was able to concentrate on preparing for the exam and acing it. (THE PAPERBOY, *a minor role, calls out while entering*) "Roster of the Successful Nanjing Provincial Examinees" for sale! Come and get it! (THE PAPERBOY *shouts repeatedly*) (SHI JIAN) Tell the servant to purchase a copy. I want to find out how many people from Yangzhou passed. (THE SERVANT *buys a copy and gives it to* SHI JIAN. SHI JIAN *says to* JIANYUN) Congratulations, my lady! Your cousin Zhang Zhongyou has passed. (JIANYUN *is pleased*) Those who are talented are bound to pass. (SHI JIAN *reads again and is shocked*) Oh, how has that ignoramus Zhou Gongmeng also passed? There must be something fishy going on there. (JIANYUN) When Zhou Gongmeng asked Mr. Wang to be his matchmaker, Mr. Cao promised to grant Zhou his daughter's hand, provided he passed the examination. Now that he has passed, I am sure Zhou will go ahead and make a formal proposal. Although Miss Cao won't be willing to betray me, if Mr. Cao gives her to Zhou, what should we do then? (SHI JIAN) I really have no idea. (JIANYUN) I happen to have thought of a plan to deal with this possibility. (SHI JIAN) What kind of plan? (JIANYUN) I heard that Mr. Cao passed the examination in the highest tier and has now entered the Hanlin Academy. Miss Cao must have gone to join him at his post in the capital. Since you will go to the capital for the palace exam next spring, I want to go with you and find a way to get in touch with Miss Cao. That way, we can put a stop to Zhou Gongmeng's sinister plot to marry Miss Cao, and at the same time, I can find a way to consummate my bond with her. What do you think, my lord? (JIANYUN *sings*)

To the Tune of *Dayagu* (Great Welcoming Drum)

> Accompanying my husband to the capital,
> I shall rekindle our poetry-inspired connection.

(SHI JIAN *speaks*) It was your naughtiness that brought me big trouble and got me demoted when the magistrate stripped me of my scholar's robes. Now that I have only just earned the robes of a provincial graduate, please don't court disaster again. (JIANYUN) Back then I was naive and acted rashly, which is why we ran into problems. Now I am much more mature and experienced. I will come up with a perfect plan, one not at all hasty and impetuous like the previous time. (JIANYUN *sings*)

> I am now seasoned, acting with caution
> I will more than make up for our past mistakes.
> Our conjugal destiny is secure,
> you need not knit your brows.

(SHI JIAN *speaks*) Normally, I don't engage in impractical ventures like this. But that cur Zhou Gongmeng behaved so viciously, practically ruining me and our whole family. Even if I fail to bring about this marriage with Miss Cao, am I going to let him go ahead and proceed with it in my place? Of course not! All right, I agree to take you to the capital. I no longer have any aspirations to marry Miss Cao, but we can't let Zhou Gongmeng get his way! (SHI JIAN *sings*)

> (*To the same tune as before*)
> You will have to wear iron shoes,
> which will make it tough to cross over ferries and bridges,
> but don't ever complain of fatigue!
> Zhou and I are like a snipe and a clam deadlocked in
>   combat,[4]
> I'd rather have you, the fisherman, reap the benefit of our
>   draw.
> Let us pack our bags, and
> make an immediate departure, without delay.

Riding in a carriage to the capital,
together we will find a way out of this quandary.
(JIANYUN *sings*)
Who knew that even a dead crab can move still,
or that a rooster knows how to fly?

SCENE 24

INTERROGATING THE MAID

Prelude in the Mode of *Zhonglü: Juhuaxin*
(The Chrysanthemums Are New)

(CAO GECHEN *enters with* THE CAO FAMILY SERVANT *and
   sings*)
Like Cai Yong I have a daughter prettier than flowers.
Like Deng You I have no son; she is all I have.[1]
My daughter, in the prime of her life, wastes away in illness.
When will she get married like everyone else?

(CAO *speaks*) I am Cao Gechen. My daughter has been sick and my
prayers have had no effect. A few days ago, the imperial physician
came to take her pulse, and he said that she is suffering from emotional exhaustion. My guess is that the root of her problems can be
traced to the Rain-Flower Nunnery. Because we were travelers in
Yangzhou, I did not have the leisure to get to the bottom of things.
Now that I have returned from the palace and have no further work
to do today, I will interrogate Yuhua's maid Liuchun and find out
the truth. Servant, summon Liuchun out here to see me. (THE CAO
FAMILY SERVANT *summons Liuchun, his daughter's maid*) (YUHUA'S
MAID *enters*) I've just sent tea to the young mistress's chambers;
now I am called to see the master in the great hall. Master, I await

your instructions. (CAO GECHEN) How is the young mistress doing these days? (LIUCHUN) She is getting worse. (CAO GECHEN) Do you know how she came to be sick? (YUHUA'S MAID) I am not an imperial physician; how should I know what caused her to be sick? (CAO) Bah! You ungrateful wench, it was you who lured the mistress into the affair that led to her illness, and yet you still try to cover it up. Tell me what really happened at the Rain-Flower Nunnery. Someone bring a rod and stand ready to apply it! (YUHUA'S MAID *kneels, saying*) Master, please don't be angry, I will tell you everything. (YUHUA'S MAID *sings*)

Passing Tune in the Mode of *Nanlü: Suochuanghan* (A Tiny Window Is Cold)

> There was nothing unusual about what happened at the
> 　nunnery,
> 　it was only a female Boya meeting her soulmate.[2]

(YUHUA'S MAID *speaks*) When we lived at the nunnery, a certain Mrs. Fan came to burn incense. She composed a poem at the temple hall, and when our young mistress heard it, she couldn't wait to show off her skills, so she wrote her own poem using the same rhyme. (YUHUA'S MAID *sings*)

> Together they harmonized in poetry;
> 　recognizing each other's talent, they exchanged praise.

(YUHUA'S MAID *speaks*) Since they hit it off so well, the two of them swore an oath of sisterhood before the Buddha. (YUHUA'S MAID *sings*)

> Their pact is as strong as metal and stone,
> 　never to be dissolved or abandoned.

(YUHUA'S MAID *speaks*) Unexpectedly, Master brought the young mistress to the capital, where not only seeing each other is out of the question, the two haven't even been able to exchange letters. (YUHUA'S MAID *sings again*)

> A pair of matching swords forced apart,
> this was the kernel of our young lady's sickness.
> Helplessly, we watch as Miss Cao's mind and body languish,
> her soul has already flown skyward.

(CAO *speaks*) Although what you have said is not a total distortion, you must have replaced a calf with a lamb. The part about composing poetry was true, but it was Mr. Fan that the mistress exchanged poems with. How can you claim it was a woman? (LIUCHUN) Heavens no, what an injustice! No man was ever seen at the nunnery! Not only has our mistress never met Scholar Fan, even I have no idea what he looks like! (CAO) This is absurd! You are saying that it was all on account of a woman that your young mistress has become this sick? What does she see in her? (YUHUA'S MAID) Miss Cao loves Mrs. Fan for her poetic talents. (CAO) Anything else? (YUHUA'S MAID) Nothing else! (CAO *laughs and says*) Is there really a girl as silly as this in all the world? (CAO *sings*)

> (*To the same tune as before*)
> I laugh at myself, having reprimanded her for nothing;
> her affliction is indeed a strange whimsy.

(CAO *speaks*) If all she wants is to find a companion to write poetry, not to say one, even one hundred wouldn't be difficult to find here in the capital. (CAO *sings again*)

> Female scribes and poets are all over this city.
> With just a single call, they will come flocking,

to sing ancient airs and strum the tunes of elegant court
lyrics.

I only fear that she will be too busy to tend to them all!

(YUHUA'S MAID) I am sure that there are many women poets in the
city, but none of them could possibly be as talented as Mrs. Fan.
(CAO) In a magnificent place like this, even if we just randomly
picked someone off the street, she would be several times better
than Mrs. Fan. (CAO *sings*)

> Unlike a frog at the bottom of a well,[3]
> these are prominent families.
> Tell the young mistress to prepare herself well;
> sound the drums for a competition of literary talent.

(CAO *speaks*) Call the servant: send a message out, declaring that I am
looking for a few female students to form a poetry club with the
mistress. Any young woman who can write poetry can come for an
audition in three days. Those who pass will be treated favorably.
(THE CAO FAMILY SERVANT) All right, I will do as instructed.

Weisheng (Closing Tune)

(CAO *sings*)
Draw up the beaded curtains in the magnificent hall,
clear away the tables and clean the windows well.
Let us see how many bright disciples
I can produce from behind the crimson screen.

SCENE 25

~~~~~~~~~~~~~~

THE EXAMINATION

Passing Tune in the Mode of *Nanlü: Xiangliuniang*
(The Lady of the Fragrant Willow)

(SHI JIAN *sings*)
I am in awe of the imperial metropolis,
how impressive this imperial metropolis is!
It is indeed gorgeous, and it's no wonder
its splendor is repeatedly recorded by successive
generations of writers.

(SHI JIAN *speaks*) My wife and I have arrived at the capital and found lodging. We inquired about Miss Cao and heard that she is not yet married. This means that we still have a chance. But the walls around noble households are high and impenetrable, making it difficult to pass a message to Miss Cao. My wife asked me to go to the Caos' front gate to observe who goes in and out of the household, so that we might ask one of them to carry a message inside. Now I am at the gate of the Cao house. Luckily, no one is standing guard, so I can wait here under the eaves for a little while. (SHI JIAN *sings*)

I find a perch here by the eaves for just a moment,
just for a moment.

(SHI JIAN *speaks*) There is no one here—why am I trembling with
fright? (SHI JIAN *sings again*)

Mr. Cao is awe-inspiring even when he's not angry,
I am scared even though he's not here.

(SHI JIAN *sighs and says*) This outermost gate is already hard enough
to breach, how many dozens of thresholds must one pass through
before finally arriving at Miss Cao's boudoir? Who would be bold
enough to do that? (SHI JIAN *sings*)

Blocked by layers upon layers of curtains,
with so many curtains, even
the most agile swallow
could only make it as far as the painted eaves of the main
hall.

(SHI JIAN *speaks*) There is a notice on the wall, let me read it. (*He
reads*) "Warning by the Scholar of the Hanlin Academy: The so-
called "three matrons and six hags" are not allowed to enter this
gate. If anyone violates this rule, she will be remanded to the author-
ities for severe punishment." Alas, who other than the "three
matrons and six hags" could deliver my message? It looks like there's
no hope for my plan. (SHI JIAN *sings*)

(*To the same tune as before*)
The "three matrons and six hags" are banned'
all are banned, and

the nine gates are all shut tight.

The phoenix bears a letter, but whom can be entrusted to
deliver it?

(SHI JIAN *speaks*) It's better to go back. What am I doing standing
here? (*He intends to leave but stop and then sings*)

> I turn my head in a huff to go back,
> now I'd better go back.
> My hands are tied, but
> my heart is not yet resigned.

(SHI JIAN *speaks*) I see someone coming out, but how do I know if it's
a visitor or someone patrolling the compound? I am both excited
and scared. (SHI JIAN *sings*)

> Who comes here?
> I'd better lower my gaze,
> hold my breath, and swallow my pride.

(THE CAO FAMILY SERVANT *enters*) The houses of officials in favor are
never deserted; who is at the gate stretching his neck out like a crane?
Who are you, peeping in through the gate? (SHI JIAN) I am a provincial graduate about to take the palace examination. I am waiting for a
friend under these eaves. (THE CAO FAMILY SERVANT) This is the gate
to the house of Mr. Cao, a scholar of the Hanlin Academy. It's not
the sort of place to use for meeting up with others. (SHI JIAN) Please
give me just a bit longer, and I will leave. (THE SERVANT) Why is it so
quiet here? Where are all the doormen? (*Two* DOORMEN, *a painted-
face and a clown role, enter together*) After enjoying three cups of wine,
a siesta is the perfect sequel. My old steward, why are you here? (THE
SERVANT) Master wants to take in some female students, and asks

you to make this known to the public: any woman who can write poetry is invited to come for an audition three days from now. (SHI JIAN *is surprised upon hearing this*) (THE DOORMEN) How did Master come up with this idea? (THE SERVANT) It is because Miss Cao composed poetry with a young lady at Yangzhou, and misses her so much, that she has become ill. (THE PAINTED-FACE DOORMAN) Oh, I see. Let's split up to spread the news. We busily convey the official's intention/ To the candidates in the inner chambers. (*Both* DOORMEN *exit the stage*) (SHI JIAN *is delighted*) How about that? It sounds like Miss Cao got sick from longing for my wife. Mr. Cao now wants to take in female students, and this is a great opportunity for us. I will hurry home to discuss this with my wife. (SHI JIAN *sings*)

> (*To the same tune as before*)
> This news is remarkable,
> it is truly incredible!
> It's all coming together nicely, and
> having to lower my head, swallow my pride, and endure
> curses—none of that was done in vain!

(SHI JIAN *speaks*) Here I arrive at our lodgings. My lady, come out quickly! (JIANYUN *enters the stage*. JIANYUN *sings*)

> The detective is back,
> now he is back!
> Seeing his cheeks bursting with smiles,
> things must have taken a turn for the better.
> (SHI JIAN *sings*)
> I have good news to report,
> wonderful news, indeed! But
> we still need to ponder this carefully,
> let's not rejoice too soon.

(SHI JIAN *speaks*) That young lady suffers from lovesickness because of
you, and she is terribly ill.

> (*To the same tune as before*)
> Longing for you,
> and badly missing you,
> Miss Cao has fallen very ill;
> her lovesickness is so grave, no doctor can heal it.

(JIANYUN *speaks*) I already guessed that she wouldn't be able to avoid
falling ill. Now that it's serious, she should tell her father the truth.
(SHI JIAN *sings*)

> She told the truth,
> the truth she did tell.

(JIANYUN *speaks*) How did her father react?

> (SHI JIAN *sings*)
> A disease caused by poetry must be healed by poetry,
> and thus, he will hold an examination for female poets.

(JIANYUN *is surprised and says*) What? Does this mean that Mr. Cao will
test women on poetry? (SHI JIAN) That is more or less what will happen. (JIANYUN) Let me ask you, did you hear this news from
others or see it with your own eyes? (SHI JIAN) I saw with my own
eyes. Mr. Cao's servant delivered the announcement to the doormen for distribution. (SHI JIAN *sings*)

> The servant holds up the recruitment poster,
> yes, he shows the poster!

(JIANYUN *speaks*) When will the audition be held?

> (SHI JIAN *sings*)
> If you ask for the date of the poetry contest,
> it will be no later than three days from now.

(JIANYUN *speaks*) In that case, this is a Heaven-sent opportunity for us to be together. (SHI JIAN) My lady, please do not get excited. Any other woman on the face of this earth can enter this contest— except, that is, for you! (JIANYUN) Why can't I go? (SHI JIAN) You are Mr. Cao's personal enemy, why would he allow you to be chosen? (SHI JIAN *sings*)

> (*To the same tune as before*)
> Why are you so obsessed?
> Why so obsessed?
> You have forgotten what came before.
> How many Qi Xi's are there in this world?[1]

(SHI JIAN *speaks*) Let's say that Mr. Cao doesn't select you, and that puts an end to it. But even if that happens, I am afraid that I would still be implicated. As of now he doesn't know about my name change. If you enter this contest and he finds out your identity, I am sure that, being the person who talked Mr. Wang into making me the "worst-behaved scholar," he can also request that the examiners fail me in the palace examination. (SHI JIAN *sings*)

> I fear this villain will sabotage my prospects,
> and land me in a thorny situation, he certainly will!
> He will reject my candidacy
> and toss away my exam papers.

(JIANYUN *speaks*) You need not worry. I have a very clever plan, and I
   will certainly not get you into trouble. (SHI JIAN *sings*)

> I will listen to you, my lady,
> My smart lady!
> I will wait to see how your miraculous machinations will
> Outdo everyone else's!

(JIANYUN *speaks*) If I win, I won't tell him that I am your wife. I'll just say
   that my parents have both passed away, leaving me alone in the
   world. Then he will take me in as his adopted daughter. I will then
   scheme with Miss Cao to elope from the inside. What else will there
   be to worry about? (SHI JIAN) This plan is too risky. (SHI JIAN *sings*)

> (*To the same tune as before*)
> The future looks precarious,
> our fate is not secure;
> thinking about it fills me with dread.
> Using you to get to her is not a long-term plan.

(SHI JIAN *speaks*) Let's say you tell him that you are unmarried, and he
   makes you his adoptive daughter. What if his daughter is unwilling
   to marry me, and they decide to marry you off to another man; what
   shall we do then? (SHI JIAN *sings*)

> Your impetuous scheme is too risky,
> it surely is risky!
> The price is too high, but the returns too low;
> don't take on such responsibility.

(JIANYUN *speaks*) It is possible to kill the commander of an army, but it
   is difficult to bend even an ordinary man against his will. If I

resolutely refuse to comply, he cannot force me. (SHI JIAN) I realize that, too. (SHI JIAN *sings*)

> I praise your wit,
>
> my lady is indeed smart! I just wonder
>
> why you are putting our marriage at stake,
>
> treating it as child's play?

(JIANYUN *speaks*) You and I should come up with a plan that works out for everyone. It will certainly not work if I let them know that I am your wife. But if I say that I am unmarried, this may make it hard to stop him, if he decides to carry out some hare-brained idea. I'll just say that when my parents were alive, I was betrothed to a son of the Shi family, but that we lost touch with one another after the two families moved apart. This will lay the groundwork for what comes later. (SHI JIAN) What will you say was given as our betrothal gift? (JIANYUN) Hualing, bring me my gold hairpin and jade toad. (JIANYUN'S MAID *brings these two items*) (JIANYUN) I will wear this gold hairpin and say this was given by you; you take this jade toad and say that it was my return gift to you. We will use these as evidence of our betrothal. (JIANYUN *sings*)

To the Tune of *Shuangdiao: Jiangshuiling* (A Song of Soup)

> The gold hairpin I accepted as your betrothal gift;
>
> this white jade toad is my return present to you.
>
> To carry out the plan, we will temporarily part ways.

(SHI JIAN *speaks*) If you go away, how will I be able to bear my loneliness? (JIANYUN) Frigid winter precedes balmy summer. Although it's cold and desolate here for now, when she and I return together to join you in matrimony, our household will be bubbling over with red-hot excitement. (JIANYUN *sings*)

> The loneliness of this present moment
> will give way to future days of joy and pleasure;
> My lord, you ought to make your best effort,
> don't allow yourself to be crestfallen,
> You and I sit for different examinations, but each of us will
> > do our best to excel.
> Husband and wife,
> you and I,
> a couple of winners each taking first place.
> Sisters in marriage,
> wife and concubine,
> We will both serve you with wifely decorum.

(SHI JIAN *speaks*) If you leave for the contest, when are you coming back?

Yuwen (Coda)

(JIANYUN *sings*)
The date of my homecoming is hard to foresee.
Only when this venture has succeeded will I pull my reins
> to turn back toward home;
even a mere top place on the exam won't shake my resolve!

SCENE 26

~~~~~~~~~~~~~

A GIFTED POETESS

(CAO GECHEN *enters with* THE CAO FAMILY SERVANT, *the secondary older man role, and* THE OLD MAIDSERVANT, *the older woman role*) (CAO *speaks*) Part the red curtains in the white jade classroom; remove the high officials to a different place. This official mansion will be used to collect spring colors; I stand watching the arrival of luscious apricots and gorgeous peaches. Longing for her poetry companion, my daughter has fallen very ill, and I have no choice but to give her some "hair of the dog" to try to counteract this infatuation. I will select some young gentry ladies to form a poetry club with her in order to lift her spirits and relieve her depression. I've already announced this event to the public, and today is the day of the contest. Listen up, manservant and maidservant: it's inappropriate for me to test the candidates face-to-face, so I entrust the two of you with the job of serving as the proctors. You, steward, shall stand at a distance and be on the lookout for anyone acting as a surrogate or passing information during the exam. You, maidservant, will patrol closely and prevent anyone from carrying in cheat sheets. You both need to be careful and must not slack off or become distracted. (THE SERVANT *and* THE OLD MAIDSERVANT) Yes, we will follow your instructions.

(CAO) I will sit and wait in the rear hall. When all of the candidates have arrived, come to ask me to shut the gate and issue the topic for writing. When rules are stringent, cheating subsides; topics should be difficult enough to separate the wheat from the chaff. CAO *exits*)

Passing Tune in the Mode of *Shuangdiao: Puxian'ge* (Samantabhadra's Song)

(*The* CANDIDATE *in a painted-face role enters and sings*)
I am the most talented woman scholar in the city,
of peach-sized characters,[1] I know a few liters' worth;
although I confuse level with oblique tones,
I will scrape together a few lines
when my sweetheart comes along to give me a topic.

(*To the same tune as before*)
(*The* CANDIDATE *in a clown role enters and sings*)
I am a female scholar, but I haven't earned an examination
    rank.
Gestating essays puts me into extreme agony.
My belly is strangely bloated,
hurting like menstrual cramps.
But after this morning's purging, there should be nothing
    left to be discharged.

(THE CLOWN CANDIDATE, *upon meeting* THE PAINTED-FACE CANDIDATE , *says*) Dear sis, have you also come for the poetry contest? (THE PAINTED-FACE CANDIDATE) Yes. (THE CLOWN CANDIDATE) In this case, you are my senior classmate. Let's walk together. (THE PAINTED-FACE CANDIDATE) I see two other people coming.

To the Tune of *Haitangchun* (Crabapple Spring)

(JIANYUN *enters with her maid and sings*)
Literary composition has had healing powers since ancient
    times,
and can quickly dispel a chronic ailment.
Chen Lin's piece treated Cao Cao's headache;[2] and
Meng Haoran's poetry remedied epilepsy.[3]

(*To the same tune as before*)
(THE DAOIST NUN, *the secondary young female lead, enters in
    Daoist attire and sings*)
All the plums and peaches have been harvested; but
there still remains a celestial apricot in the divine realm.
What is stored in my medicine basket
can transport you to a place of tranquility.

(THE OLD MAIDSERVANT *speaks*) I will ask Master to provide the top-
ics for the contest; you will be in charge of closing the gate. (THE
SERVANT *closes the gate*) (THE OLD MAIDSERVANT *enters with a box*)
(THE PAINTED-FACE CANDIDATE *and* THE CLOWN CANDIDATE
speak) The topic has not been given yet, but the refreshments are
already here. (THE PAINTED-FACE CANDIDATE *opens the box*)
Pooh! It turns out to be a couple of paper balls. (THE OLD MAID-
SERVANT) These are the poem topics. Each one of you pick one.
(*Each of the candidates picks up one paper ball and opens to read*)
(JIANYUN) My topic is "Ban Ji Continues the *History of the Han
Dynasty*."[4] (THE DAOIST NUN) Mine is "Red String Handles Fil-
ing."[5] (THE PAINTED-FACE CANDIDATE) My topic is "Phoenix
Writes Verse on a Red Leaf."[6] (THE CLOWN CANDIDATE) Mine is
"Lady Su Weaves the Brocade."[7] (THE OLD MAIDSERVANT) Now

that you have all picked your topics, you should sit quietly and compose your thoughts. You may not speak to one another. (*Everybody sits down*)

Passing Tune in the Mode of *Zhenggong: Yufurong* (Jade Hibiscus)

(JIANYUN *sings*)
The Ban family produced talented scholars;
many wonders were achieved during the Han dynasty.
I envy its splendid history of four hundred years,
all written down by the Ban siblings.

(JIANYUN *speaks*) Ban Ji was able to ensconce herself, a lowly woman, in the position of Grand Historian in the imperial court, an opportunity that comes along only once in a thousand years. This was, of course, partly due to her powers as a scholar of all things ancient, but it was also made possible by the Han emperor's benevolence in making a special exception for her. Were Bao Zhao living in our era, who today would allow her to achieve her ambitions in this manner? (JIANYUN *sings*)

> If Ban Zhao had not met a ruler who appreciated her
>   talents,
> she could only have achieved minor fame within the
>   feminine domain.
> How fortuitous! It's no wonder her good fortune and fine
>   looks draw the envy of many, for
> without much effort,
> her fame is on a par with Zuo Qiuming, Sima Qian, and
>   Ban Gu![8]

(*To the same tune as before*)

(THE DAOIST NUN *sings*)

The general was not good at writing.

Who would he hire to join his advisory staff?

It was the female clerk, extremely dashing;

a girl of extraordinary competence.

Red String was also capable of brandishing the sword.

(THE DAOIST NUN *speaks*) When General Xue Song was stationed at Luzhou, his territory was coveted by Tian Chengsi, the commander of a neighboring region. If it weren't for Red String, who else would have been able to defuse the tensions between the two of them, and how could Xue Song have kept Luzhou for so long? (THE DAOIST NUN *sings*)

Drawing a line in the sand, the general didn't allow a
    powerful neighbor to swallow up his
territory, but survived only thanks to a female knight who
    swept away armies with her pen.

(THE DAOIST NUN *speaks*) Red String was originally a goddess who occasionally came down to the human world to have some fun. After she successfully completed the task that General Xue assigned to her, she flew up to Heaven in broad daylight. Her story has convinced me that immortal beings are not made up, but do actually exist. (THE DAOIST NUN *sings*)

She deserves reverence.

We respect her remarkable achievements;

just imagine how, presented with a cup of wine at the
    celebratory banquet,

she answered with a smile before quickly ascending to
Heaven.

(THE PAINTED-FACE CANDIDATE *speaks*) "Phoenix Writes Verse on a
Red Leaf" is the story about floating leaves in the moat outside the
imperial palace. If it weren't for the fact that I love reading and
watching operas, I would fail this topic today. Mr. Cao gave me such
a romantic topic, he must be an old flirt. Let me write a salacious
poem in return. (THE PAINTED-FACE CANDIDATE *sings*)

(*To the same tune as before*)
A poem written on a single leaf
sealed the poet's love for three lifetimes.
Phoenix's story teaches us that
every talented woman since ancient times
knew how to seduce men with her verses.

(THE PAINTED-FACE CANDIDATE *speaks*) Only because Phoenix
wrote a poem on a leaf and the leaf was found by a man, the two of
them became husband and wife. If Phoenix had not shown off her
talent, she would have died an old maid inside the palace without
ever seeing the face of a man. (THE PAINTED-FACE CANDIDATE
sings)

This tells us that not all marriages are predestined by fate,
sometimes
one has to dig tunnels or climb over walls for a tryst.

(THE PAINTED-FACE CANDIDATE *speaks*) She wrote a poem on one
red leaf, then she met a man. If she had known that red leaves make
such good matchmakers, she should have written a few more.
(THE PAINTED-FACE CANDIDATE *speaks*)

> She felt lonely all walled in,
> so she used leaves as her matchmaker;
> if only she had written on a few more of them,
> who could have competed with her?

(THE CLOWN CANDIDATE *speaks*) "Lady Su Weaves the Brocade." This must be the story of the wife of Su Qin, who when weaving a piece of silk does not step away from her loom even when Su Qin returns home. Could there be another Lady Su besides her?[9] (THE CLOWN CANDIDATE *sings*)

> (*To the same tune as before*)
> Lady Su wove with diligence,
> only because her household was dirt poor.
> Seeing her husband return home empty-handed,
> she couldn't rest her shuttle.

(THE CLOWN CANDIDATE *speaks*) I think this anecdote is the right one, but the word "brocade" needs to be elaborated further with more facts, or else Mr. Cao will laugh at me for being ignorant. (*She ponders a bit*) All right, I have an idea. I need not look elsewhere but the anecdote itself. The old saying, "returning to one's hometown in brocade robes," would be perfect for this line. (THE CLOWN CANDIDATE *sings*)

> My lord, please don't blame me for being heartless,
> I wait for you to return in broad daylight wearing brocade robes.

(THE CLOWN CANDIDATE *giggles and says*) Who but me could come up with such a clever idea? There is no doubt that I will take first place. (THE CLOWN CANDIDATE *sings*)

Who could be on a par with me?
I will be placed high at the top.
How can those three women of minuscule talent compete
with me?

(THE OLD MAIDSERVANT *exits after collecting all of the exam papers*)
(THE PAINTED-FACE CANDIDATE and THE CLOWN CANDIDATE
speak) Are you all happy with what you wrote? (JIANYUN and THE
DAOIST NUN) How can anyone write well in such a short time and
in such a drafty place? We just barely managed to write something. Were you two able to write some nice lines? (THE PAINTED-
FACE CANDIDATE) There is nothing special about my poem, but I
did come up with something clever for the word "loom." (THE
CLOWN CANDIDATE) My poem is also ordinary; I succeeded in
fully addressing the topic, without leaving anything out. But that
was about it. (THE DAOIST NUN *turns her back to* JIANYUN) These
two are so boastful! I wonder how good they really are. Let me test
them a bit. (*She turns to everyone*) Since Mr. Cao is now reading
our poems and we have nothing to do, why don't we improvise
some linked verses? (THE TWO CANDIDATES) We haven't got a
topic. (JIANYUN) We can just link the four topics together into one
poem; it would be fine as long as the lines make sense together.
(THE TWO CANDIDATES) In that case, please come up with the
opening rhyme. (JIANYUN *recites*) Having just put down her bamboo brush to edit some chapters of history, / (THE DAOIST NUN)
Now she receives the general's letter to be in charge of taking
notes. / (THE PAINTED-FACE CANDIDATE) But she ran out of paper,
so she had to find some red leaves to write on, / (THE CLOWN CAN-
DIDATE) She wove the red leaves into fabric and made clothes
with it. (THE DAOIST NUN *asks the first candidate*) Would you
please tell me how to interpret the third line? (THE PAINTED-FACE

CANDIDATE) The two of you! One needs paper to edit history, the other needs paper to take notes; where can I find so many sheets of paper for you both? So, I had to collect some red leaves together to make up for this shortfall. (JIANYUN) All right, that will do. But how does the fourth line follow? (THE CLOWN CANDIDATE) You all have not studied the ancient customs. In prehistoric times, people did not wear clothes made of fabric; they used leaves to cover their bodies. This is why I wrote about gathering red leaves and weaving them into clothes. (JIANYUN *and* THE DAOIST NUN *laugh at her*) Now that is something we never would have thought of! (THE OLD MAIDSERVANT *enters with the exam papers*) Who wrote "Ban Ji Continues the *History of the Han Dynasty*?" (JIANYUN) I did. (THE OLD MAIDSERVANT *reads out loud*) "Following in the footsteps of her older brother, she completed the Han History that he left unfinished, / among all the writers in a thousand years, who could rival Ban Zhao? / Although every dynasty has its share of talented female scholars, / Lady Ban was the only one who received an exceptional promotion from the emperor." This poem is exceptional in both literary skill and insight; its style is also unique and belongs in the rank of Zuo Fen and Xie Daoyun.[10] This poem is ranked number one. Who is the author of "Red String Handles Filing?" (THE DAOIST NUN) I am. (THE OLD MAIDSERVANT *reads the poem out loud*) "A beautiful goddess ventured into the army; / with grace she managed filing instead of needlework; / in order to stop the enemy from waging war, / Red String employed a minor art to counter a big threat." This poem is vigorous and graceful, very similar to Yu Xuanji's style.[11] Mr. Cao selected this poem as number two. Who wrote the poem on the topic of "Phoenix Writes Verse on a Red Leaf?" (THE PAINTED-FACE CANDIDATE) I did. (THE OLD MAIDSERVANT *reads the poem out loud*) "Phoenix married a man after writing a poem on a leaf, / she languished alone in an empty house after her man left; / if she had known one leaf would bring her one man, / she should've written a dozen a day." My master said this is in the style of romantic folk songs from Suzhou and cannot be regarded as proper poetry. Therefore, this piece was not selected. (THE PAINTED-FACE CANDIDATE) When Confucius revised *The Classic of Poetry*, he included the folk songs from Zheng and Wei. Mr. Cao should also select poems with sensual overtones. (THE OLD MAIDSERVANT *says to* THE CLOWN CANDIDATE) "Lady Su Weaves the Brocade" must be written by you. (THE CLOWN CANDIDATE) Who other than I could have written such a poem?! (THE OLD MAIDSERVANT *reads the poem out loud*) "The wife of the statesman of six countries did not stop weaving; / it was rare for someone like her to work so hard; / she did it during moments of leisure for times of need, / preparing for her husband's victorious homecoming." My master said that this poem is decent, but the author made a mistake of identifying the wrong anecdote. "Lady Su" in the topic refers to Su Hui, who was the wife of Dou Tao. Su Hui wove a brocade for a love palindrome when her husband was away from home. How did you end up writing about the wife of Su Qin? You interpreted the topic incorrectly; you wouldn't pass even if you had composed a good poem. (THE CLOWN CANDIDATE) Many examination candidates have passed the civil exam even if they wrote about the wrong topic. As I see it, as long as the poem is good, the master should pass me. Why be so inflexible?! (THE OLD MAIDSERVANT) Will the two women who passed the examination please take a seat. My master will come out to meet you, then he will take you to see our young mistress. Those of you who failed will now please leave. (THE PAINTED-FACE CANDIDATE and THE CLOWN CANDIDATE) Talented poets like us failed the examination; those who passed should be ashamed of themselves. (*They both exit the stage*)

To the Tune of *Pozhenzi qian* (Breaking Through Enemy Lines, Before)

(CAO GECHEN *enters and sings*)
My hope to select unusual talents has not been
   disappointed;
I have snagged two gifted women poets.

(CAO *meets them, then turns his back to them and says*) How come there is a Daoist nun among the two? I made it clear that the "three matrons and six hags" were forbidden to enter the house; it's bad form to relax the rules that I myself set. I will now call the servant to prepare ten taels of silver to send her off. (*He speaks to* THE DAO- IST NUN) I originally wanted you to keep my daughter company; but since you have already cut yourself off from worldly affairs, I cannot tie you down again with such matters. Here are ten taels of silver to compensate you for your writing; I hope to meet you again another day. (THE DAOIST NUN *thanks him*) A hermit ought not to sojourn among the gentry; let me return to the mountains and rest among the clouds. (*She exits*) (CAO *asks* JIANYUN) Young lady, may I ask for your provenance and name? Are your parents still with us?

To the Tune of *Yanlaihong* (Wild Geese Coming in Red) [*Yanguosha* (Wild Geese Passing Sands)]

(JIANYUN *sings*)
It's been long since my parents withered away,
my hometown is green only in my dreams.
I am from the Cui clan and Jianyun is my name.

(CAO *speaks*) Have you been spoken for?

(JIANYUN *sings*)
Although I was once engaged to a gentleman,
we completely lost contact because of separation.

(CAO *speaks*) You lost your parents, and yet have not married; now that
you have drifted to an unfamiliar land, how can you manage all this?

To the Tune of *Hongniangzi* (Crimson Maiden)

(JIANYUN *sings*)
Despite my misfortune,
floating around like duckweed,
I resign myself to the misfortune of being a woman.

To the Tune of *Shangdiao: Cuyulin* (A Thicket of Imperial Forest)

(CAO *sings*)
It turns out that you are a rootless traveler,
accompanied only by your shadow, your lot deserves my pity,
for talented people I have sympathy, and
to challenge Heaven's will, I want to change your destiny.

(CAO *speaks*) I only have one young daughter and she has no companion in her daily activities. If you are willing, please stay in my house
and become an adopted sister to her! (JIANYUN) If you will allow me,
it would be my great pleasure. In that case, let me kowtow to you as
my adoptive father. (*She kowtows to* CAO)

(CAO *sings*)
I am pleased that the jade tree is planted next to the
fragrant orchid.[12]

I will treat her like my own child, and
who will dare to say she is adopted?

Weisheng (Closing Tune)

(JIANYUN *sings*)
Could I be luckier?
I came for a mentor but received a father,
you are truly the arbiter of literary fate.
(CAO *points to the back of the stage and sings*)
You also have a literary sister,
who now waits for you in the inner chamber.
(CAO *sings*)
I often blame prevailing fashions for failing to value virtue,
people may claim to love talent, but it never goes beyond
        mere talk.
(JIANYUN *sings*)
Your generosity to an orphan has revived my spirits,
giving me faith that people can master their own destiny.

SCENE 27

SURPRISE MEETING

Prelude in the Mode of *Nanlü: Boxing* (Unfaithful)

(YUHUA *enters with the assistance of her* MAID, *Liuchun, and
    sings*)
My body lingers on in the physical realm, but
my name is already inscribed on the roster of the dead.
Everything here seems foreign and temporary to me, as
I pack my belongings and wait for my final departure.
It is only because I have yet to pay my remaining debts, that
I cannot break free once and for all.
(YUHUA'S MAID *sings*)
Please don't feel so miserable.
In just a moment, you will meet your soulmate, and
unleashing your tautly bound heartstrings to each other,
the soothing strains of your strumming will bring you
        comfort and relief.

[*Langtaosha* (*Waves Washing the Sand*)] (YUHUA'S MAID *recites*) Spirit and
    body have grown apart; dwelling amidst tombstones, / my days are
    forever enshrouded in a dusky gloom. / In my dreams, I cannot feel
    my body; I only pray that I will be reborn as a man. / Doctors

frequent our house in vain; they labor much, yet while they can heal whole kingdoms, they cannot cure our patient. (YUHUA'S MAID *speaks*) I stand and watch the newly adopted daughter enter the family; hopefully she will help revitalize my mistress. Young Mistress, the servant said that Master accepted a new female student, and he will bring her here to chat with you and relieve your boredom.

To the Passing Tune: *Luojiangyuan*
(Luo River Lament)

(YUHUA *sings*)
Weary and weak, I am waiting to die;
I can hardly wield the duster.
In this life, I cannot be anyone's classmate.
To whom can I untangle the knotted secrets that torment
　　my breast?
Going to the netherworld alone,
I await my companion in the next life.

(YUHUA'S MAID *speaks*) Young Mistress, why don't you also compose a poem on one of the topics given to the candidates outside?

(YUHUA *sings*)
I am already in poetic debt,
deep in debt from poetry.
The luxury of contributing another lyric is not mine to have.

To the Tune of *Yijianmei* (A Plum Blossom Cutting)

(CAO GECHEN *enters and sings*)
In searching for literary steeds, I have come upon a
　　peerless mare;

now that my stable is no longer empty,
I hope my daughter will also be happy.
(JIANYUN *enters with her* MAID *Hualing and sings*)
In order to study the *Classic of Poetry* and *Book of Rites*,
I have found a new home:
for *Rites*, I want to read the piece on marriage ceremonies;
for *Poetry*, I ask about the opening poem about love birds.

(CAO *speaks*) Daughter, your father has taken in a very promising new student. She has already asked me to be her adoptive father, so you and she are now sisters. Liuchun, please help your young mistress to come down and meet her sister. (*The two young ladies meet and greet each other.* YUHUA *is surprised*) (*She turns to her* MAID) Liuchun, look! This young lady looks exactly like Mrs. Fan! (YUHUA's MAID) Not only does the young lady look like Mrs. Fan, but her maid also resembles Hualing.

To the Double Tune: *Yuanlinhao*
(The Garden Is Good)

(JIANYUN *sings*) Young Mistress,
from a poor family, I am low in status.
How could I possibly qualify to join your exalted household?
Meeting you for the first time today,
already you shower me with kindly, affectionate glances;
with time, our relationship can only grow stronger,
we will certainly grow close!

(*Delighted,* YUHUA *turns her back to* JIANYUN *and speaks*) Not only does her face resemble Mrs. Fan, her voice is also exactly the same. She must be Mrs. Fan herself! I shall respond to her decorously for now. Once father leaves, I will get to the bottom of things. (YUHUA *smiles to* JIANYUN *and sings*)

To the Tune of *Jiaqingzi* (A Felicitous Celebration)

> Sister,
>
> you and I feel just like old friends though it's our first meeting,
>
> unlike those who exchange pleasantries, without sincere
>   feelings.
>
> From today on,
>
> you will be my bosom friend, and I will pour my heart out
>   to you;
>
> we are as equal as siblings, never will we go against one
>   another,
>
> intimate as blood relations we shall be!

(CAO *laughs joyfully and says*) She is a divine healer! Indeed, she is! Such marvelous medicine! It has been three years since we came to the capital, and my daughter has never smiled once. But today when she saw this Miss Cui, not only did her frown turn to a smile, even her color has changed for the better. How is Papa's prescription working? (CAO *laughs again*) Liuchun, take good care of these two young mistresses. Today I learned of an effective treatment for a child; I shall pass it on to other parents in this world. (CAO *exits while still laughing*) (YUHUA *asks* JIANYUN) Are you Sister Fan? (JIANYUN) Yes, I am!

To the Tune of *Kuxiangsi* (Tearful Longing)

> (JIANYUN *and* YUHUA *sing*)
>
> Long I thought we would only meet again in the
>   netherworld,
>
> how fortunate that we are now happily reunited!

(YUHUA *speaks*) Older sister, where did you fly in from? Where is my brother-in-law? Why are you dressed as an unmarried maiden? (YUHUA *sings*)

To the Tune of *Yinling* (Song of Yin)

I ask her: Where has she suddenly come from?
I ask her: Where is her groom?
I ask her: Why is she wearing her hair down, like an
unmarried girl?
This has made me suspicious even in the midst of my joy:
Could it be that you are all alone now, having drifted here
like a solitary migrating goose?

To the Tune of *Pinling* (Song of Pin)

(JIANYUN *sings*)
Please rest assured,
nothing untoward has happened.
My husband has passed the provincial examination,
and I have come along with him here, where he will
compete in the metropolitan examination.

(YUHUA *is elated and says*) So, brother-in-law has passed after all! Congratulations! (JIANYUN) We offended your father with our marriage proposal three years ago. Before he left Yangzhou, Mr. Cao asked Mr. Wang of the school to report my husband as "the worst-behaved scholar" and stripped him of his scholar's status. We were forced to return to his ancestral home and reassume his original family name. Luckily, he passed at the top of the provincial examination. If I had told the truth, (YUHUA *sings*)

I fear that your father would be infuriated,
And bring up the bad blood from the past.
The old wounds are still fresh and must not be
reopened.

This is the reason that I got rid of my high-standing
    chignons signifying my wifely status, and
    Redid my hair into the buns of a young maiden.

(YUHUA *speaks*) How lovingly considerate you have been. You've shown
me that I didn't fall this sick in vain! (YUHUA *sings*)

To the Tune of *Douyehuang* (Bean Leaves Are Yellowing)

When people talk about being crazy in love,
women certainly outdo men.
Men tend to be fickle, and
I laugh at their fickleness;
they have a habit of abandoning a woman halfway
    through their journey together.
You fully deserve to be praised as a skirted hero,
a knight among women.
Separated by ten thousand mountains and rivers,
oh, ten thousand mountains and rivers,
you crossed them all
to reach me while I still clung to life.

To the Tune of *Yujiaozhi* (Crisscrossed Branches of Jade)

(JIANYUN *sings*)
I am to blame for having prolonged her suffering,
her beautiful, delicate frame is nothing like what it was
    before;
my first glance at her inspired fear for her life,
but happily, her spirits are well on the way to recovery.

(YUHUA *speaks*) Since we parted, my story of suffering is endless. I don't even know where to begin!

> (JIANYUN *sings*)
> Your face has turned into the portrait of a woman's lament,
> there is no need to put your deepest feelings into words;
> this joyful meeting has let us both relax our frowning brows,
> oh, let's relax our sorrowful brows!

(YUHUA *speaks*) Older sister, now that you are here, how will we realize our plan for the future? (YUHUA *sings*)

To the Tune of *Jiang'ershui* (River Water)

> I fear that our clever ruse will run afoul, and
> our cheerful laughter turn into painful lamentations.
> Snatching the pearl from underneath the dragon's neck,
>   we risk waking the monster.
> Stealing a bell while covering our ears is futile.
> Saving a person from a burning house, we put our own
>   lives on the line.
> At this time of rejoicing we still need to be cautious:
> if we are not, then although you and I may be reunited as
>   sisters,
> We will risk husband and wife being torn apart.

(JIANYUN *speaks*) Let's wait for my husband to complete the metropolitan exam first, and then we'll figure out a way to get out of this situation. You and I have suffered for three years. Now that we are together, let's enjoy ourselves. Please don't start worrying again. (JIANYUN *sings*)

To the Tune of *Chuanbozhao*
(Plying Oars on the River)

Don't worry about the future,
now that we're reunited let's have some fun.
A channel is formed where water flows,
oh, how the water flows!
I believe Heaven will not betray us,
let's drive away the memories of former sorrows, and
from this day forward, bask in the happiness of being
    together.

Weiwen (Closing Words)

(YUHUA *sings*)
I am in high spirits, back to my old self.
Where has my illness gone?
(JIANYUN *sings*)
Spending this first night here together
we share the same pillow and quilt.

SCENE 28

CURTAIN BLOCKADE

Passing Tune in the Mode of *Zhonglü: Tiyindeng*
(Trimming a Silver Lamp)

(ZHOU GONGMENG *enters with a servant, a silent character
in the secondary clown role, wearing the round collar
scholar robe*) (ZHOU *sings*)
Smiling that I was born into such fortunate circumstances,
I passed the exams without even cracking a book.
I shall wear an official hat made of black gauze,
I will take a wife first, and then add concubines to my
harem.
Buying good farmlands,
building fancy gardens,
fulfilling my dreams of luxury—
it all starts here and now.

(ZHOU *speaks*)There's no need to be diligent; I have a better way to seek fame and wealth. No one could have expected my promotion from the worst- to the best-behaved; even spirits cannot prevent me from carrying out outrageous schemes. Swapping another's exam paper without leaving a trace, the expenditure for doing this

was quite a bargain. I had another man take my slot as an examinee, and he wrote the exam essay for me. It's not that I regularly
commit such shameful deeds; it's simply that wealth and fame
keep me busy day and night. After this purchase of the degree
entitling me to a spot at the provincial examination, I went to sit
for it. It turned out to be my lucky day, and I ran into an old exam
proctor to whom I wrote an IOU. He cut off one of the best
essays and pasted it onto my exam paper. Who knew that thanks
partly to human effort, and partly to Heaven's will, when the
report came out, I indeed passed? I then went around to different
government offices making use of my connections to exact bribes,
and used the bribe money to pay off the debt. In the end, I got the
juren title without paying a penny of my own money. Isn't that a
great deal? However, the metropolitan exam is a wholly different
story from the provincial exam. I will have to figure out another way
to cheat. The cutting-and-pasting method cannot be reused; it's
also impossible to have someone deliver me a ready-made essay.
This time I need to carry cheat sheets into the exam. I've already
copied out a few hundred essays and a volume of past successful
essays from the second and third rounds. Year after year, the examiners tend to recycle these same shopworn topics, and probably
won't go into the "Five Books and Six Classics."[1] Moreover, for
the last round, no matter short or long, I expect they'll stick to the
same handful of themes. I doubt they would ask us to compose
poetry or rhymed prose. There is only one thing: as the old saying
goes, every wine shop sells bad wine, but only the expert gets away
with it. It all depends on finishing the job without leaving a
trace! I wrapped the cheat sheets into a bundle that looks like a roll
of firecrackers. Before I go inside the exam room, I will insert it into
my anus. Even a spirit wouldn't be able to find it there. What a marvelous idea! It's a good thing that I used to enjoy cavorting with
men, and opened up this territory for development, so that now it's

capacious enough to hide the cheat sheets. I rehearsed this yesterday; it was as easy as traveling on a familiar road in a light carriage,
entirely unlike trying to push something through goat entrails or
some other narrow chute. If anyone decided to take up this method
at the very last moment without such preparation, even with five
strong men working hard, it would still take a lot of chiseling
and hacking to bore a wide enough tunnel. (ZHOU *laughs and sings*)

In the Mode of *Zhenggong: Sibianjing* (Quiet in All Four Directions)

Neither a bag nor a sac, this receptacle for hiding cheat
    sheets is truly marvelous;
I will carry essays into the exam cell
undetected by the proctor!
If the topic chances to coincide with the essays,
all I need to do is copy it out.
This comes straight out of my belly;
    it's my genuine talent and learning!

(ZHOU *speaks*) It is still a few days away from the metropolitan exam;
I need to take care of something important first. Mr. Cao Gechen
promised me his daughter's hand if I passed the exam at the provincial level. Now is the perfect time to get down to business and
wrap up this marriage proposal. If I marry Miss Cao, after I take my
official post, I would not need to hire any special advisors. In addition, I'd have a father-in-law in the Hanlin Academy at court, who
would shield me from any superiors who might try to lord it over
me. This will be crucial to my future career. In addition, I have heard
that Fan Jiefu changed his name to Shi Jian and also passed the
provincial level examination in Zhejiang. If he hasn't given up his
diabolical plan to marry Miss Cao, I'm afraid he might start

foolishly dreaming of seeking her out again now that he is in the capital. I need to let Mr. Cao in on this secret, so I won't be cheated out of Miss Cao by Shi Jian. I now ask my servant to prepare a calling card signed "your student." I will sign "your son-in-law" soon enough, but I'll leave it at "your student" for now. Cao will hold me in high esteem when we meet again; in rushing out to greet me, he will put on his shoes backwards.[2] (ZHOU *exits with his servant*)

Prelude in the Mode of *Xianlü: Fanbusuan* (Foreign Divination)

(CAO GECHEN *enters wearing casual attire, with his*
        SERVANT *and sings*)
My daughter has recently recovered from her illness;
this father feels relieved from stress.
Now is the time to seek a good son-in-law,
Whom will I select as the lucky fellow?

(CAO *speaks*) Ever since I brought in Jianyun to be my daughter's companion, I've been overjoyed to see my daughter recover completely from her illness and revive her radiant good looks. This is the year of the metropolitan examination; among the three hundred successful examinees, there will certainly be a few who are still unmarried. I shall pick a son-in-law from the roster. Now that the exam period is approaching, based on my experience and my rank and salary, I ought to be one of the examiners. But many officials will try to pull strings to be chosen as examiners, and I am not sure if I will have a chance. I'll just leave it up to Providence. As the saying goes: don't rush to be the first in following the tide, instead be content with your fate and stay relaxed. (ZHOU GONGMENG *and his servant enter*) A precious son-in-law has come from thousands of miles away; there ought to be magpies announcing his arrival at your door. (*The servant hands* ZHOU's *calling card to* CAO) (CAO *reads the card*) Oh, Zhou Gongmeng has passed the provincial level examination. This reminds me that Mr. Wang Zhongxiang acted as his matchmaker a few years ago, and I promised that I'd approve if he passed the exam. If he brings it up now, how should I respond? (CAO *hesitates*) (THE MESSENGER, *in the clown role, enters in a hurry*) Announcement! Announcement! (THE SERVANT) What are you announcing? (THE MESSENGER) I am here to announce that Mr. Cao is summoned to be one of the examiners. (*The servant reports the news to* CAO, *who says*) Since I am summoned to be an exam reader, I should avoid seeing anybody. Please tell the doorman to close the gate. (CAO's SERVANT *answers and goes out to see* ZHOU) My master is summoned to be an examiner, and therefore he has to excuse himself from seeing any guests. Sir, please go back for now, and Mr. Cao will see you after the exam period is over. (CAO's SERVANT *closes the gate*) (CAO) Don't blame me for tightly guarding the pass; he should know the emperor's rules are strict. (CAO's SERVANT *follows* CAO *to exit*) (ZHOU) If only I had come a few minutes earlier, then when Mr. Cao received the order to serve as an examination judge, we could have agreed on a code with which to identify my exam. In that case, not only a marriage, but also examination success would have been mine. What an unfortunate coincidence! (ZHOU *sings*)

In the Mode of *Zhenggong: Fumalang*
(Lad with a Lucky Horse)

Bad luck, bad luck, such bad luck!
A few minutes too late and
I missed my chance.

Now I won't be able to reap the advantages of
having a father-in-law as my examiner!

(ZHOU *speaks*) Go ahead and avoid other people, but what's wrong with
seeing your own son-in-law? (ZHOU *sings*)

> You need not be so pretentious,
> you and I will be like blood relations,
> no need to fear people talking behind our backs.

(ZHOU *speaks*) Well, now that I have a belly full of essays ready to
excrete, why do I need anyone's help? After I have passed the exam,
I will come and discuss the marriage with him. He won't be able to
reject me then! (ZHOU *sings*)

> I am so talented that I do not need my father-in-law's aid;
> I will seek Miss Cao's hand after I've risen in the ranks;
> let me now sharpen my sword to go slay the dragon,
> I shouldn't wait around idly for good fortune to drop into
> > my lap.

SCENE 29

SEARCHING THE CRACK

(THE LOVE MESSENGER[1] *enters and says*) Don't say that marriages happen by chance; a red string of love secretly ties everything together. Let the villain devise his devious plots, they'll all be in vain; the Bronze Sparrow Tower was never able to lock up the two Qiao sisters.[2] I am the love messenger. Since I secretly guided Miss Cui and Miss Cao into tying their marital knot at the Rain-Flower Nunnery, Zhou Gongmeng has managed to break up the pair of lovebirds with a wicked scheme. Now that that scoundrel Zhou has piled up a veritable mountain of villainous deeds, and Shi Jian will soon acquire fame and success, I must discuss this matter with the Star of Literature and the Divine Arbiter of Exams: first as retribution, we should expose Zhou's cheating and have him severely beaten; then we will ensure that Shi Jian's exam essays are delivered to Cao Gechen for grading, and eventually turn them from teacher-and-student into father-and-son-in-law. Today is the first day of the exam period. I ought to pay a visit to the exam arena. It's just as the saying goes: when one's wicked deeds have piled up to heaven, it's finally time to pay for them. How could predestined marriages not be Heaven's will? (THE LOVE MESSENGER *exits*)

Passing Tune in the Mode of *Xianlü: Xiaopenglai* (A Minor Paradise)

(THE SUPERINTENDENT *of the capital, an older man role, enters dressed in official attire; a group of actors playing doormen, guards, and yamen runners enter with him as he sings*)

As the imperial Superintendent,
My prestige is as lofty as the tallest mountain;
supervising the examination adds to my renown.
Lighting a torch to peer into the dark depths, this I pledge:
I will relentlessly root out any and all counterfeits;
the true dragon will then emerge.

(THE SUPERINTENDENT *speaks*) I am the Superintendent of the capital, and I am following the emperor's order to monitor the examination precincts. Externally I need to stop the examinees from currying favor with the examination officials; internally I ought to prevent the examiners from providing clues to their students. The civil examination is an important ritual of the state, the source of fairness in recruiting court officials. Not only must I work hard without complaining, but I must also overcome difficulties with great caution. Guards! (*Many voices respond*) (THE SUPERINTENDENT) In the past the metropolitan examination was different from the provincial examination, and body-searches were only conducted perfunctorily. As a result, both "dragons and ordinary fish made it through together," bringing charlatans as well as genuine talents into the ranks of successful graduates. Today we must be strict and not repeat such previous negligence. (*Many voices answer affirmatively*) (THE SUPERINTENDENT) Now open the gate and let the examinees in, one by one. (*Drumroll and trumpet, the gate opens*) (*A staff member holding a placard brings in* SHI JIAN) The examinee whose name is on the first placard is entering! (THE SUPERINTENDENT) Search him carefully! (*Many voices answer loudly;* SHI JIAN *is searched*) The search is complete, and no contraband has been found. (SHI JIAN *receives his exam paper and exits*) (*A staff member holding a placard brings in* ZHANG ZHONGYOU) The examinee whose name is on the second placard is entering! (THE SUPERINTENDENT) Search him carefully! (*Many voices answer loudly,* ZHANG *is searched*) The search is complete, and no contraband found. (*The second examinee receives his exam paper and exits*) (*A staff member holding a placard brings in the third examinee, in the clown role*). The examinee whose name is on the third placard is entering! (THE SUPERINTENDENT) Search him carefully! (*Many voices answer loudly and search the examinee*) Search is complete, nothing suspicious is found. (*The third examinee receives his exam paper and exits.*) (*A staff member holding a placard brings in* ZHOU GONGMENG) The examinee whose name is on the fourth placard is entering! (THE SUPERINTENDENT) Search him carefully! (*Many people answer loudly, and are flabbergasted when they pat down* ZHOU's *rear*) What's this? How come this gentleman has a tail? (ZHOU) I have a hemorrhoid there. It hurts a lot, please don't touch it! (*People find the essays on* ZHOU) It turns out to be a volume of essays. (*Many voices shout out*) We have found contraband! (THE SUPERINTENDENT) Bring the evidence here. (*People spread out the essays on his desk*) (THE SUPERINTENDENT *sniffs around*) Where is that foul smell coming from? (*Many voices*) Master: We found this volume of essays inside someone's anus. (THE SUPERINTENDENT *covers his nose and retches*) Take it away! Bring the accused to me. (ZHOU *kneels in front of him*) (THE SUPERINTENDENT) You obviously do not know a thing about writing essays, and that's why you stowed away these cheat sheets. Let me ask you: where did you obtain the title of provincial graduate? (ZHOU) I achieved it by writing essays. (THE SUPERINTENDENT) Where did you get the essays? (ZHOU) My essays came out of my belly. (THE SUPERINTENDENT) You still won't confess? Bring me the finger squeezers! (ZHOU) How could you apply finger squeezers to a provincial graduate?[3] (THE SUPERINTENDENT) If you don't want to be clamped, then I shall give you the exam face-to-face. (ZHOU) I can't take that punishment; I would rather be clamped. (THE SUPERINTENDENT) In that case, clamp him! (*People clamp his fingers*) (ZHOU *shouts*) I can't take clamping either! I will confess. (THE SUPERINTENDENT) All right, confess right now!

Passing Tune in the Mode of *Zhonglü: Zhumaqi* (Halting the Horse to Sob)

[ZHUMATING (HALTING THE HORSE TO LISTEN)]

(ZHOU *sings*)
With a small ruse,
I earned my scholarly titles with ease.

(THE SUPERINTENDENT *speaks*) Was it by asking someone to take the exam in your place? Or by receiving the answers from someone else? Or, did you bribe the examiner into providing you with the questions?)

(ZHOU *sings*)
No one took the exam for me,
or delivered the answers to me,
I didn't bribe anyone, either.

(ZHOU *speaks*) I bought off an old exam proctor, who cut off someone's essay and pasted it on my exam paper. It was like (ZHOU *sings*)

stealing a bag of fruit by snipping its string, and
making a straw rain-cape by stitching the pieces together.

[QI YAN HUI (CRYING FOR YAN HUI)]

I therefore snatched my title in the exam last fall.
Who could have guessed that my true identity would be
    exposed this spring?[4]

(THE SUPERINTENDENT *speaks*) I see! The officers in charge of the
    provincial exams are utterly laughable for letting someone like him
    get away with his tricks undetected. (THE SUPERINTENDENT *sings*)

(*To the same tune as before*)
It is all because of those pedantic numbskulls, who
allowed a bunch of puppeteers to hijack our hallowed exam
    precincts.
They confuse deer with horses,
substitute sheep for cows, and
mix up fishes with dragons.

(THE SUPERINTENDENT *speaks*) That student labored for countless
    nights and wrote seven excellent essays at the provincial examina-
    tion, only to have them stolen by you. Is there no justice in this
    world? (THE SUPERINTENDENT *sings*)

Such a pity that he practiced ten years of needlework,
only to have someone else steal his wedding dress.[5]

(THE SUPERINTENDENT *speaks*) Call the attendants to drag him away
    and give him fifty strokes of heavy bamboo, then put him in the
    cangue. (THE SUPERINTENDENT *sings*)

You, a beast in human clothing, deserve to die,
an essay-stealing bandit shouldn't be allowed to live!

(*Attendants deliver the lashings to* ZHOU) (THE SUPERINTENDENT *speaks*)
Lock him up in front of the exam compound; I will deal with him
after the exam is over. (*Attendants lock* ZHOU *with the cangue*) (THE
SUPERINTENDENT) Discipline the examinees to boost their morale;
initiate reforms and root out corruption to show our gratitude to
the emperor. (*Music rises and the gate is closed; the group of attendants
follows* THE SUPERINTENDENT *to exit*) (*As a theatrical transition
ensues,* ZHOU *yells, "Ouch!"*) (SHI JIAN'S STEWARD *in a clown role and*
ZHANG'S STEWARD *in an assistant painted-face role enter and recite*)
When our masters enter the exam hall, we servants share in their
glory. / We will become the senior stewards, serving our first-place
masters. (SHI JIAN'S STEWARD) I am the steward of Mr. Shi from
Jiaxing. (ZHANG'S STEWARD) I am the steward of Mr. Zhang from
Yangzhou. Our young masters went in for the exam; we are waiting
to meet them in front of the exam compound. (SHI JIAN'S STEW-
ARD) Oh, that's Zhou Gongmeng. Why is he locked up there?
(ZHANG'S STEWARD) We recognize him, but he doesn't know us;
let's go up to him and ask. Old chap, why are you wearing this
cangue? (ZHOU *sighs*) Unlucky, damned unlucky, I obtained the
juren title all for nothing. I passed the previous exam by cutting off
and stealing someone's essays, but this time I was found smuggling
in some notes. I spent a great deal of time and energy copying sam-
ple essays, bundled them up in wax paper, and stuffed them up my
arse. It was only because the officers' loud voices startled me into
farting that things went awry. This bundle of damned essays was
bound to make trouble; how could it have withstood the force of
my passing wind? At first, the bundle only protruded an inch or so,
and I tried really hard to hold it in. But those damned security people pulled out the whole fragrant lump. The guards brought it in to

demonstrate their diligence and ask for a reward; but it was mistaken as a sweet Osmanthus fan pendant, and when they opened it up, the foul smell spread everywhere in the hall, leading the examination clerks to flee and their supervisor to nearly vomit. He recited a couple of lines from *The Story of the Lute* to the effect that I have nothing in my belly but a pile of crap. The supervisor then threw down ten bamboo slips[6] and condemned me to fifty flesh-gouging strokes of the bamboo cane. Then he ordered me to be locked up outside the gate, with the charges to be determined after the exam is over. (*Both stewards roll over laughing*) That is hilarious! The caning and the cangue, all of it! Marvelous, marvelous, indeed marvelous! Old chap, do you recognize us? (ZHOU) No, I don't. (SHI JIAN'S STEWARD) My young master is called Shi Jiefu. (ZHANG'S STEWARD) My young master is Zhang Zhongyou. (ZHOU) Oh, I see. They are both good friends of mine. (SHI JIAN'S STEWARD) Good friend? Good friend, indeed! In days past, he suffered at your hands. First you slandered him to Cao, and later badmouthed him at the school. Although my master couldn't avoid your stab in the back, today you yourself cannot escape when retribution is due. Old Zhou, Old Zhou, let me tell you this: (SHI JIAN *sings*)

> (*To the same tune as before*)
> You have committed so many evil deeds;
>> surely you cannot escape from the net of Heavenly justice
>> in which you have landed.

(SHI JIAN *speaks*) You schemed so hard against my master. Now that he is doing well, what has happened to your proud demeanor? (SHI JIAN *sings*)

>> Even if your Mouth is as venomous as snakes and
>> scorpions, and
>> your heart is as vicious as jackals and wolves,

> you can do nothing to my young master,
> who aspires to soar high like the legendary roc.

(ZHANG'S STEWARD *says to* SHI JIAN'S STEWARD) You should not make fun of Zhou Gongmeng. Who says he's not basking in glory even now? Look at him, (ZHANG'S STEWARD *sings*)

> he alone is congratulated at his very own imperial banquet,
> surrounded by onlookers tightly squeezed together.

(ZHANG'S STEWARD *speaks*) He'll be locked up here for a day or two; when Mr. Cao hears of this, he will come to his rescue. Zhou has (ZHANG'S STEWARD *sings*)

> a prospective father-in-law as virtuous as Confucius.
> How can he allow his son-in-law to be shackled as a
> common criminal?

(*A bugle call is heard from inside the stage*) (BOTH STEWARDS *speak*) It is probably time for the gate to be opened. Let's leave here for now and come back with our masters. (*They both leave*) (ZHOU *sighs and says*) With their servants I've already been utterly humiliated. When they themselves come out, how will they insult me? I want to hit my head against the wall and put an end to my suffering, but the cangue keeps me from going anywhere. I'm stuck here with no way out. (SHI JIAN *and* ZHANG *enter together*) A ten-thousand-word essay has exhausted both heavenly and human matters; let's wait and see who will be praised as today's Dong Zhongshu.[7] (BOTH STEWARDS) Masters, you have come out. We have a very delightful piece of news. Gongmeng was given fifty strokes of the cane for smuggling in essays, and now he is locked in a cangue in front of the compound. We made sport of him just now, but we still haven't had our fill of fun. Young Masters, let's go together and thoroughly humiliate him to get even. (SHI JIAN) No, we cannot do that. Although he wronged me before, after all, it's thanks to his goading that I've gotten to where I am today. Besides, he has already been punished by Heaven; we should be magnanimous. (ZHANG) What my cousin-in-law says is correct. (*They walk by* ZHOU *covering up their faces*) Although we are not as lofty-minded as He Wu, we should certainly hold to Liu Kuan's tolerant attitude.[8] (ZHANG *and* SHI JIAN *exit*) (BOTH STEWARDS *point and curse at* ZHOU) This time we let this bastard off lightly. (*They exit the stage*) (ZHOU) I fully expected them to insult me, but who knew that they simply covered their faces and passed me by? (ZHOU *sighs and says*) Now I realize that Shi Jian is indeed a gentleman and I am a petty scoundrel. (ZHOU *sings*)

> (*To the same tune as before*)
> Kind and charitable,
> he could tolerate people like me a hundred times over.
> Ashamed that I was crafty but not sensible,
> going against my conscience I had eyes but failed to see.
> I spent half my life dreaming to become Duke Zhou;
> now I have finally awoken from this pipe dream.

(ZHOU *speaks*) I have made such a fool of myself. How will I face others? It would be better to find a way to end my life. (ZHOU *sings*)

> I have left a bad reputation in my native place.
> What face do I have to return?
>
> I planned to have the last laugh but ended up in tears,
> chasing after fame I have reaped only shame;
> this started off well but went nowhere,
> I may not be dead yet, but I'm already in my casket.

SCENE 30

IMPORTUNING A MATCHMAKER

To the Prelude of *Shuangdiao: Yeyouhu*
(Drifting on the Lake at Night)

(CAO GECHEN *enters wearing his cap, accompanied by* CAO'S
SERVANT)
With one glance Bo Le[1] was able to pick out all the best
steeds;

lofty talents vie with one another at court.

The list of those passed has been announced,

the exam cells have been dismantled.

One after another, phoenixes all gather around.[2]

(CAO *speaks*) I was invited to be an examiner for the oral examination,
and during my labors, I often worried that the candidates assigned
to me wouldn't make it through all of the subsequent hurdles and
succeed. But when the list of winners was announced, who would
have expected that some of the top-placed scholars came from
my division? In the first place is Shi Jian, a scholar who passed
the provincial exam at Jiaxing; the second place is Zhang Sanyi,
also known as Zhang Zhongyou from Yangzhou. I have known
him since before the examination. But because of the marriage

proposal, we had a falling out and I feel quite awkward seeing him today. Tell the servants: if my students come to pay me a visit, let me know immediately. (CAO'S SERVANT *gestures his assent*)

(*To the same tune as before*)
(SHI JIAN *and* ZHANG ZHONGYOU *enter dressed in official
     attire.* SHI JIAN'S STEWARD *and* ZHANG ZHONGYOU'S
     STEWARD *enter with them*)
(SHI JIAN s*ings*)
I fell into the abyss in my former days, but
now I have risen up thanks to your kind patronage;
·the same hands that threw stones at me
now help me climb up the ladder into the sky.
(ZHANG ZHONGYOU)
Who could have expected that a tumbleweed
would turn into peaches and plums that,
though they cannot speak, transform the ground around
     them into paths trod by eager visitors.³

(SHI JIAN *speaks*) I am a second-tier *jinshi*⁴and my name is Shi Jian. (ZHANG ZHONGYOU) I am a third-tier *jinshi* and my name is Zhang Sanyi. Cousin-in-law, a few years ago, you and I offended Mr. Cao for proposing to his daughter. You were slandered and I was cursed to my face by him. Who would have expected that now, our exam papers were assigned to him for grading? Now we owe him our gratitude for recognizing our talent and selecting us as *jinshi*; we can put all of that bad blood of the past behind us. (SHI JIAN) Since you were once Mr. Cao's good friend, and have now reconnected with him as his student, it is perfectly natural for your former antagonism to have dissipated. As for me, I have suffered a wrong that has yet to be made right, while his misunderstanding is still unexplained. Therefore, at our first meeting with him today, we absolutely must not tell him the truth. Let's find a way to deal with all of this after we have heard from your cousin. (ZHANG) What you have said makes sense to me. (CAO's SERVANT *announces the arrival of* SHI *and* ZHANG) (CAO *meets the two of them;* SHI *and* ZHANG *greet* CAO *with respect*) Shallow in knowledge and lacking talent, we are but pedantic bookworms. You have turned our stone into gold, and helped us to trade our scales for feathers, transforming us from earthbound fish into eagles soaring up into the skies.[5] Your kindness to us is as great as the universe, your benevolence dearer than that of our parents. (CAO) Now, I have taken you two prominent students under my wing. Both of you are of exceptional talent, standing high above your peers. Though I am but a feeble old man with limited understanding of the world, I have been lucky to enjoy a decent reputation among my contemporaries, and was able to grow close to the emperor, becoming the recipient of honors and glory in my advanced years. (CAO *invites both young men to sit down*) Mr. Shi, for such a young man, your writing is quite mature. How old are you this year?

To the Tune of *Zhuomuer* (Woodpecker)

(SHI JIAN *sings*)
Ashamed to compare myself to Zhong Jun, Jia Yi,[6] and
    Ziqi,[7]
I am already twenty years of age.
(CAO *sings*) Are you married?
(SHI JIAN *sings*)
People laugh at me—
Like Liang Hong, I am old and still single,[8]
Like Sima Xiangru, I am[9]—
A wanderer with no one to depend on.

(SHI JIAN *speaks*) When my late father was alive and serving in various official posts around the country, he made an engagement for me with the daughter of a colleague. But later the two families moved away from one another, and we lost contact. This is why I've put off my wedding, and still remain unmarried to this day. (CAO) Youth passes quickly; a reunion between you and your former fiancée seems implausible at this point. You should seek another good match. (SHI JIAN *sings*)

> In my humble days, it was hard to find my old sword.[10]
> Now I still haven't prepared another jade mirror;[11]
> therefore, I often resemble a lonely goose flying with only
> its own shadow as a companion.

(CAO) Mr. Zhang, it has already been three years since we parted at Yangzhou. I had an irascible temperament back then and greatly offended you with my inconsiderate words. I hope you won't bear me any grudge. (ZHANG) I shouldn't have poked my nose into that business and offended you greatly. For that I still feel regret, even now. (ZHANG *sings*)

> (*To the same tune as before*)
> I often look back,
> remembering past mistakes of
> offending your honor;
> for this I am deeply regretful.

(ZHANG *speaks*) I hope that my esteemed teacher will be generous and forgiving, and let bygones be bygones; only then can I be at ease. (ZHANG *sings*)

> Please forgive me for my brash ignorance, and overlook
> my petulant bluster,

take pity on this unenlightened fool, and your benevolence will command the respect of all.

(CAO *speaks*) What happened to that Mr. Fan then?

(ZHANG ZHONGYOU sings)
He has long shed his scholar's cap and gown like a cicada's shell;
He hides among fisherfolk, draped under a straw rain-cape;
Who knows on which outcrop he perches, peering out over the fog-drenched shore?

(*A staff member enters holding a report in hand and says*) The ministers presented their memorials at the royal court; the emperor sends out his edicts from the palace. The Ministry of War has issued an official newsletter, which I now deliver for Your Honor's perusal. (CAO *reads the newsletter*) This document from the Ministry of War is about the conferment of vassal status to the Ryukyu Islands. The imperial edict says: The Ryukyu Islands is a large nation in the Southeast; the conferral ceremony should be conducted by an experienced official. The historian-scholar Cao Gechen from the Hanlin Academy possesses excellent rhetorical skills, and is also seasoned and reliable. I therefore order him to accept this edict and immediately proceed to the Ryukyu Islands to carry out the conferral ceremony. (CAO *looks surprised*) Huh, why the sudden mission? (SHI JIAN *and* ZHANG) Teacher, you have received an order directly from the emperor, to represent him as an imperial envoy to a great vassal state. This is an auspicious and magnificent event in a time of great peace. Why do you look troubled? (CAO) You might not know this, but the Ryukyu Islands are located in the Eastern Seas, and one can only get there by boat. When I was in Shandong last year, I met the envoy of the Ryukyu Islands who had come to request conferment. He ran into a typhoon and was almost shipwrecked. Only someone young and in his prime will be competent to perform this task. I am old and timid and cannot endure the hardship of traveling at sea; this is why I am troubled. (SHI JIAN *turns his back to* CAO) The Ryukyu Islands are not far from China, and the conferral ceremony is a plum assignment. Why is he so scared? If I want to ask for his daughter's hand, then I must first get on his good side. I have an idea. (SHI JIAN *turns back to face* CAO) Teacher, ever since I was little, I was fond of reading books about exotic places, and I often felt ashamed of having stayed close to home without achieving anything out of the ordinary. Now that you have selected me as a *jinshi*, I would like a chance to repay your kindness. Let me write a memorial to the emperor and ask to replace you on this mission. (CAO) If you can do this for me, that would be wonderful. (SHI JIAN *and* ZHANG) We will be leaving for now. (CAO) Mr. Shi, goodbye for now. Mr. Zhang, would you please remain behind so that I can have a word with you? (SHI JIAN) Volunteering for battle is not a routine event during a flourishing dynasty; to be a diplomat one has to learn the rituals of a peaceful age. (SHI JIAN *exits*) (ZHANG) Teacher, what did you want to talk about? (CAO) I offended you in the past all because of my daughter's marriage. Fortunately, my daughter has not yet married. May I ask you to be a matchmaker for her in order to fix my mistake? (CAO *sings*)

To the Tune of *Sanduanzi* (Three Suites)

> It is not too late to atone for my offense,
> my daughter is still waiting to be engaged.

(ZHANG ZHONGYOU) I would be happy to help you with anything but this. As soon as you mentioned the word "matchmaking," I got a headache. Ever since I was rebuked by you, I posted a warning note on my door and swore in front of the gods: never again will I try to make a match for others.

> I swore off matchmaking many years ago.
> Having been there, I will not stray into that territory again.

(ZHANG *gets up and says*) I bid you farewell for now. (CAO *tries to keep* ZHANG *there and says*) You should not be so stubborn. (CAO *sings*)

> This matchmaking is much anticipated and hardly unintentional,
> the one who started it all should finish it.
> (ZHANG *sings*)
> I would rather be called shallow and stubborn,
> than give myself cause for regret.

(CAO) At that time, Mr. Fan already had a wife; you can hardly blame me for rejecting the marriage proposal. This time I already have someone in mind, and I only want to ask you to be the matchmaker for a readymade union. Is that really too difficult for you? (ZHANG) May I ask who you have in mind? (CAO) It is Mr. Shi who just left. (ZHANG) Although we two are both your disciples, I do not know him well. According to what he just said, he is already engaged. This is the same situation as before with Mr. Fan. (CAO) You don't have to worry about this. I want to take him in as my son-in-law to care for me in my old age. As long as he agrees, it will all be thanks to you. Whatever may have happened before or might yet happen after this matchmaking is not your responsibility. (ZHANG) I don't dare carry out this task until I have your word on this. (ZHANG *sings*)

To the Tune of *Guichaohuan* (Happy to Be Back at Court)

Entrusted with this task,

how can I refuse a second time?

I will have to temporarily put my rule on hold.

(CAO *sings*)

Don't be such a stickler for rules,

seize the moment.

This marriage is quite different from last time!

(ZHANG *sings*)

May I ask you, teacher, if Brother Shi agrees to this marriage, then

when do you expect the wedding day to be?

(CAO *sings*)

The nuptial ceremony would be carried out tomorrow.

(*They sing together*)

Let us make this teacher-student pair turn into father-in-law and son-in-law

in a match already made.

(*They both exit the stage*)

SCENE 31

GRANTING THE MARRIAGE

Prelude in the Mode of *Yuediao: Zhu Yingtai jin*
(Zhu Yingtai Draws Near)

(JIANYUN *enters and sings*)
We made a surprise attack, and
deployed a risky stratagem,
thank heavens we were victorious.
I've heard that my adoptive father
has fallen for our clever scheme.
(YUHUA *enters*)
How can the younger sister marry first,
thereby delaying her elder sister's marriage?
I am much chagrined by such a plot twist.

(JIANYUN *speaks*) Younger sister, Shi Jian has become father's student;
isn't this a case of Heaven's will according with man's desires? Yesterday when selecting a son-in-law from among the successful
graduates, father coincidentally picked him and asked my cousin
Mr. Zhang to act as the matchmaker. It looks like this marriage will
soon come about. (JIANYUN *sings*)

To the Tune of *Zhu Yingtai* (Zhu Yingtai)

This means that
the heartbreak of these past several years and
the tears shed at three different places
can all be mopped up and put away, as of today.
Let's hurry up and prepare ten brocaded flags, and
one stick of holy incense,
To show our gratitude to the spirits of the Rain-Flower
    Nunnery.

(JIANYUN *speaks*) Younger sister, now that we are together, thinking
    back to when we first formed our alliance, it was indeed quite silly.
    (JIANYUN *sings*)

Looking back,
if Heaven had not allowed our wish to come true today,
would we really be fated to wait it out till our next lives?
This foolish business of ours
in the end relied entirely on heavenly help!

(YUHUA *speaks*) You are happy for me, but I am now very worried for
    you. (YUHUA *sings*)

To the tune of *Di'er huantou* (Second Variation)

I am vexed.
Although you are keen as an impartial outside observer,
when you are caught up in the situation on the inside, can
    you get to the bottom of things?
How many times have we seen that when saving someone
    who has fallen into a well,

the victim reaches safety first while the rescuer sinks down
to the bottom?
You and I swore we would
hold this Fan family broomstick together.
But should one of us be in front and the other at the back?
Does this mean I will make you sleep on a lonely pillow,
going to bed late, and gazing up at the Altair Star, a boy
pulling his ox across the sky?[1]

(YUHUA'S MAID, *Liuchun, enters*) The wedding day approaches; conjugal bliss we must not delay. Young Mistress, just now Mr. Zhang came to tell us that the marriage proposal has been accepted by Mr. Shi, and the wedding ceremony will be conducted tonight. (JIANYUN *is elated*) Thank Heavens! From now on we will have no further worries whatsoever. Younger sister, it is time for you to do your make up and get dressed. (YUHUA *sits silently still*) (JIANYUN) What's the matter? I have taxed the limits of my ingenuity to finally win this piece of good news. Now, you are apparently not happy to hear it; on the contrary, you are looking very sad. What is this about? (YUHUA) Originally, I agreed to marry you, not him; even when I agreed to marry him, it was all for you. But as of now when your own fate has yet to be settled, how can I go on ahead all by myself? (JIANYUN) Well, in that case, then what do you want to do? (YUHUA) I will go ahead with this only if we tell my father the truth, so that I can be together with you . . . (JIANYUN) Together to do what? (YUHUA *appears bashful and* JIANYUN *smiles*) For someone as smart as you, that is a silly thing to say. Do you think the truth is something we can so easily explain to that father of yours? If we do tell him, we'll have to start from the very beginning and explain all of its twists and turns. (YUHUA'S MAID) It is time! Young Mistress, you need to do your makeup and dress up for the wedding now. (JIANYUN) Liuchun, please bring me the makeup box, and I will help your Young Mistress with her makeup. (JIANYUN *combs* YUHUA's *hair and sings*)

To the Tune of *Disan huantou* (Third Variation)

> Shiny and luminous,
> no need for pomades,
> your hair is naturally lustrous.

(JIANYUN *speaks*) The color of your brows is just perfect, neither too heavy nor too light, and hence there is no need to pencil them in. I will just shape the tips a little higher. (JIANYUN *paints* YUHUA's *brows and continues to sing*)

> Even if I could draw brows as stunning as the far
>   mountains,
> or as gorgeous as painted moths,[2]
> they would still pale next to your natural eyebrows!

(YUHUA's MAID *exits the stage. She reenters with the wedding gown and says*) Here I have the Young Mistress's newly sewn wedding gown. (JIANYUN's MAID *enters and* JIANYUN *takes a look at the gown*) This dress is too big for your svelte waistline. Let me draw it in a few stitches. (JIANYUN *sews and sings*)

> To narrow your wedding gown,
> today I'll take the measurements for your waistline,
> so that in a few years we shall see if you've lost or gained
>   weight.
> (JIANYUN *has completed* YUHUA's *makeup and takes a long
>   look at her*)

Look closely at your delicate, tender beauty;
you're a perfect gift for that man to accept and enjoy!

(*To the same tune as before*)
(YUHUA *sings*)
Listen to me,
If that person asks about your whereabouts,
How do you want me to respond to his inquiries?

(JIANYUN *speaks*) If he asks about me, just tell him to rest assured and stop worrying; I have a plan to take care of things.

(YUHUA *sings*)
Do you think that by telling him to "rest assured" and
"stop fretting," you will relieve him of his anxiety?

(JIANYUN *speaks*) You worry too much! He and you will soon be in the thrall of nuptial pleasures. Do you think that he will have time to ask about me?

(YUHUA *sings*)
I feel embarrassed, as
I am afraid that the new wife is too ugly to look at, and
the groom will soon wish he could have the old one back.

(YUHUA *speaks*) Elder sister, you may talk all you want, but you ought to come up with a concrete plan soon, so that the three of us can be together again and free of all of these worries. (YUHUA *sings*)

I urge you to imitate Lin Xiangru, and quickly return the
jade intact to the State of Zhao.[3]

To the Tune of *Gewei* (Apart at the End)

(YUHUA *and* JIANYUN *sing together*)
Rejoicing face to face,
lips smiling to one another,
worries and misgivings are all discarded;
we prepare to celebrate one sweet wedding after another.

Prelude in the Mode of *Zhonglü: Juhuaxin* (Chrysanthemums Are New)

(CAO GECHEN *enters wearing official attire and sings*)
My daughter got herself a wonderful groom today,
it was all worthwhile for me to be picky.
Ice and jade are equal in their purity,[4] but
I am embarrassed that my student has surpassed me.

(CAO *speaks*) The young Shi has accepted a position in the Ministry of Defense. I've heard that the emperor issued an imperial edict, granting him first-rank official attire and appointing him as the imperial envoy to the Ryukyu Islands. I wonder when he will depart? I shall worry about this after the wedding ceremony.

(*To the same tune as before*)

(SHI JIAN *enters dressed in a brocade wedding robe and cap.* ZHANG ZHONGYOU *enters with* THE CAO FAMILY SERVANT. *Both act as* SHI JIAN's *entourage; one carries the imperial edict; the other holds the tally. A group of people enter playing gongs, horns, and drums*) (SHI JIAN *sings*)

With the emperor's tally stick in hand, I take leave of the capital.
Dare I tarry for my wedding ceremony?

Granted an additional three days to stay,
I am deeply thankful for the emperor's generosity.

(SHI JIAN *meets and greets* CAO) (CAO) Dear son-in-law, when will you be taking off? (SHI JIAN) One ought not to delay even overnight when he receives an imperial order, so I should take my leave immediately; but since I reported to the emperor that I am getting married, His Majesty kindly gave me three days of leave. (CAO) This is great! (CAO *invites* SHI *to enter the house with courtesy*) (YUHUA *enters*) (*They greet each other casually*)

Passing Tune in the Mode of *Zhonglü: Dahuanzhuo* (Wearing a Big Ring)

(*They sing in unison*)
This good marriage is made in Heaven, and it is
    indeed
a marriage of divine destiny!
The groom and bride are equally attractive,
their minds are similarly creative, and
they both come from families of great distinction.
The groom is young and dressed in brocade, and
the bride, having just reached sixteen,
has already been conferred with the Five-Flower
    Colors, as well as the Seven-Perfumed Carriage.[5]
Are they a common couple from the mundane
    world?
They must be two immortals from the Daoist realm!
Bubbling with laughter, guests move in throngs.
The evening haze and fragrant incense form auspicious
    clouds,
rising up in plumes signifying luck in love.

Weisheng (Closing Tune)

Gauze lanterns, precious candles, and gigantic flowers,
the sumptuously decorated hall is lit up bright as day.
We can expect that
such an imperially bestowed night of bliss shall be
repeated more than once.

(*Everyone exits the stage except* JIANYUN'S MAID, *who says to herself*)
Falling low, falling low, [my Young Mistress] lost her advantage and
broke the rules, too. I've only heard of the man who sells his wife
and throws in a pillow, but not of a woman who sells her husband and then serves as his wife's maid. My Young Mistress was
so out of line! She yielded such a good husband to someone else,
and on top of that, she even helped the bride get ready from head
to toe. Now that the newlyweds have entered the wedding chamber together, she sits in her room all alone. How can I swallow
such indignation? I must call her out and make fun of her! Young
Mistress, please come here quickly! (JIANYUN *enters in a hurry*)
Why are you making such a commotion, calling me out like this?
(JIANYUN'S MAID) The second Young Mistress is calling for you.
(JIANYUN) What for? (JIANYUN'S MAID) The two of them
undressed and climbed into bed, then she made "oh, ah" sounds a
few times, and she suddenly got up and called for Hualing, saying: Go tell your mistress that if she wants to help me, she should
follow through to the end. Just now, she combed my hair, washed
my face, and dressed me in my wedding gown. Now she should
also come to endure this pain for me, too! (JIANYUN *laughs and
strikes her maid*) (JIANYUN'S MAID) It is not that I dare to make
fun of you, it's just that if I don't crack a joke, how will you make
it through this night?!

(Jianyun's maid)

The maid keeps her company, counting the sands in the
hourglass;

tonight she lost her bearings, bringing on new sorrow.

(jianyun)

It is not that I am playing coy and prefer to be alone,

but that I have a mind most unusual, and a romance most
unconventional.

SCENE 32

COVETING BEAUTY

Passing Tune in the Mode of *Nanlü: Qiuyeyue*
(Autumn Night Moon)

(WEI KAI, *a clown role, enters dressed luxuriously; a group of
actors playing his entourage enter swaggering and shouting
to clear the way*) (WEI *sings*)

As a spoiled young playboy,

my circumstances are fortunate indeed.

Although when I began my studies I was virtually
illiterate,

I advanced smoothly through the civil service
examinations to the very highest level.

By this I can say,

even Heaven and its deities each have their own private
interests, quite apart from their "public" duties. (WEI
speaks)

My name is Wei Kai, and my father is the current chancellor in charge
of royal affairs. My relatives are all noblemen and marquises, and my
family wealth rivals that of Shi Chong and Wang Kai.[1] By nature,
I disdain smart people; my head is often in a fog. Poetry and history

are my irreconcilable enemies; brushes and ink-stones are only good for concocting a toxic brew. I rushed through my studies of the classics, without understanding a single word. I underlined and circled everything in the texts, and my teacher did not dare to make any corrections. I received a passing score in the last examination and became a petty scholar of no particular distinction. I turned in seven essays without bothering to check for mistakes or infelicities. Who would know that my rich and powerful background opened doors for me, adding even more embellishments to the array of brilliant insignia already weighing down my epaulets? I got my *juren* title without pulling any strings; I acquired my *jinshi* rank without spending even a single penny. The examination officers wanted to curry favor with the rich and powerful; they volunteered to take care of me like a dutiful son pleasing his parents. Once they found my essays in the exam hall, the principal examiner praised them, shouting "bravo!" Apples don't fall far from the tree; who can stop the scion of a family of generals from declaring victory? After the results of the examination were published, my townsmen were all shocked. Celebration gifts and wines were sent to our house one after another; the affairs of human life suddenly changed: the hat of the official is as soft as its gauze wings, while the round collars of the official's robe are as hard as the robe's lower hems. My two hands constantly stroke the silver belt at my waist; my feet repeatedly kick back and forth in their expensive black boots. The three-layered parasol remains unfolded over my head even when I am on the toilet; the manes on my horses are braided into five-petal flowers even when I visit my parents. Dapper, I am indeed dapper! Unrestrained, no doubt, and who can restrain me? Considering all of this, I now have everything, except a ready-made missus who is most sweet, charming, and alluring. (WEI *laughs*) Before I passed the exam, I was engaged to the daughter of a rich family. But she wasn't lucky enough to become my wife, and died before the wedding. Although I am now happily listed on the exam passers' golden registry, I have yet to enjoy a night in the wedding chamber. I've heard that Mr. Cao from the Imperial Academy has a daughter called Yuhua who is most talented and beautiful. I want to send someone to do some matchmaking on my behalf. I am calling my servant to prepare a red calling card. (WEI'S SERVANT, *a secondary older man role, enters and responds*) Master, if you are arranging to have someone deliver a marriage proposal to the Caos, which of their young ladies do you have in mind? (WEI) Miss Yuhua. (WEI'S SERVANT) In that case, Master, forget about it. Someone has already beaten you to it. (WEI KAI) Who did? (WEI'S SERVANT) It was Mr. Shi from Jiaxing who passed together with you in the same class. He married into the Cao family and the wedding was last night. (WEI) How can that have happened without my knowledge? (WEI *stomps his feet and sings*)

To the tune of *Tusi'er* (Baldy)

I stomp my feet, repeatedly lament,
for missing the opportunity and regretting it's too late.
Like visiting Luoyang hearing that the peonies are
blooming everywhere,
I, proud as the spring, wanted to go pluck some flowers
like a bona fide top-ranked thief.
But how could I have expected that wherever I went on my
fancy saddle, I failed to see a single spray?

(WEI'S SERVANT *speaks*) Master, please don't panic. Mr. Cao has one more daughter. (WEI) What? Another one? (WEI'S SERVANT) He has two daughters. The one who married Mr. Shi is the second one. The first one has not been engaged yet. (WEI KAI) Do you know what she looks like? (WEI'S SERVANT) Both daughters are equal in beauty and talent. (WEI'S SERVANT *sings*)

(*To the same tune as before*)
No need to lament,
the opportunity is still yours;
there's still time.
Fortunately, Luoyang still has plenty of flowers;
although it has already been visited by one flower thief,
luckily, the highest branch was left alone because there was
no ladder.

(WEI KAI *speaks*) In that case, I will ask someone to deliver
a proposal to Mr. Cao immediately. (WEI KAI *sings*)

The younger sister is already a newlywed;
the elder sister is still an old maid.
Like me, an old bachelor,
every day she must be suffering, too.

SCENE 33

To the Tune of *Bei zuitaiping*
(Northern Intoxicated with Peace)

(THE KING OF THE RYUKYU ISLANDS, *the painted-face role,*
enters, leading his entourage and sings)
The curled dragon shapes our coastline,
the sea mist rises, endless and vast,
billowing waves surge forth toward the brilliant horizon.
Our borders are secured by a vast expanse of water.
The blades of our swords rise high over frothy surf, and
our reputation for doughtiness reaches China's distant
    shores.
If we are provided with the Zhou ritual implements and
    Han regalia,[1]
we will be monarchs sharing in the glory of the imperial
    Chinese.

(THE KING *speaks*) I am the king of the Ryukyu Islands. Since I sent
    my prime minister to China to request to become a vassal, I have
    relied on the Chinese emperor's august power to fend off our neigh-
    bors' provocations. Thanks to this approach, Siam and Japan have

not encroached on our islands, instead keeping careful watch over the situation. Yesterday a scout came to report: our prime minister has come back with an envoy from China, bringing the emperor's edict with them. I have already sent a royal order throughout the islands for our officials to put everything in order, prepare festive decorations, and solemnly wait for the envoy's arrival. I shall now go down to the port to personally welcome them. (*He repeats the last two lines above*) (SHI JIAN *enters dressed in official attire, leading a group of people*) Wind sends banners billowing, and rosy clouds part open; our neighboring utopian island sets up a sacrificial altar. Stomping on the dragon palace and breaking through sea mist, I carry the imperial edict to the coast where the sun rises. I am Shi Jian, an official from the Office of Scrutiny for War. I was given the status of a first rank officer by the emperor, and I have brought the imperial edict here to confer upon the Ryukyu Islands the status of a vassal nation. I have been traveling by boat, and now I have reached the coast. (*A minor role actor playing the customs officer enters leading a boatman*) Mr. Shi, the customs officer from Haicheng County of Zhangzhou Prefecture has prepared the ship and will help you embark. (SHI JIAN *and his entourage step onto the ship*)

To the Tune of *Nan putianle* (Southern Universal Joy)

(SHI JIAN)
I carry the imperial proclamation;
leading the celestial procession,
catching a heaven-sent breeze,
we ride over turbulent waves.
Our corvette is sailing, oh how it sails!
Over vast expanses of tempestuous seas,
with light sails fluttering in the air.
(*All sing together*)

O! Revere the celestial kingdom,

its bounties are as boundless as the ocean waters.

See how the people of these barren lands and remote islets

have all changed from their scaly costumes into proper
headdress and attire.

(*All exit*)

To the Tune of *Bei chaotianzi* (Northern Paying Respects to the Son of Heaven)

(THE KING *enters with his entourage*)

Display the peacock feathered flags,

hold the pearl beaded saddles and colored reins,

set foot on the sandy dike, and

welcome the celestial procession with music and dance!

All the men and women of the city have come out to

admire the splendor of China.

Filled with joy,

people fix their gazes upon

the colorful sails stretching in the distance, and

the brocade flags fluttering in the sky.

Hazy, foggy, and misty!

China's heavenly raft comes near,

sound the divine music!

O, such heavenly music!

This small vassal state is filled with happiness and joy! O,
how we delight on this day!

To the Tune of *Nan putianle* (Southern Universal Joy)

(SHI JIAN *enters with his entourage*)

Five-colored flowers spreading,[2]

covering the green peaks;

dragon-horses are marching,

flanked by red flags.

The green islet draws near.

O! It draws near!

When the parapet walls of the city emerge in the distance,

my poem of this heroic trip will be complete.

(THE KING *kneels down to welcome the envoy from China and says*) Shang Bazhi, His Majesty's subject in the land of Ryukyu, reverently welcomes the celestial edict. (SHI JIAN) Your Highness, please dispense with these formalities! Let's line up and enter the city, where we will assemble for the reading of the edict. (*They march forward*) (*All sing in unison*)

Its bounties are as boundless as the ocean waters.

See how the strange creatures of these barren lands and

remote islets

have all donned fancy costumes.

(*They all cross the bridge and enter the city gate.* SHI JIAN *reads out loud*) "It is Heaven's will and the Emperor's command that I was given the Mandate of Heaven to extend my grand authority over illimitable lands, reaching the far corners of the ocean. Not once was my voice unheeded; wherever I spread my instructions and leadership, awards were fairly bestowed on those who deserved them. Your nation of the Ryukyu Islands is located on the remote southeastern flank of China, and it has been paying tribute to China for many generations. The monarch Shang Bazhi, the most virtuous and capable of your people, sent your envoy to China, braving long distances to plead on behalf of your people. You have demonstrated extreme respect and submission. I will now recognize you as the

Zhongshan King of the Ryukyu Islands,[3] and confer on you the royal crown and gown, the jade belt, and other objects. All of the officials at court along with elders over the age of sixty are allowed to upgrade their clothing accordingly. Let us forever maintain the serenity of your islands and enjoy a peaceful world together." Please thank His Majesty for his favor. (THE KING *and his entourage thank the emperor, don new robes, and celebrate with dancing as they sing*)

To the Tune of *Bei chaotianzi* (Northern Paying Respects to the Son of Heaven)

> Much obliged to the grace of the celestial court,
> we bow humbly before His Majesty's edict and the general
>   who has borne it here from afar,
> sending excitement and delight throughout the Ryukyu
>   Islands.
> The hat with gold gauze wings and green silk ribbons
> replaces the hat made of fur and pelt;[4]
> donning this glowing red gown embroidered with a
>   curled-up dragon,
> I can hardly bear to have turned so handsome and elegant.
> And such imposing regality!
> This little state, this tiny islet of a country,
> receives China's beneficence,
> our road is wide and the future is bright.
> "Long Live His Majesty!" we mightily shout,
> "Long Live His Majesty!" we mightily shout!

(SHI JIAN *and* THE KING *greet each other*) (THE KING *speaks*) Our barbarian land is far off the mainland, and we are blessed to receive a visit by the envoy from the celestial kingdom. It brings great honor to our barren land to be able to pay obeisance to His Majesty's imperial countenance. (SHI JIAN) I, a mere low official, have been received with such respect, and given the opportunity to observe local customs and meet such a benevolent king. This is indeed the chance of a lifetime. (THE KING) Our seaside land is bleak and desolate; I have nothing worthy to offer you. We have prepared some coarse rice wine to give you a welcoming banquet. (SHI JIAN) Thank you for your kindness! (THE KING *takes* SHI JIAN *to the banquet*)

To the Tune of *Nan putianle* (Southern Universal Joy)

> (SHI JIAN *sings*)
> On this eastern side of the ocean
> the breeze is crisp and invigorating;
> the gorgeous Middle Mountain[5] of the islands
> is of a most impressive extent.
> Fine wine flows,
> Giving off a lovely, fermented aroma;
> drinking till faces are all flushed pink,
> laughing banter resounds across the hall. (*He repeats these lines*)

(THE KING *speaks*) My country has a few boorish girls who can lighten things up with singing and dancing. I wonder if they will be good enough to please your eyes and ears? (SHI JIAN) Young ladies from the south are a different breed. Since you have some talented performers, I would be more than pleased to take a look. (*The young female lead and the secondary young female lead play the young female islanders. They sing and dance, pouring wine for the guests*)

To the Tune of *Bei chaotianzi* (Northern Paying Respects to the Son of Heaven)

(THE KING *sings*)
With faces clumsily powdered,
giggling while holding up the purple goblets,
these lady marines mingle noisily among the ceremonial
    guards.
Their local tongue is clamorous,
but it lights up the mood of the ranks of celestial officers.
Bungling and oafish, their presence is graceless,
one would not expect songs lovely enough to reverberate
    among the rafters, or
dances soaring and airy like floating rainbows.[6]
From this far, far, far distant territory,
we revere China's civilization.
Although we are no doubt as different as heaven and
    earth,
to our hearts' content we enjoy ourselves.
O, let's enjoy our pleasures!

(SHI JIAN *speaks*) Thank you for your warm and hospitable reception. We now have dined and wined to satiety and would like to return to our lodgings. We shall bid you farewell tomorrow. (THE KING) I have not even begun to fulfill my obligation as a proper host! How can you speak of leaving so soon? (SHI JIAN) The duties of an imperial envoy are pressing; I do not dare stay long. (THE KING) In that case, tomorrow I will write a memorial expressing our gratitude, prepare some local products, and select ten young girls from our islands as gifts to His Majesty. I will again send our prime minister to accompany you back to China to formally thank His Majesty for his kindness.

To the tune of *Nan putianle* (Southern Universal Joy)

(SHI JIAN *sings*)

I have enjoyed your boundless hospitality,

received a great many rarities.

Counting the days till my return

makes me sad and depressed.

Though we have only just viewed, oh, we just viewed the
     scenic beauty of your seaside domain,

already we long for the tingling sounds of jade pendants.[7]

(SHI JIAN *sings*)

Carrying the imperial edict, I hurriedly traveled to the
     eastern sea.

(THE KING *sings*)

A literary star from China, he is a guest I cannot keep for
     long.

(SHI JIAN *sings*)

Going back, I will report to His Majesty and conclude my
     mission,

meeting my fellow officers, I will tell them all about the
     Ryukyu Islands.

SCENE 34

CHASTITY PLEDGE

Prelude in the Mode of *Zhenggong: Yan'guiliang ban*
(Swallows Return to the Beam, Half)

> (CAO GECHEN *dressed in casual clothing enters with his
> servant and sings*)
> I rid myself of a big concern, yet there is a smaller one:
> the younger sister has married, but the elder sister
> remains.

(CAO *speaks*) Ever since I had Shi Jian marry into my family and go in
my stead as the imperial envoy to the Ryukyu Islands, not only have
I been blessed with an outstanding student, I also will have someone on whom to rely in my old age. Nevertheless, my adopted
daughter has not married yet. Today, my fellow metropolitan classmate Wei sent a matchmaker for his son, and I have already given
him my consent. Now I will tell my daughter to inform her sister.
Someone ask the second mistress to come out. (*The servant goes to
call for* YUHUA)

> (*To the same tune as before*)
> (YUHUA *enters with her* MAID *and sings*)

No sooner had we married than my groom took off on a
distant journey,
leaving this shy bride to fend for herself.

(YUHUA *speaks*) Father, what instructions do you have for me? (CAO) My
child, although you found a good husband, your sister has not yet
secured a good match. This has been weighing on my mind. I have
now selected a husband for her, so why don't you go tell her this
good news so she can stop worrying? (YUHUA) I was just going to
tell you something, father. My elder sister is engaged to the son of
the Shi family, and she has sworn not to marry anyone else. (YUHUA
sings)

Passing Tune in the Mode of *Nanlü: Lanhuamei* (Too Lazy to Paint One's Brows)

She has already accepted a betrothal gift,
one red string cannot tie two grooms.

(CAO *speaks*) She told me the same thing when she first came to our
house. But I have also heard that they lost contact many years ago.
Who knows where the young man is now?

(YUHUA *sings*)
The osprey has already arrived at the islet,
but the fair lady frowns in vain.[1]
Meanwhile a lewd fellow has butted in on this perfect
pair!

(CAO *speaks*) Well, where did you manage to find him? (YUHUA) Right
here in our house. (CAO *is shocked*) What, right here? Who is he? Tell
me! (YUHUA) Years ago, when her father was the assistant to the

prefectural magistrate, and the father of my husband was a correctional officer, they decided to go from colleagues to in-laws. The Shi family gave her a pair of gold bracelets as the engagement gift, and her family reciprocated his gift with a jade toad. Later on, the two families moved to different places and their parents all passed away, resulting in their losing contact for many years. A few days ago, I saw my husband wearing a jade toad and asked him where it came from. He told me that it was an engagement gift from the Cui family. I then took it with me. When my sister saw it, she recognized it as her family heirloom and took out a pair of gold bracelets. That was when I realized that she was actually my husband's original betrothed. (CAO) How could there be such an amazing coincidence?

> (*To the same tune as before*)
> (YUHUA *sings*)
> They are destined to meet after being separated by
>   thousands of miles from each other.
> How can we rip them apart just when they have come face
>   to face?

(YUHUA *speaks*) My elder sister is unwilling to become an unchaste woman; I also don't want to put my husband in the position of having to violate his moral duty. (YUHUA *sings*)

> I can't possibly let him drive out the old turtledove, who is
>   not at all at fault,
> while I take over the magpie's nest, turning into a thick-
>   skinned, shameless squatter![2]
> Therefore, I often leave the left side of the bed empty,
>   covered with the other half of the quilt.[3]

(CAO *speaks*) This is nonsense! You have already married Shi Jian; am I to marry your sister to him as well? Let me ask you this: If both of you married him, who would be the principal wife and who would be the secondary one? (YUHUA) Since she was engaged to him first, as she is also older than me, naturally she should be the principal wife. (CAO *becomes angry*) Nonsense! How can you have so little self-respect? Back when I was just an old scholar, I didn't allow you to marry as a concubine; now that I have become a *jinshi* and entered the Hanlin Academy, how can you say something so spineless?! Tell Hualing to call the young lady out, so that I can talk some sense into her. (YUHUA's MAID *makes a gesture to call to her*) (JIANYUN *enters with* MAID) Father's summons comes with the sound of clappers; he calls the daughter who stays in the shadow of the bamboo curtains. Father, what instructions do you have for me? (CAO) My daughter, just now your younger sister told me about your relationship with the Shi family. It is indeed remarkable! But we are finding this out a few days too late. If we had known this before your sister's wedding, I could have found another groom for her so you and Shi Jian could consummate your marriage. However, now that your sister has already married him, we cannot have this both ways. I have already selected a good husband for you, someone who passed the examination with Shi Jian. He has prepared a bridal trousseau and wants to marry you in a few days. You must obey my wishes. Please don't be stubborn. (JIANYUN) Father dearest, hear me out: (JIANYUN *sings*)

> (*To the same tune as before*)
> When I was little, I studied the Confucian textbooks for
>   girls;
> admiring the ancient paragons, I cultivated my womanly
>   virtue.

(JIANYUN *takes out the gold bracelets*)
These jewelries have already sealed my fate for a life-long
    marriage;
we will stay committed as long as I live and breathe.
How can I betray this love and jump ship?

(CAO *speaks*) If you also marry Shi Jian, what kind of position are you
putting your sister in? (JIANYUN) Father, you need not worry. There
is no way that I will marry Mr. Shi. (JIANYUN *sings*)

(*To the same tune as before*)
Although this is not a case
of what's done cannot be undone,
I also know that it is dishonorable
to disrupt the domestic pecking order that regulates
    relations between wife and concubine.

(CAO *speaks*) Since you refuse to marry another man, and won't wed Shi
Jian either, do you mean to stay unmarried for the rest of your life?
(JIANYUN) Father, I will not trouble you. I have my own way of get-
ting out of this. (JIANYUN *sings*)

By a cedar boat, I shall take the Mercy Ferry and
leave this dusty, impure world behind, washing off all my
    rouge and powder;
I shall cut off all my hair, put an end to my troubles, and go
    practice Buddhist vows.

(JIANYUN *exits with her* MAID) (YUHUA *speaks*) Alas! My elder sister is
about to chop off her hair! I have taken her husband from her and
made her homeless. Now she has become a martyr for her chastity.

But what face will I have when people start talking about me? That's it!

> (YUHUA *sings*)
> I also would rather cut off all my hair, put an end to my troubles, and go practice Buddhist vows. (YUHUA *exits with her* MAID)

(CAO *is stupefied and says*) Now what do I do about this? (JIANYUN'S MAID *and* YUHUA'S MAID, *enter in a hurry*) Terrible! Terrible! The two young mistresses are both cutting their hair off! If they become nuns, there is no way that I can still keep these few strands on my head. What is to be done? (CAO *panics*) Hurry up and stop them! Tell them that they can both marry Mr. Shi and I will no longer raise any objections. Hurry, go! Go! (THE MAIDS *answer together and exit*) (CAO) Can you believe that children could make one's life so difficult?! [Who else's daughter can't I adopt? What other *jinshi* can't I take as my son-in-law?] How is it that I happened to bring this couple into my house, and upset myself so? If I marry both of them to Shi Jian, I will have to face two problems: first, it is hard to rank them; second, I have already given my consent to the Wei family. What do I tell them now? (CAO *mutters to himself*) All right! I will write a memorial to the throne about these events and submit it to the court. I will let His Majesty make the final decision on this dilemma. (CAO *sings*)

> If I want to marry both daughters to the same son-in-law, then His Majesty must be asked whether this accords with the rites.

SCENE 35

<hr>

CO-CONFERRAL

(SHI JIAN *enters dressed in his official robe and holding his court tablet*[1])
(SHI JIAN *speaks*) Like the Han envoy Zhang Qian who just returned
to China,[2] I arrive at the capital still damp, with traces of the foggy
mirage lingering on my clothes. Paying respects to His Majesty I
have rigorously adhered to court protocol, and counted the days till
my marriage could be consummated. I am Shi Jian, sent to the
Ryukyu Islands as imperial envoy by His Majesty. I now return to
the court to submit my report to His Majesty. The audience has not
been held yet; I shall wait a while in the adjoining room. (THE
ENVOY *of the Ryukyu Islands, the secondary older man role, enters
holding a court tablet. The girls from the Ryukyu Islands enter with* THE
ENVOY) China and its neighbors are now united as one family; this
vassal has visited the capital twice. With my own eyes, I have seen
the magnificence of the crown; upon returning I shall flaunt my
knowledge to my subordinates. I am the prime minister of the
Ryukyu Islands. My king was conferred the status of vassal king by
the celestial kingdom, and he sent me to escort beautiful women
and deliver our local products here, to express his gratitude to the
emperor. I shall accompany the Chinese envoy into the court. (CAO
GECHEN *enters wearing his official robe and carrying the court tablet*)
Managing the state and regulating family affairs should be the same

in nature; and yet, it seems rather harder to be a father. When one can no longer pretend to be deaf or mute regarding family affairs, he shall yield the matter to the all-knowing emperor. I am Cao Gechen. I wrote a memorial to the throne over the issue of my two daughters' marriage. I will read this to His Majesty at the regular court audience. (*A voice from behind the stage announces the court audience*) All of the officials in front of the palace steps, please read your memorials one by one.

Adagio in the Mode of *Yuediao: Rupo*
(Entering the Break)

(SHI JIAN *sings*)
Entrusted with an imperial errand, I, Shi Jian, now report:
Not long ago I received Your Majesty's edict instructing
    me to
deliver the imperial order,
confer recognition on the Ryukyu court,
grant them a noble title, and
permanently fortify our maritime borders.
Off to the Ryukyu Islands I went on this mission,
exhausting all my strength.
With luck your humble servants
rode the wind and crossed the waves.
Thanks to your Celestial Majesty,
the sea waves seemed to spur us on in carrying out our
    mission,
and we arrived at the islands ahead of schedule.
I read the imperial edict, and presented the royal
    garments;
everyone at the vassal court was overjoyed to hear its
    generous pronouncements;

the whole kingdom from king to subjects faced north,
    shouting "Long Live His Majesty" at an earthshaking
    pitch.
As I unrolled the edict,
countless exotic creatures of that strange land crowded
    around, like ants, to listen.

To the Tune of *Podi'er* (Entering the Break, Two)

They praised the Han official
for his charming and dignified manner.
Seeing how different our customs are,
they finally realized the crudeness of their local practices.
From this day forward, they will adopt Chinese clothing
    for generations to come,
and purge themselves of their malodorous habits.
Even in old age when their toothless mouths can scarcely
    utter a coherent word,
they will extoll the refinement of Your Majesty's sagely
    pronouncements.

To the Tune of *Gundisan* (Imperial Robe, Three)

My mission completed,
within a day
I had packed my bags for the return journey.
Blessed by the God of the Wind,
like a floating reed,
my voyage home was smooth and swift.
I am afraid that I have neglected to perform my duty with
    competence;

now kneeling at the base of these palatial steps
I respectfully deliver my report and wait for Your Majesty
   to penalize me for my errors.

To the Tune of *Xiepai* (Resting the Beat)

(THE ENVOY *sings*)
The celestial envoy has completed his report,
This vassal would like to make a statement:
having been treated with such great benevolence,
my king wants to thank Your Majesty from afar.
I was also entrusted to present some items of tribute
in baskets laid out on the palatial steps.
I humbly ask Your Majesty to please accept these small
   gifts,
as it would bring my king much contentment and
   happiness.

To the Tune of *Zhonggun diwu* (Middle Imperial Robe, Five)

(CAO *sings*)
Currently serving in the Hanlin Academy,
this petty minister reports to Your Majesty:
In my old age I am quite lonely;
I am indeed miserable, as
my wife passed away,
leaving me with no male heir.
Without a flourishing family,
I only fathered a daughter, and
with Shi Jian she has completed her matrimonial vows.

To the Tune of *Shawei* (Rounding Off)

It's just that in former times I also adopted an orphan as
    another daughter,
but it turns out that her late parents had already betrothed
    her, and then
having moved away, she lost contact with her prospective
    mate.
After careful investigation, she was found to be Shi Jian's
    original fiancée.
Although the circumstances were extraordinary,
what caused all this was hardly out of the ordinary;
consequently, it is impossible to rank my two daughters.

To the Tune of *Chupo* (Leaving the Break)

Who should take the title of concubine? I beg Your
    Majesty to rectify their names.
Forgive me for being old and inadequate
to bringing order to my family matters, a circumstance of
    which I am deeply ashamed.
If this inept subject inadvertently has brought offense to
    your kind benevolence,
I tremble, thoroughly mortified!

(THE EUNUCH, *secondary young male lead, enters holding the emperor's
    edict*) The imperial edict is issued and it reads: "As a young officer
who successfully carried out the imperial mission, Shi Jian demonstrated his skills and effectiveness, and not only should he be com-
mended for his achievements, he should also be awarded with a
promotion. The King of Zhongshan[3] sent his envoy to express his
gratitude for the conferral; the imperial secretariat will write an

edict to thank him for his service and make an announcement to the nation. The marital issue about which Cao Gechen has inquired is an important matter of moral concern; naturally, the original betrothal should be upheld. Cao's adopted elder daughter is steadfast in her chastity and should be praised for her virtue; his younger daughter willingly yields the principal seat to another, and should be regarded as a role model. The two young ladies should not be distinguished by ranks, but rather both should be conferred with the title of principal wife. Each will receive a foreign maidservant to serve her in her new home. Now please thank His Majesty for his kindness. (*Everyone kneels and kowtows.*(THE EUNUCH *sings*)

Passing Tune in the Mode of *Huangzhong: Diliuzi* (Going Round and Round)

The royal graciousness spreads across the land,
oh, it is widespread,
and everyone is pleased to have achieved his desires!
After shouting "Long Live His Majesty,"
oh, after that earthshaking cry,
the sounds of cheering reach the sky.
How remarkable this story is!
One edict is issued from top down:
two wise women are matched in beauty and in virtue.
This is a marriage tale that shall
be told in the four corners of the world.
(SHI JIAN *sings*)

How unusual it is, for a bride to take foreign maidservants
along with her;
it assuages the shame of marrying off princesses to avoid
fighting one hundred battles.[4]
(CAO *sings*)

Tomorrow we will hold a grand wedding banquet.

(THE ENVOY *sings*)

Will you allow a guest from the Eastern Isles to play a
trick or two on the groom?

SCENE 36

<span style="text-align:center">~~~~~~</span>

HAPPY REUNION

Passing Tune in the Mode of *Yuediao: Lihua'er*
(Pear Blossoms)

(THE MASTER OF CEREMONIES, *the clown role, sings*) I was
    born to be a wedding master of ceremonies;
from luxurious mansions to squalid alleyways, I have seen
    it all;
yet never in my life have I seen two women marrying one
    man.
Upon whose bridal bed should I cast auspicious fruits?[1]

(THE MASTER OF CEREMONIES *speaks*) I am the most popular master
of ceremonies for weddings in the capital. Not long ago, Mr. Cao
from the Hanlin Academy married his younger daughter to Mr. Shi
Jian from the Ministry of Defense. Today he will marry his elder
daughter to him. His Majesty issued an imperial edict, saying the
two wives shall not be differentiated between wife and concubine,
but both given the title of "First Lady." Today is the wedding day
selected by His Majesty, and I have been invited to serve at the
ceremony.

Prelude in the Mode of *Huangzhong: Nüguanzi qian* (Female Daoist, Before)

(CAO GECHEN *enters in formal attire*)
Royal favor falls from Heaven, and
the three phoenixes, male and female, are bathed in
morning light.[2]

(THE MASTER OF CEREMONIES *speaks*) The master of ceremonies kowtows to you. (CAO) No need, please just offer a regular congratulatory gesture, that will be fine. (THE MASTER OF CEREMONIES) In that case, let me invite the groom and bride to come out. (*He clears his throat as he prepares to call her out*) (JIANYUN *rushes in and sings*)

To the Tune of *Nüguanzi qian* (Female Daoist, Before)

This marriage has already been consummated,
a fact that cannot be concealed indefinitely.
I will come out without having been called;
please forgive my brashness in revealing our secret.

(THE MASTER OF CEREMONIES, *turning his back toward* JIANYUN *and giggling, speaks*) I have been a master of ceremonies for my whole life, but never have I seen such an unconventional bride like her. She popped out on her own without my invitation. (JIANYUN *greets* CAO) Papa, I wish you great happiness! (CAO *sees her and is surprised*) Daughter, you have always behaved properly, but why are you so brazen today? You walked out on your own before the master of ceremonies called for you. This is certainly against protocol. (JIANYUN) I have something to tell you, Father in private. Please send away the master of ceremonies, so that I can tell you everything in detail. (CAO) Do you have still more objections to this marriage? This time you are marrying on His Majesty's orders, so there is no way you can get out of it. (JIANYUN) I do not dare to object, but there are some special circumstances that I should tell you about. (CAO) You and your special circumstances! All right, I will ask the master of ceremonies to step aside for the moment, and I'll call him back to resume the ceremony after our talk. (THE MASTER OF CEREMONIES) This bride will surely get married on her own, no master of ceremonies is necessary. For this bride, coming out was so easy; it certainly won't be difficult for her to get into the wedding bed! (THE MASTER OF CEREMONIES *exits*) (CAO) Now tell me what all of this is about. (JIANYUN *kneels down*) I beg your forgiveness for my grave sins; I dare not reveal the truth unless I have your pardon. (CAO) Get up, you may as well tell me everything. (JIANYUN *gets up*) Father dearest, here is the truth: I have already been married to Mr. Shi Jian for several years. It is because he was adopted by his maternal uncle that he took on the last name of Fan. I met your daughter in the Rain-Flower Nunnery and we fell in love with each other's talent, and went on to swear an oath of sisterhood in front of the Buddha. Who would expect that you, Father, would then suddenly take my younger sister away with him to the capital? And as a result, her longing turned into illness. Later on, Shi Jian was stripped of his *xiucai* title; as a result, he returned to his birthplace, and had the good fortune to pass the provincial examination under his original family name, Shi. I accompanied him here to the capital and made inquiries about my younger sister. Fortunately for us, Father, you held the audition for female students, which enabled me to enter your household. If I had told you the truth then, you definitely would not have accepted me. If I hadn't gotten in, my sister's illness would not have been cured. This was why I made up a story to answer your questions about my background. Now thanks to your kind protection, my fervent wish has already been fulfilled. And now that the imperial edict has been issued, if I do not tell the truth now, I would be guilty of deceiving His Majesty, and that is an unforgiveable offence. I therefore venture to reveal the truth to you now and beg for your forgiveness. (CAO *is shocked and raises his voice*) What? It was you who composed poetry with my daughter in the nunnery? (JIANYUN) Yes, it was me. (CAO GECHEN) Fan Jiefu is none other than Shi Jian? (JIANYUN) Yes, that is he. (CAO *is furious and says*) This is terrible! So, it looks like the three of you have played me like a puppet, all along manipulating me this way and that, down to this very day! If I did not know the truth, that might be the end of it. But now that I have found out the truth, do you think that I can just swallow it all and continue to let you have your way? (CAO *turns his back to* JIANYUN *and thinks before he speaks*) Hold on. My daughter has already been hooked, and I was the one who requested the imperial edict. The rice has been cooked; what is done cannot be undone. What else can I do now? It would be wiser to just play the nice guy. (*He turns toward* JIANYUN *and speaks*) All right, all right! Let it be! A person becomes incompetent when he is old; a deity loses his power when he is elderly. This was all because of my own stupidity. I cannot blame others for it. Now why don't you three go have your happy ending. (JIANYUN) My lord, younger sister, hurry and come out!

To the Tune of *Nüguanzi hou* (Female Daoist, After)

(SHI JIAN *dressed in wedding attire enters the stage.* YUHUA *enters with* SHI, *accompanied by her maid. Women from the Ryukyu Islands—the older woman role, the painted-face role, and the clown—enter with* SHI JIAN *and* YUHUA) (SHI JIAN *sings*)

> This wedding has become a farce,
> the bride calls for her groom on her own;

No need for the master of ceremonies!

(YUHUA *sings*)

Now that the truth has come out,

as a co-conspirator, I hurry to take my share of the blame.

(JIANYUN *speaks*) I have already explained everything clearly to father; now let's all go ask for his forgiveness. (*They all kneel down in front of* CAO) (SHI JIAN) Father-in-law, your son-in-law makes his deepest apologies to you! (JIANYUN *AND* YUHUA) Father dearest, your unfilial daughters ask for your forgiveness! (CAO) You don't need to apologize to me. I just ask you not to come up with some other clever scheme to sell me out like this again! (*He laughs*) (SHI JIAN *and everyone else kowtow to* CAO)

To the Tune of *Huameixu* (Prefatory to Painting One's Brows)

(CAO *sings*)

It is hard to guard against a thief inside the household,

lifting the curtains and leading the robber straight into my home;

I even bowed to her thankfully.

I adopted a female spy as my own daughter!

(CAO *speaks*) Though I may complain, your marriages must be destined from a previous lifetime. Otherwise, as I am no fool, how could I have been duped to the very end? (CAO *sings*)

It is all because of your secret strategy of keeping everything under wraps

that prevented this half-deaf dotard from hearing anything about it.

(*They sing in unison*)

On the wedding night the groom expects to meet a new
    companion.

Who knew she would turn out to be the old wife who has
    shared his hard lot?

(*To the same tune as before*)

(SHI JIAN *sings*)

Twice through examinations,

both husband and wife were taken in by the Caos.

Happily, Heaven acceded to our wishes,

and we both bluffed our way inside the Cao household.

I thank you for recognizing my talent despite our difficult
    history,

you should know that I was in the wrong but through no
    fault of my own.

(*In unison they repeat the above lines*)

(*To the same tune as before*)

(JIANYUN *sings*)

To avoid courting disaster, I confessed my crime,

my confession can be rewritten as a romantic play.

Lovesick from longing for talent

surely that reads better than the grave illness caused by
    rivalry among beauties.

I am thankful that my brilliant plan to bring her back
    from death's door

was effective enough to completely fool her father.

(*In unison they repeat the above lines*)

(*To the same tune as before*)

(YUHUA *sings*)

My offenses are more numerous than all the hairs on my
    head;
it is no exaggeration to charge me with rebelling against
    my father and deceiving Heaven.
My love is for my female companion,
not for the sake of a man.
This sinful karma has brought our marriage to fruition today,
our feelings were kindled years ago when I itched to show
    off my poetic skills.

(*In unison they repeat the above lines*)

(THE MASTER OF CEREMONIES *enters and says*) I report to the Master: All of the officials from the Hanlin Academy and the Court of Censors have arrived, and they are now waiting to congratulate you and the newlyweds in the main hall. (CAO) It's been a while since you two saw each other; why don't you enjoy each other's company and let me go entertain the guests. Staying here I will only get in the way of their conjugal diversions; finding an excuse to leave, I will volunteer for the labor of entertaining guests. (CAO *exits*) (SHI JIAN) Maids, light up the lanterns and lead us to the bedroom. (*A group of foreign maids kneel down and ask*) Master, please tell us: which lady's bedroom would you like to enter? (SHI JIAN *laughs*) All you need to do is light the way and follow me. We Chinese have our own system. (*The maids light up the lanterns.* SHI JIAN *takes* JIANYUN *in his left hand,* YUHUA *in his right hand, and starts walking*) (SHI JIAN *sings*)

To the Tune of *Baolaocui* (Old Bao's Urgings)

The wedding chamber dimly lit,
brocade quilts embroidered with mandarin ducks and
    lotus flowers;
bamboo bedsheets ripple under gold-threaded curtains.

To the left, skin as soft as jade,
to the right, flesh of warm scent.
In the middle, love unfolds.
Let's prepare two sets of baby clothes for boys,
for a year from now a pair of pearls shall be born,
as we welcome two bright boys into this household.

Weisheng (Closing Tune)

The scent of a beautiful woman has always been prized,
only jealous women do not find it attractive.
In this world how many are like Mrs. Fan, who broke the
    rules in pursuing her love of talent?
Nine out of ten romantic plays are about unrequited love;
they speak of passion yet are not passionate.
Only these marvelous events have yet to be told:
breaking from convention, I bashfully compose their
    lyrics.

APPENDIX: MODES AND TUNES

A song suite, the basic organizational component of each scene in a *chuanqi* play, consists of one to three "modes" (*gongdiao* 宮調)[1] and multiple "tunes" (*qupai* 曲牌) that follow the modes that a playwright has selected. For instance, Li Yu used two modes in scene 6, "Praising the Scent in Verse": *shuangdiao* 雙調 and *nanlü* 南呂. In the *nanlü* mode, he included the tunes "Too Lazy to Paint My Brows" (*lanhuamei* 懶畫眉), "Fragrant Silk Belt" (*xiangluodai* 香羅帶), "Ascending, Notch by Notch" (*jiejiegao* 節節高), "Joy of Great Victory" (*dashengle* 大勝樂), and others.[2] All of the arias in the same scene or mode follow one rhyme.

Premodern Chinese musical modes correspond to the musical keys of C (*gong* 宮), D (*shang* 商), E (*jue* 角), F (*bianzhi* 變徵), G (*zhi* 徵), A (*yu* 羽), and B (*biangong* 變宮); the music in *gong* mode (*gongdiaoshi* 宮調式) is based on the key of C, for example, and the music in *shang* mode (*shangdiaoshi* 商調式) is based on the key of D. Whereas Yuan *zaju*, features northern music (*beiqu* 北曲), Ming *chuanqi* plays follow the tradition of southern music (*nanqu* 南曲): northern and southern music are distinguished by meter (*banshi* 板式), notation (*pushi* 譜式), suite (*taoshu* 套數), and mode. According to Shen Jing's 沈璟 (1553–1610) *Guide to*

Nine Southern Modes (*Nan jiugong pu* 南九宮譜), there are nine modes in addition to four variants in southern music.

In composing the singing parts for a play, the playwright selects *qupai* (tunes); for each tune the musical scores, tonal patterns, rhymes, lengths of sentences, and number of characters are fixed; the playwright fills in lyrics that accord with the musical and language requirements of the tune in question. The 1746 *Compendium of Nine Modes* of *Northern and Southern Plays* (*Jiugong dacheng nanbeici gongpu* 九宮大成南北詞宮譜) includes 2,094 *qupai* or tunes found in both northern and southern dramas. In a play script, the mode of a certain act is usually given before the name of a tune. For instance, in Li Yu's *The Fragrant Companions*, the first song sung by the male lead in scene 2 is in the mode of *nanlü* 南呂 and set to the tune of "Longing for a Fragrant Spring (*lianfangchun* 戀芳春); this is noted in the phrase, "Prelude in the Mode of *Nanlü: Lianfangchun* (Longing for a Fragrant Spring)." The tunes vary by place of origin, meter, rhyme, musical form, and other features, but the song title remains the same as the title the original singer chose.

Modes and tunes are ordered in a sequence of "prelude" (*yinzi* 引子); "passing tunes" (*guoqu* 過曲) or "collected tunes" (*jiqu* 集曲); and "closing tune" or "coda" (*shawei* 煞尾, *weisheng* 尾声) or (*yuwen* 餘文). The prelude or *yinzi* is used to introduce or give rise to the main mode, which is followed by multiple passing tunes, or *guoqu*, which are varied as adagio (慢曲), flat (平曲), and allegro (快曲). The collected tune, or *jiqu*, is one type of passing tune that is "cut and pasted" from several different tunes. The closing tune, or *weisheng*, ends the whole scene. The expressions *yaopian* 幺篇 and *qianqiang* 前腔 mean to continue the same tune used before or to repeat the same tune. A tune can be repeated several times in one scene. If the number of words are increased or reduced in a tune, the expression *huantou* 換頭 (variation) will appear at the place where a tune name is given. Modes and tunes are still meaningful to modern readers because they indicate the musical and linguistic features of a play; they also serve some structural and sequential functions, which an audience would experience in a live performance.

To translators of traditional Chinese drama, the decision of how to deal with modes and tunes is a difficult one, and to date most translators have either not translated them at all or made a minimum effort (for instance, only translating the tune names into English). We have chosen to provide more information about the modes and tunes to the reader: first, by translating the names of the modes and tunes in the play into English; second, by attaching an index of the modes and tunes, including Chinese characters and pinyin, as an appendix; and third, by including this general discussion on modes and tunes.

LIST OF MODES AND TUNES WITH CHINESE CHARACTERS

Modes

Beixianlü 北仙呂

Huangzhong yinzi 黃鐘引子

Nanlü yinzi 南呂引子

Nanzhonglü 南中呂

Shangdiao yinzi 商調引子

Shuangdiao yinzi 雙調引子

Xianlü guoqu 仙呂過曲

Yuediao manci 越調慢詞

Yuediao yinzi 越調引子

Zhenggong guoqu 正宮過曲

Zhonglü yinzi 中呂引子

Tunes

Basheng Ganzhou 八生甘州

Baolaocui 鮑老催

Bei chaotianzi 北朝天子

Bei diezier fan 北疊字兒犯

Bei fendieer 北粉蝶兒

Bei pudeng'e fan 北撲燈蛾犯

Bei shiliuhua 北石榴花

Bei zuitaiping 北醉太平

Boxing 薄幸

Buchan'gong 步蟾宮

Bushilu 不是路

Changxiangsi 長相思

Chaoputianle 朝普天樂

Chuanyan Yunü qian 傳言玉
　女前

Chuduizi 出隊子

Chupo 出破

Chuanbozhao 川撥棹

Cuipai 催拍

Cuyulin 簇御林

Dahuanzhuo 大環着

Dashengle 大勝樂

Dayagu 大迓鼓

Di'er huantou 第二換頭

Dianjiangchun 點絳唇

Diliuzi 滴溜子

Disan huantou 第三換頭

Dong'ouling 東甌令

Douyehuang 豆葉黄

Erlangshen 二郎神

Fanbusuan 番卜算

Fengma'er 風馬兒

Fumalang 福馬郎

Gewei 隔尾

Guazhen'er 掛真兒

Guichaohuan 歸朝歡

Guizhixiang 桂枝香

Gundisan 袞第三

Haitangchun 海棠春

Han'gongchun 漢宮春

Hongnaao 紅衲襖

Hongniangzi 紅娘子

Huameixu 畫眉序

Huanglonggun 黄龍袞

Huangying'er 黄鶯兒

Huatangchun 畫堂春

Hudaolian 胡搗練

Hunjianglong 混江籠

Jiaqingzi 嘉慶子

Jiang'ershui 江兒水

Jianghuanglong 降黄龍

Jiangshuiling 漿水令

Jiechengge 解酲歌

Jiejiegao 節節高

Jiesancheng 解三酲

Jinlongcong 金瓏璁

Jinluosuo 金絡索

Jinwutong 金梧桐

Jishengcao 寄生草

Jixianbin 集賢賓

Juhuaxin 菊花新

Kuxiangsi 哭相思

Lanhuamei 懶畫眉

Langtaosha 浪淘沙

Lianfangchun 戀芳春

Lihua'er 梨花兒

Linjiangxian 臨江仙

Liu Po mao 劉潑帽

Luojiangyuan 羅江怨

Lülüjin 縷縷金

Maoerzhui 貓兒墜

Nan putianle 南普天樂

Nan Qi Yan Hui 南泣顏回

Nan shangxiaolou fan 南上小樓犯

Nanwei 南尾

Nezhaling 那吒令

Nüguanzi qian 女冠子前

Paige 排歌

Pinling 品令

Podi'er 破第二

Pozhenzi qian 破陣子前

Pudeng'e 撲燈蛾

Puxian'ge 普賢歌

Qi Yan Hui 泣顏回

Qingbeixu huantou 傾杯序換頭

Qiuyeyue 秋夜月

Queqiaoxian 鵲橋仙

Quetazhi 鵲踏枝

Rupo 入破

Sanduanzi 三段子

Sanhuantou 三換頭

Sanxueshi 三學士

Shawei 煞尾

Shanpoyang 山坡羊

Shengchazi 生差子

Shengruhua 勝如花

Shuazixu 刷子序

Shuangtian xiaojiao 霜天曉角

Sibianjing 四邊靜

Suochuanghan 瑣窗寒

Suonanzhi 鎖南枝

Taishi weizui 太師圍醉

Taishi yin 太师引

Tiyindeng 剃銀燈

Tianxiale 天下樂

Tusier 禿廝兒

Weisheng 尾聲

Wugongyang fan 五供養犯

Xidijin 西地錦

Xijiangyue 西江月

Xiaopenglai 小蓬萊

Xiaoshunge 孝順歌

Xiaotaohong 小桃紅

Xiangliuniang 香柳娘

Xiangluodai 香羅帶

Xiepai 歇拍

Xinshuiling 新水令

Xingxiangzi 行香子

Xiudaier 繡帶兒

Xiutaiping 繡太平

Xueshi jiecheng 學士解醒

Yan'guiliang ban 燕歸樑半

Yan'guosha 雁過沙

Yan'guosheng huantou 雁過聲換頭

Yanlaihong 雁來紅

Yaopian 幺篇

Yichunle 宜春樂

Yichunling 宜春令

Yijianmei 一剪梅

Yijiangfeng 一江風

Yizhihua 一枝花

Yinling 尹令

Yejinmen 謁金門

Yexingchuan 夜行船

Yeyouhu 夜游湖

Youhulu 油葫蘆

Yubaodu 玉胞肚

Yufurong 玉芙蓉

Yujiaozhi 玉交枝

Yuwe 餘文

Yuanlinhao 園林好

Yue shang haitang 月上
　　海棠

Zaojiaoji 皂角幾

Zaoluopao 皂羅袍

Zhegutian 鷓鴣天

Zhonggun diwu 中袞第五

Zhu'nu'er 朱奴兒

Zhuyunfei 駐雲飛

Zhumaqi 駐馬泣

Zhumating 駐馬聽

Zhuyingtai 祝英台

Zhuyingtai jin 祝英台近

Zhuansha 賺煞

Zhuomu'er 啄木兒

Zuifugui 醉扶歸

Zuitaiping 醉太平

NOTES

INTRODUCTION

1. Patrick Hanan, *The Invention of Li Yu* (Cambridge, MA: Harvard University Press, 1988), 35.
2. Li Yu wrote about male same-sex desire and love in two short stories "Cui ya lou" (House of Gathered Refinements) and "Nan Mengmu jiaohe sanqian" (A Male Mencius's Mother Educates His Son and Moves House Three Times); in *Naihe tian* (You Can't Do Anything About Fate) he also included some elements of sexual innuendo between the two wives of the unsightly male protagonist.
3. For a more detailed explanation of the song suites and musical components of *chuanqi* plays, see "Modes and Tunes," the appendix of this book.
4. Cyril Birch, "Introduction: *The Peach Blossom Fan* as Southern Drama," in *The Peach Blossom Fan*, trans. Chen Shih-Hsiang and Harold Acton with Cyril Birch (New York: New York Review of Books, 1976), xxiv–xxv.
5. Li Yu, *Li Yu quanji* (Hangzhou: Zhejiang guji chubanshe, 1991), vol. 3, 9. Patrick Hanan, trans., *The Invention of Li Yu* (Cambridge, MA: Harvard University Press, 1988), 45.
6. Li Yu, *Li Yu quanji*, vol. 3, 14.
7. Li Zhi, "Tang Shouwangfei yangshi," in *Cangshu*, vol. 2 (Shanghai: Zhonghua shuju, 1959), 1055.
8. Patrick Hanan, *The Invention of Li Yu*, 26.
9. This is a rewriting of two earlier plays: *Liu Yi chuan shu* 柳毅傳書 (Liu Yi Delivers a Letter for the Dragon King's Daughter) and *Zhang Sheng zhu hai* 張生煮海 (Scholar Zhang Boils the Sea).
10. Li Yu, *Lianxiangban*, annotated Du Shuying (Beijing: Zhongguo shehui kexue chubanshe, 2011), 24–25.

11. For detailed discussions of the prominent roles played by women writers, including both Wang and Huang, in the mid-seventeenth century, see Wai-yee Li, *Women and National Trauma in Later Imperial China* (Cambridge, MA: Harvard University Press, 2014). Of these two women who wrote prefaces for Li's plays, Wang Duanshu's life and writings are better documented, but both were well known for their poetry and paintings.

12. In recent years, the term "cultural prisons" has become a popular expression for describing the examination halls in Ming and Qing times, echoing the "examination hell" coined by the historian Miyazaki Ichisada. See Benjamin A. Elman, *Civil Examination and Meritocracy in Late Imperial China* (Cambridge, MA: Harvard University Press, 2013), 226.

13. Laura H. Wu, "Through the Prism of Male Writing: Representation of Lesbian Love in Ming-Qing Literature," *Nan Nü* 4, no. 1 (2002): 5.

14. This expression is used by Tze-Lan D. Sang in her book *The Emerging Lesbian: Female Same-Sex Desire in Modern China* (Chicago: University of Chicago University Press, 2003), see especially 86 and 88.

15. Qingyun Wu, "Introduction," in *A Dream of Glory: Fanhua meng*, trans. Qingyun Wu (Hong Kong: The Chinese University Press, 2008), 18.

16. Qingyun Wu, "Introduction," 22.

17. Tze-Lan D. Sang, *The Emerging Lesbian*, 21.

18. Laura H. Wu, "Through the Prism of Male Writing," 16.

19. S. E. Kile, "Transgender Performance in Early Modern China," *Differences: Journal of Feminist Cultural Studies* 24, no. 2 (November 2013): 138.

20. Tze-Lan D. Sang, *The Emerging Lesbian*, 49.

21. Tze-Lan D. Sang, *The Emerging Lesbian*, 74.

22. S. E. Kile, "Sensational *Kunqu*: A Performance Review of the May 2010 Beijing Production of *Lian Xiang Ban* (Women in Love)," *CHINOPERL Papers* 30, no. 1 (July 2013): 225.

23. Benjamin A. Elman, *Civil Examination and Meritocracy in Late Imperial China*, 97.

24. Benjamin A. Elman, *Civil Examination and Meritocracy in Late Imperial China*, 97.

THE RELATIONSHIP BETWEEN ROLE TYPES AND CHARACTERS

1. A. C. Scott, "Chapter V: The Performance of Classical Theater," in *Chinese Theater: From Its Origins to the Present Day*, ed. William Dolby (Honolulu: University of Hawaii Press, 1988), 123.

2. Scott, "Chapter V: The Performance of Classical Theater," 123.

3. H. Laura Wu, "Through the Prism of Male Writing: Representation of Lesbian Love in Ming-Qing Literature," *Nan Nü* 4, no. 1 (2002): 4.

4. D. C. Lau, trans. *The Analects* (London: Penguin, 1979), 86.

5. Here, the last name 魏 is a homonym of and a pun for "fake" ("wei" 偽), and the meaning of Kai 楷 is "role model" in Chinese. Putting the last and first name together in Chinese order, it means "fake role model."

SCENE 2

1. *Huazhuan*, translated as either "flower biography" or "Flower Registry," may refer to the social mores of judging and selecting beautiful prostitutes and actors in premodern China. Such a practice can be traced back to the Tang dynasty (618–907) and became quite popular in the competitions to select the best female impersonators in the Ming and Qing dynasties. Both *Rulin waishi* (The Unofficial History of Scholars) and *Pinhua baojian* (The Mirror of Judging Flowers) include episodes of such social gatherings and events. Here, Li Yu wants to indicate that Fan Shi's appearance would stand out even in such a competition among good-looking actors.

2. "Stroking the stringless zither" alludes to Tao Yuanming (c. 365–427) who, though he did not understand music, often imitated musical performance by "playing" a zither without strings after drinking wine. Here the allusion is used to indicate that the character shares the worldview of Tao Yuanming and imitates his reclusive lifestyle.

3. This line refers to two famous stories in Chinese literature. According to "The Biography of Pan An" in *Official History of Jin Dynasty* (*Jinshu*), Pan An was famous for his handsome appearance. He lived in Luoyang in his youth, and whenever he rode in a carriage on its streets, women threw fruits at him to express their admiration and affection. The second part of the line is about the precocious and talented poet Jiang Yan (444–505), anecdotes of whom are included in both the *History of Southern Dynasties* (*Nanshi*) and Taiping Imperial Encyclopedia (*Taiping Yulan*). According to these stories, Jiang demonstrated extraordinary literary talent when he was very young, but his writings lost their sparkle when he grew old. The famous idiom, "*Jiang lang cai jin*" (The young Jiang's creative powers are now exhausted) derives from these stories. Here, the two stories are used to imply that other men are all jealous of Fan Shi because of his handsome appearance and literary talents.

4. The story of Zhang Chang painting his wife's eyebrows is often used to indicate a man's romantic sentiments and caring manner toward the

woman he loves. Zhang's story is recorded in "The Biography of Zhang Chang" in *History of the* [*Former*] *Han Dynasty* (*Hanshu*).

5. "White Snow" or *baixue*, often paired with "Spring Time" or *yangchun*, are two highbrow songs from the Warring States period (475–221 BCE). Only a small number of people who had musical talent and the best training could sing and appreciate them. Here, this allusion emphasizes Fan Shi's high self-esteem.

6. The six marriage rituals include: (1) a prospective groom's family proposes a marriage to a woman's family through a matchmaker; (2) the matchmaker, on behalf of the young man's family, asks about his prospective wife's name, birthday, and horoscope; (3) the groom engages in a divination at a temple on the future of the marriage, by providing his prospective bride's birthday and horoscope; (4) the groom's family sends a dowry or betrothal gifts to the bride's family; (5) the groom's family selects the date of the wedding and seeks agreement from the bride's family; and (6) on the wedding day, the groom goes to the bride's house to fetch her and take her back to his home.

7. According to Chinese traditional customs, before the wedding the groom's and bride's respective family members and friends congratulated the couple by writing *cuizhuang shi* or "poems urging the bride to dress up for the wedding."

8. "Shallow," because in Chinese the Milky Way is known as the "Silver River" (*Yinhe*). To say that the "Silver River" is "shallow" suggests that it is an opportune moment for the legendary lovers Shepherd Boy and Weaver Girl (see note 9 below) to meet by crossing over the barrier separating them. Fan Shi's implication here is that this is a good moment for him to wed his bride.

9. This alludes to the fairytale of the Shepherd Boy (a human being, symbolizing Altair) and Weaver Girl (a fairy from the celestial realm, symbolizing Vega). The Shepherd Boy and the Weaver Girl fall in love with each other, marry, and are forced to separate and remain apart at different ends of the Milky Way. Out of compassion for them, on the seventh day of the seventh lunar month each year, flocks of magpies fly to form a bridge with their bodies over the Milky Way, allowing the Shepherd Boy and Weaver Girl to meet each other. This story, to some extent, reflects a desire to pursue the freedom of love and marriage. But here the fairytale is used to describe the feelings of the male character as he remains separated from his soon-to-be wife, and his anxiety over and impatience for the wedding day.

10. The Sui dike refers to the dikes along the Grand Canal from Beijing to Hangzhou, built in the Sui dynasty (581–618). Also note that the smaller font size for the words "I ask" indicate *chenzi*, extra words or phrases within sung parts that allow for some flexibility to account the rules for fixed tonal patterns and rhyme schemes in *chuanqi* lyrics (see further explanation at the end of the introduction.

11. "Making havoc in the wedding chamber" (*nao dongfang*) is an old Chinese custom that is still popular and practiced in today's China. This custom can be traced back to Qin (221–207 BCE) times. It was meant to drive away evil spirits and ensure that the new couple would remain on good terms with each other and with their family members and other relatives. The specific manner of "making havoc" varies and can be either verbal or physical, mainly involving playing tricks on the groom and bride.

12. "Repaying with peaches a gift of plums" is an expression taken from the "Odes" (*Guofeng*) of the *Classic of Poetry*. It means to requite someone's aid or kindness with something even more valuable and signifies profound friendship as well.

SCENE 3

1. The aspiration to rise to the "lofty clouds" refers to the ambition of a Confucian scholar. Usually it means to climb to the top of officialdom by passing civil service examinations and serving the imperial court.

2. The reference to "Confucian Five Classics" here is an abbreviation for the Confucian Four Books and Five Classics: The Four Books include *Great Learning, Doctrine of the Mean, Analects*, and *Mencius*; the Five Classics are *Classic of Poetry, Book of Documents, Book of Rites, Book of Changes*, and the *Spring and Autumn Annals*.

3. This phrase may recall the Chan (Zen) Sixth Patriarch Huineng's famous gatha about dust (i.e., impurities of the mind): "There is no Bodhi tree / and the bright mirror has no stand; / since all in the end is void, / where can dust alight?"

4. The name of the nunnery is actually a homonym of and thus a pun for the character's name. Miss Cao's name, Yuhua 語花 (meaning "talking flower"), is identical in pronunciation and tones to the name of the nunnery Yuhua 雨花 (meaning "rain flower"). The image of flowers raining down from above, sticking only to those with desirous hearts, comes from the *Vimalakirti* sutra.

5. Gautama refers to Gautama Buddha, which is the original name for Sakyamuni, the founder of Buddhism.

6. Song Yu (c. 319–298 BCE), a writer of the late Warring States period (475–221 BCE), is known as the author of a number of poems in the *Songs of Chu* (*Chuci*). Song Yu was both handsome and talented, and he gained fame in the literary circles of his time while still very young.

7. "An apricot stretching out of the partition/wall" is an oft-used expression to describe a woman having an extramarital affair with a man.

8. These lines are an adaptation of the first two couplets from Tao Yuanming's (365–427) poem titled "Drinking Wine, #5": "Though I've built my hut in the mundane world, / yet I hear no racket from carts or horses. / you ask how this could be so? / When one's mind is detached, his place is distant, too."

9. This line parodies one of Gao Shi's (704–765) two poems titled "Saying Farewell to Dong Da." The poem includes these four lines: "Yellow clouds covering a thousand *li* and the sun setting dim, / in whirling snow the north wind drives south the wild geese. / On the road ahead surely will be friends dear and true; / throughout the land is there anyone who knows you not?" Here, Cao contrasts himself, as someone who has not established his reputation through the civil examination and is thus unknown to the world (or to Dong Da in Gao Shi's poem), and the alluded-to lines are to be read as self-mockery.

10. This line is adapted from Du Mu's (803–852) poem titled "Sent to Yangzhou Judge Han Chuo." Du's original poem reads: "Green Mountains fade into endless flowing waters, / autumn ends at Jiangnan where vegetation has yet to wither. / Whereas the bright moon still shines over the Four and Twenty Bridge, / where is the jade-like person now to teach the flute?" Since Du Mu's original poem was written in memory of his old friend Han Chuo, here Cao Gechen borrows the line to imply that he is meeting an old friend (Wang Zhongxiang) in Yangzhou.

SCENE 4

1. Imperial officials wore black gauze caps, so here the term is used to refer to official status.

2. "Snow cape" means white beard, and the "meat sack" carried on the back means humpback.

3. A reference to orchids and jade trees, which suggests the promise of offspring, was first found in "The Biography of Xie An" in *History of the Jin Dynasty*.

4. The afterglow that the setting sun sheds on the elm and mulberry trees is often used as a metaphor for old age.

5. The Lord of Scholars refers to Confucius. Scholars usually worshipped Confucius for good luck in the mid-spring or -autumn before taking the examinations. The sacrificial food can be eaten after the ceremony is complete. Thus Wang Zhongxiang intends to use this meal of meat dishes for two purposes—worshipping Confucius and treating his guests.

6. The official title given to those scholars who passed the district level of the civil service examination is *xiucai* (budding scholar). The two higher titles are *juren* (elevated scholar), awarded to passers at the provincial level, and *jinshi* (advanced scholar), given to successful graduates of the metropolitan examination.

7. Here, the character uses the image of Nian (time or year) riding on a horse as a metaphor to describe the swiftness of the passing of time.

SCENE 5

1. "A scholar from East Mountain" alludes to Xie An (320–385), a famous statesman of the Eastern Jin dynasty, who lived in seclusion in a cottage on Dongshan (East Mountain) in Shanyin County, Zhejiang Province, before rejoining officialdom to rise to the rank of prime minister of the Eastern Jin. Here the allusion refers to Fan Jiefu's uncle, who once used the premises as a villa, and later had it converted into a temple.

2. Anāthapindika was the donor of Jetavana, one of the most famous of the Buddhist monasteries in India.

3. Deng You (?–326 CE, with the sobriquet Bodao) fled home with his son and nephew during a time of war. In these dire circumstances, he abandoned his son to save his nephew. This was regarded as a selfless deed in Chinese culture, as Deng gave up his own heir to spare his brother's. Eventually Deng died with no heir. This is why Sakyamuni, the character, complains here about the error made by Heaven.

4. Yao and Yu were two wise and benevolent rulers of the semi-legendary Xia dynasty. Yao abdicated his throne in favor of an unrelated but worthy successor, Shun, rather than passing it to his son Danzhu (see note 5); Yu similarly was chosen by Shun to succeed him, in recognition for his achievements in flood control.

5. Danzhu is Yao's son and Taijia is the grandson of Shangtang, the founder of the Shang dynasty (1600–1046 BCE). Both were morally corrupt and, as a result, were passed over in the imperial succession.

6. According to Liu Yiqing's (403–444) *Youming lu* (Record of Nether World), during the Han dynasty, two young men named Liu Chen and Ruan Zhao got lost on Tiantai Mountain. They then met two fairies who invited both men to live with them in the immortal world for half a year. When Liu and Ruan returned to the human world, seven generations had passed. Here Liu and Ruan are used as ideal lovers for all women, even for the presumably chaste female immortals.

7. See scene 2, note 4.

8. The "shrike and swallow [who will soon] take off in opposite directions" (or "laoyan fenfei") is an oft-used expression to imply the parting of loved ones and friends in China. It originally appeared in Guo Maoqian's (1041–1099) "Dong fei Baolao ge" (The Song of East-Flown Baolao) in *Yuefu shiji* (The Collection of Yuefu Poetry).

9. "The Red Star of Love" (*hongluan* or *hongluanxing*) is responsible for marriage in the celestial realm according to Chinese folklore and mythological tales.

10. According to the Daoist theory of Yin and Yang and the Five Elements (medal, wood, water, fire, and earth), the white tiger represents the animal spirit of the west, belonging to the season of autumn, and it is portrayed visually as a demon. Hence, the interference of the White Tiger Star means that misfortunate and unlucky events will happen to the characters.

11. See scene 2, note 9.

12. This sentence is adopted from a poem of Tang Yin (1470–1524), a famous painter and poet of the Ming dynasty. The line refers to the mystery surrounding the death of the legendary beauty Xi Shi, imagining that she died tragically during a dark, stormy night. Read together, the last two lines of the lyrics mean that if one could have a love like that of the Shepherd Boy and Weaver Girl it is even worth suffering a horrible death.

SCENE 6

1. This line is taken from the poem "Tender Peach" ("Taoyao," no. 6) in the *Classic of Poetry*. The original lines read: "The peach tree is turning red, / its blossoms are luxuriant; / this is the high time for a flower-like belle to wed, / she would make a household peaceful and exuberant." Here Jianyun implies that she got married at just the right age.

2. Qingdi (or Dongjun), who resides in the east, is regarded as the "God of Spring" in Chinese historical and literary writings. One example

can be found in Huang Chao's (835–884) poem "Ti juhua" (On Chrysanthemums): "If I will be the Qingdi in another year, / I will make chrysanthemum and peach bloom together."

3. This metaphor is also borrowed from a poem from the *Classic of Poetry*. The original piece, titled "Falling Plums" ("Biaoyoumei") reads: "The plums are falling, / seven out of ten are still on the tree; / young fellow who is interested in marrying me, / now is the right time to propose. / The plums are falling, / three out of ten are still on the tree; / young fellow who is interested in marrying me, / you no longer have the time to waste. / The plums are falling, / they now have to be gathered by dustpan; / young fellow who is interested in marrying me, / you only need to open your mouth." Here Jianyun's maid borrows the metaphor of "fallen plums" from the poem to indicate that she is already an old maid and her time to wed has long passed.

4. Yuhua has not been provided with the name of Cui Jianyun yet at this point. Thus, she is referring to her as someone like the heroine of *Romance of the Western Chamber* (Xiiang ji), Cui Yingying, who is famous for her astonishing beauty.

5. Cao E's father, Cao Xu, was a shaman who presided over local ceremonies at Shangyu. In 143 CE, while presiding over a ceremony during the Dragon Boat Festival, Cao Xu accidentally fell into the river. Cao E, in an act of filial piety, decided to try to find her father in the river, searching for three days before disappearing. After five days, she and her father were both found drowned in the river. Eight years later, in 151 CE, a temple was built in Shangyu dedicated to the memory of Cao E and her filial sacrifice. And, to this day, Cao E River, a tributary of the Qiantang River, is named after her. Here Cao Yuhua mentions the name of Cao E to indicate that she is from an eminent and virtuous family, who can be traced to the legendary Cao E.

6. See note 3.

7. The image of "a man leaning against his horse" is meant to evoke quick-witted literary talent. When Yuan Hu (fl. fourth century) was ordered to produce an edict, he filled seven sheets of paper immediately, all the while leaning against a horse. Yuhua uses this masculine imagery here to indicate that Jianyun's self-confidence and literary skills are comparable to those of men.

8. When the Tang poet Li Bai (701–762) worked at the Imperial Academy, he was invited to write three poems for the imperial concubine Yang Yuhuan. These poems use the images of a cloud, evening glow, spring

breeze, a peony flower decorated with dew, and a legendary belle to describe Yang's beauty. The poems are admired by many for their creative imagination and poetic wording. Here Cao Yuhua compares Cui Jianyun's poem with Li Bai's, indicating her admiration for Cui's literary talents.

9. The expression *wan zhong you gui* (demons are clinging to my wrist) is probably taken from the Ming literatus Wang Shizhen's (1526–1590) *Yiyuan zhiyan* (Casual Talks in the Artistic Garden), in which Wang uses the phrase to self-deprecatingly claim that his writing skill doesn't match his lofty aspirations or standards.

10. This alludes to a story of the Tang poet Li Bai, found in Wang Renyu's (880–956) *Kaiyuan Tianbao yishi* (The Incidents of Kaiyuan and Tianbao Times). According to the story, Li Bai dreamt of having flowers blooming on the tip of his brush when he was little, a sign that he would become a famous writer when he grew up. Here this allusion is used as an indication of literary talents. To say that flowers do not sprout from her brush is Yuhua's expression of modesty.

11. According to Song Yu's (298–222 BCE) "Dui Chuwang wen" (Responding to the King of Chu's Inquiry), when the songs (such as "Spring Snow") are lofty, fewer people can sing them; when the songs (such as "Song of Rustic Poor") are earthy, more people can sing them.

12. This refers to the talented female poet Xie Daoyun of the Eastern Jin dynasty (317–420). She is famous for using the image of a catkin to describe wind-blown snow.

13. Yu Xin (513–581) was a well-known poet of the Liang and the Northern Zhou Dynasties, and Bao Zhao (c. 414–466) was one of the best poets of the Southern Dynasties.

14. According to "The Biography of Shi Chong" in *History of the Jin Dynasty*, both Shi Chong and Wang Kai were fabulously rich and often competed in extravagant displays of their wealth. Here the concept of competition is retained, but the content of the competition changes from material treasures to poetic talents.

15. Buddhist temples in China have always attracted both the faithful and more casual visitors. It was common for famous poets to inscribe their poems on the walls of a temple they visited, which could spread or increase the fame of the poets as well as that of the temple. Here Jingguan refers to this common practice, although a woman's poetry was not supposed to be exposed to public view.

16. Lu and Wei were neighboring states during the Spring and Autumn period (771–476 BCE) that were comparable in size and political power.

Here the compatibility of the two states is used to suggest the equality of poetic talents between the two young ladies.

17. It is said that the cry of the cuckoo sounds like *buru guiqu* (why not go home) in Chinese. Thus hearing the cry of the cuckoo stirs up feelings of homesickness.

18. This line refers to Yu Boya and Zhong Ziqi's story. Yu Boya was famed for his skill on the lute (*qin*). Zhong Ziqi was a discerning listener of Boya's music. When Boya thought of high mountains while playing, Ziqi would say, "How towering like Mount Tai!" When Bo Ya's mind turned toward flowing water, listening to his playing Ziqi would say, "How vast are the rivers and oceans!" Whatever thoughts inspired Boya's playing, Ziqi would never fail to understand. Boya said, "Amazing! Your heart and mine are the same!" When Ziqi died, Boya broke the strings of his lute and vowed never to play it again. Thus was born the idiom known as "Soul-mates of High Mountains and Flowing Water." This allusion here compares the friendship between Cui Jianyun and Cao Yuhua to that of Boya and Ziqi.

19. "Chu prisoners grieving over their common misery" is an idiom originally referring to Zhong Qi, a citizen of the state of Chu but taken as prisoner by Jin during the Spring and Autumn Period. As a captive of Jin, Zhong often cried with his fellow Chu prisoners over their shared misfortune. Later, this idiom was used as a general expression for those who have suffered a great loss but are helpless and can do nothing but lament over their desperate situation.

20. The words *bang he* refer to the staff (*bang*) wielded by a Chan master on a disciple which, accompanied by a loud shout (*he*), are thought to spur sudden illumination (translated here as "enlightening blow").

SCENE 7

1. According to Daoist mythology, the Queen Mother of the West has three blue birds that deliver messages for her.

2. Yingzhou is one of three legendary paradises or celestial mountains. The other two are Penglai and Fangzhang.

3. This line is an adaptation of the Tang poet Li Shangyin's (813–ca. 858) line "Chang'e must regret stealing the elixir." Chang'e is the Goddess of the Moon, and according to myth she was said to have married to Houyi, the archer, but she later stole his elixir of immortality and flew off to the Moon. Finding herself alone there, Chang'e felt lonely and regretted what she had done. Here the allusion mainly refers to Cui

Jianyun's visit to the temple and her regret for possibly having to leave Fan Shi behind.

4. See scene 6, note 18.

5. Whereas "flower" is usually used as a metaphor for a beautiful woman, "butterfly" and "bee" are often used to imply her male suitors. Here "flower" means Miss Cao, and "butterfly" and "bee" point to Fan Shi, Cui Jianyun's husband.

6. According to a story from Zhong Rong's *Shi pin* (Poetics), the famous poet Xie Lingyun (385–433) of the Eastern Jin dynasty produced his famous couplet "Spring grasses sprout all over the pond, / bird-warbling turns the garden-willow green" in a dream. The "pond-grass" poetry is an allusion to Xie's story.

7. According to a story told in "Mu, King of Zhou State" found in the pre-Qin work *Liezi*, a person from the state of Zheng killed a deer and hid it under plantains. When he returned to collect it later, nothing was there. He thus believed that he had killed the deer in a dream. Here this allusion is used to suggest Fan Shi's favorable dream.

8. For "Pen-Flower," see scene 3, note 4. "Talking-Flower" usually refers to a beautiful woman, and it points to Miss Cao here. In the play, Miss Cao's given name, Yuhua, means "talking-flower" if translated literally.

9. Jianyun, Mrs. Fan's given name, which literally means "Paper-Cloud" (here a self-reference by Mrs. Fan). At the same time, it also implies her poem (a romantic poem written on a piece of paper). The "Romantic Cloud" refers to the mythical story of the King of Chu's tryst with a fairy at Gaotang Mountain. The mythical story is told in Song Yu's *Gaotang fu* (Rhapsody on Gaotang), in which Song describes the encounter between King Huai of Chu [r. 328–299 BCE] and a female divinity of Mount Wu to the king's successor, King Xiang of Chu [r. 298–263 BCE] during their visit to the mountain.

10. See note 9.

11. Ehuang and Nüying were the daughters of the sage-ruler Yao, whom he gave as concubines to his successor Shun. Here their names imply that Cui Jianyun intends to have Cao Yuhua become Fan Shi's second wife, and thus she and Yuhua would form a sisterhood in imitation of Yao's daughters.

12. The brothers Lu Ji (261–303) and Lu Yun (262–303) were both talented poets of the Jin dynasty (265–420). "Pan" refers to Pan Yue (247–300), or alternatively Pan An, who was famous for his literary talents and handsome features.

13. "Tender home" or "tender village" is a term often used to describe feminine love and caring.

14. According to fascicle 703 of *Taiping yulan* (Taiping imperial encyclopedia), Xun Yu (163–212), an official of the Han dynasty, liked to wear
scented clothing. Wherever he went, the scent lingered for days. Here
Xun Yu's story is borrowed to refer to Miss Cao's lingering bodily scent.
Xun Yu is used to refer to Fan Shi himself.

15. See scene 2, note 5.

SCENE 8

1. See scene 4, note 6.

2. The Chinese original, *baodu* or *doudu*, covered the chest and abdomen,
something akin to a Japanese *obi* (though unlike the latter, worn beneath
outer garments).

3. Zhou Gongmeng's name can be read and translated as either "the dream
of Duke Zhou" or "Duke Zhou's dream." Zhou Gong (fl. ca. 1100 BCE)
represents a pinnacle of wisdom and strategic ability, and his deferral of
personal ambition during the founding of the Zhou dynasty (1046–256
BCE) helped to secure his place as a sage with few equals in the Confucian pantheon of statesmen. The phrase "dream of Duke Zhou" refers to
a passage in *Analects* VII.5 that reflects Confucius's admiration for him.
The irony of naming such a depraved and petty villain after Duke Zhou
is obvious.

SCENE 9

1. In ancient China *fu* was a type of descriptive prose interspersed with
verse. Here it is used to refer more generally to literary composition.

2. "Sitting on the cold stool" is an oft-used phrase meaning "being
neglected" or "to be given the cold shoulder."

3. This alludes to the passage in Chapter 1 ("Xiaoyaoyou") of *Zhuangzi*, in
which a carpenter ignores trees that are unsuitable for making timber.

4. The image of rotten wood as a metaphor for uselessness comes from *Analects* V.9.

5. "No good will come to the middle part" in the Chinese original is
zhōngyòng nán, a homophone for *zhòngyòng nán* (hardly useful at all),
both written with the same characters 中用難. Here, the expression
is used as a pun for "hardly useful." By saying this, Zhang Zhongyou is
expressing his modesty.

6. Yan Hui (521–481 BCE) and Min Sun (536–487 BCE) were two of Confucius's seventy-two disciples. They are both famous for their moral integrity and self-cultivation. Yi Yin and Lü Shang were famous statesmen, thinkers, and military strategists of the Shang dynasty (c. 1600–1046 BCE).

7. The five cardinal duties refer to a man's duty in the five cardinal relationships. In the five cardinal human relations, a ruler should act benevolently to his subjects and a subject should be loyal to his ruler; a father should be strict but caring, and a son should be obedient and filial; fraternal bonds and affection are expected between brothers; although mutual respect is required between husband and wife, the husband is dominant and the wife is submissive; and trustworthiness and personal loyalty are the qualities valued between friends.

8. "Borrowing a flower to worship Buddha" or "presenting Buddha with borrowed flowers" is an idiom often used in a situation where one borrows something to make a gift of it, or one gives a present provided by someone else.

SCENE 10

1. According to "The Biography of Su Qin" from *The Records of the Grand Historian (Shiji)*, Wei Sheng waited for his lover under a bridge. His lover did not show up, but the water level rose. Wei Sheng did not leave and died waiting for her.

2. This is the legendary tragic love story between Zhu Yingtai, a female scholar, and her male classmate, Liang Shanbo. It is known as the "Butterfly Lovers" story or also as a Chinese version of *Romeo and Juliet*. It tells of Zhu falling in love with Liang when she is disguised as a man in an all-male school, their secret engagement, the breakup of their marriage by Zhu's father, and the tragic death of the lovers. One can find this story in both written and oral folk literature. The earliest written form of this story can be seen in *Shidao zhi* and *Xuanshi zhi* of the Tang dynasty (618–907). The most detailed version of the story can be found in Yu Yue's (1821–1907) "Zhu Yingtai xiaozhuan," in his *Chaxiangshi conggchao*. This story has a folkloric version and has been performed on stage in various local operas for a very long time, up to the present.

3. This line is virtually identical to that spoken by Liu Mengmei to Du Liniang in *Mudanting (The Peony Pavilion)*. In scene 10 of *Mudanting*, Liu Mengmei also says "I love you to death" to Du Liniang before making love to her in her dream.

4. Pan An of the Jin dynasty (265–420) and Song Yu of the Warring States period (specifically during the time frame from 298 to 222 BCE) were legendary for their handsome looks. For Pan An, see scene 2, note 3; and for Song Yu, see scene 3, note 6.

5. For Zhang Chang, see scene 2, note 4.

6. Wei Jie (286–312) of the Jin dynasty was another famously handsome man who died at the young age of twenty-seven. One legend has it that because Wei was extraordinarily good looking, he was followed by people and stalkers everywhere, putting him in a state of continuous tension that led to his death from exhaustion.

7. This line refers to the mythical story of the King of Chu visiting the Gaotang Mountain and making love with the Goddess of Wu Mountain in a dream. See scene 7, note 9.

8. "A *shi* could die for his soul mate" is the first part of a famous Chinese couplet. The second part is "A woman would beautify herself for the man who loves her." A *shi* refers to a scholar, official, and/or military officer in ancient China. The couplet indicates how important it is to be truly appreciated or understood by another person, both for a *shi* and for a woman.

9. This alludes to the story of King Cheng (r. 1055–1021 BCE) of the Zhou who, when he was little, playfully used a tree leaf to enfeoff his younger brother. In the story, the king was told that since a ruler's words will not be taken as a joke or a jest, they must be truthful and authoritative and beyond doubt, and thus he would have to carry out his childhood promise to his brother.

10. Operas of the Ming and Qing usually had one or two actors, whether male or female, conclude the act after the other actors had exited the stage. Alone or together, they would recite a poem, sing a few lines, or say a few words in monologue or dialogue, and then exit the stage, leaving it empty.

11. This is a euphemism for sexual activities between two women. Here "twig," like "flute," suggests a man's sexual organ. Thus "not a single twig is at hand" means the sexual activity is lacking the participation of a man. The "itch of a flower" suggests a woman's sexual desire.

SCENE 11

1. Shang Bazhi is the name of the first Ryukyan king (r. 1424–1439) to unite the entire archipelago, in 1429. Although the events of the play

seem to reflect this development, the conferral of vassal status on Ryukyuan kings by the Chinese court actually began several decades earlier, during the reign of the first Ming emperor, Zhu Yuanzhang (r. 1368–1398).

2. After Qin Shihuang, the first emperor of the Qin dynasty (221–206 BCE), had completed the unification of China, he also unified the writing and road systems that until then lacked such uniformity. These policies were considered to be beneficial for the nation's subsequent cultural and economic progress by historians of multiple later eras.

3. At the end of the Han dynasty (206 BCE–220 CE), China was divided into three kingdoms by three major contenders for imperial power. After a long period of military and political contention, Wei, Shu, and Wu were declared to be independent states respectively in 220, 221, and 222, thereafter officially entering an era of tripartite confrontation. This is called the Three Kingdoms period, which lasted from 220 to 280.

4. The "nautilus" allusion here is to a seashell-shaped mountain.

5. Cangzhou City is 240 kilometers south of Beijing in the southeast area of present-day Hebei Province. The city, which literally means "Ocean Prefecture," gained its name from its proximity to the Gulf of Bohai, which lies to the east. Legend has it that Pangu, the god credited with separating the sky from the earth, settled there after performing his great deeds. A local temple dedicated to him dates from as early as the Han dynasty.

6. Red Dust refers to the mundane world of human society, and though its first use predates the introduction of Buddhism, Buddhists often employed it as a metaphor for illusory passions.

7. The tiger-shaped tally was a kind of commander's tally stick, often with notches or markings as a means of documentation, used by a ruler to confer the authority to lead troops on military commanders.

8. Lantian jade, produced in Lantian County, Shanxi Province, about 40 kilometers south of the city of Xi'an, is considered to be one of the four best jades in China. The other three types are Hetian jade from Xinjiang, Dushan jade from Henan Province, and Xiu jade from Liaoning Province.

SCENE 12

1. "Double Ninth" Festival, or Double Yang Festival, is a traditional Chinese holiday that occurs on the ninth day of the ninth month of the lunar calendar. According to traditional custom, on the Double Ninth day

people climbed a high mountain, drank chrysanthemum liquor, and donned sprigs of *cornus officinalis*, as both plants were considered to have cleansing properties.

2. Here she means to drink wine and eat crabs. To Chinese literati, this symbolizes attaining the most pleasurable, satisfying life possible. The line in Jianyun's speech to follow, "hold a wine-cup in your right hand, and a crab claw in your left," has the same meaning.

3. Xi Shi, the classical paragon of beauty of the Warring States period (476–221 BCE), was a village girl from Zhuji of Zhejiang Province. The king of the local state of Yue, Gou Jian (520–465 BCE), who had been captured by the king of Wu, Fuchai (528–473 BCE), used her in a plot to take revenge on his former captor. Gou Jian presented Xi Shi to Fuchai in the hope that Fuchai would indulge in women, wine, and extravagance, and forget his kingly duties. This scheme turned out to be successful, and the state of Wu was defeated by Yue as a result of Fuchai's moral and sensual corruption and neglect of his duties. Yang Yuhuan, often known as Yang Guifei, was the beloved consort of Emperor Xuanzong of Tang (r. 712–756) during his later years. Yang is also known as one of the most beautiful women in Chinese history. She and her family were blamed for corrupting the court and indirectly causing the An Lushan Rebellion (757–763). After fleeing the capital to escape the rebels, Emperor Xuanzong reluctantly acceded to his imperial guard's demand to put Yang to death. Here, Jianyun mentions these two legendary beauties to indicate that Yuhua is a peerless beauty of her time.

4. According to "Empresses and Their Clans" in *Records of the Grand Historian*, Lady Xing and Lady Yin, consorts of Emperor Wu of the Han dynasty (157–87 BCE) were both favored by the emperor, but the emperor always summoned them separately to his presence, fearing their mutual jealousy and rivalry.

5. *Xiaolian* (literally "filial and incorruptible"), interchangeable with *juren* ("Elevated Scholar"), is a title conferred on those who passed the provincial level of the civil examinations during the Ming and Qing dynasties.

6. "The two daughters of the Qiao clan" refers to the two legendary sisters of the Qiao family in the Three Kingdoms period (220–280). The elder sister married the crown prince of the state of Wu, Sun Ce; the younger sister married Zhou Yu, the most famous and heroic general of Wu.

7. This refers to Fan Shi, who is both handsome and talented.

8. Liu Bang and Xiang Yu were two contenders for power during the late Qin dynasty. They swore a pact of nonaggression that established

Honggou (canal) as the border between their respective territories. But the two armies they led eventually became enemies and fought a deadly battle at Wu River where Liu Bang's troops defeated Xiang Yu's, leading the latter to take his own life. Here Fan Shi uses the story of Liu Bang and Xiang Yu as a metaphor to suggest that Jianyun's friendship with Yuhua could turn into a rivalry like that of Liu Bang and Xiang Yu's.

SCENE 13

1. Incense-burning is a ritual of Buddhist worship (of the Buddha as well as multiple other deities) that started during the Six Dynasties (222–589) and continues to the present.

2. Here the colloquial term "real pickle" alludes to the word "sour" as one possible translation of "*hansuan*," which usually means miserable and shabby. "Sour" can also mean pedantic. The oft-used description of a poor scholar is "*qiongsuan*" (literally, poor and sour), which can be translated as "poor and pedantic."

3. For *jinshi*, please see scene 4, note 6.

4. Yamen runners (*yayi*) were locally hired employees who served the officials appointed by the imperial bureaucracy such as the magistrate. They were responsible for menial tasks such as enforcing summons and arrest warrants, conveying messages or other communications, and multiple other functions of daily administration.

5. Here the expression "young maiden" is used as a metaphor for young scholars who are about to take examinations.

6. Sima Xiangru (179–118 BCE) was a writer of the Han dynasty famous for his handsome looks as well as for literary talent. But as a young man his talents were not recognized and he was mired in poverty, and there is a story of him trading his white fur coat for some wine.

7. Su Qin (?–284 BCE) was a famous strategist during the Warring States period. He once went to the state of Qin to seek a position in the Qin government; while waiting for employment there, he spent all of his money, and his coat was in shreds and tatters.

8. Both Zhao Xinchen and Du Shi were governors of Nanyang in the Western Han dynasty (206 BCE–8 CE) and the Eastern Han dynasty (25–220), respectively. They were considered to be benevolent and accomplished officials and were highly praised by local people. See "Xunli zhuan–Zhao Xinchen" (Biographies of Upright Officials: Zhao Xinchen) in *Hanshu* (*History of the Han Dynasty*) and "Du Shi zhuan"

(Biography of Du Shi) in *Hou Hanshu* (*History of the Later Han Dynasty*).

9. See scene 10, note 10.

10. Here this alludes to the ideal marriage between the younger daughter of the Qiao family and Zhou Yu, the heroic general of the state of Wu in the Three Kingdoms period. See scene 12, note 6. Zhou Gongmeng uses this allusion because he thinks that Yuhua's beauty is equivalent to that of the younger Qiao, and he is as talented as Zhou Yu. Needless to say, the only thing he shares with Zhou Yu is the same surname.

SCENE 14

1. "Encountering Sorrow," or "Lisao," is the representative work of the poet Qu Yuan (c. 340–278 BCE) of the Warring States period. He is known for his patriotism and contributions to several genres of classical poetry through the poems of the *Chuci* anthology (also known as *The Songs of the South* or *Songs of Chu*). "Encountering Sorrow" is the best-known of the *Chuci* poems.

2. This expression is taken from one of the Confucian classics, *Mencius* (XI "Gaozi shang," 10). Both fish and bear's paw were considered to be delicacies in ancient times. Not only is it excessively greedy to want to have both, but it would be almost impossible to have them both. It is like the English saying: one wants to sell the cow but still be able to drink its milk after selling it.

3. "A small magician in the presence of a great one" or *xiaowu jian dawu*, is an idiom used to express feeling inferior or insignificant in comparison with another person.

4. Wang Wei (701–761) was a famous poet and painter of the Tang dynasty (618–907). One of his paintings shows plantains with snow in the background. People criticized this painting for not making sense, since it places things from two different seasons (plantains and snow) in the same picture. Here this allusion is used to indicate the extraordinary character of the romance between Jianyun and Yuhua.

5. See scene 2, note 9.

6. Cao Cao (155–220) was a warlord and the penultimate chancellor of the Eastern Han dynasty who rose to great power in its final years. As one of the central figures of the Three Kingdoms period, he laid the foundations for what was to become the state of Wei (sometimes also known as Cao-Wei), and he was posthumously honored as "Emperor Wu of Wei."

One story claims that Cao Cao waged a war against the state of Wu, located to the south of Wei, partly because he desired to capture and lock up the two Qiao sisters in Tongque Tower, so that he could possess these two peerless beauties for himself.

7. The Battle of the Red Cliff (*Chibi zhi zhan*) was a decisive battle fought at the end of the Han dynasty, about 12 years prior to the beginning of the Three Kingdoms period. It was fought in the winter of 208–209 CE between the allied forces of the southern and western warlords, Sun Quan and Liu Bei, on one side, and the numerically superior forces of the northern warlord, Cao Cao, on the other. Liu Bei and Sun Quan successfully frustrated Cao Cao's effort to conquer the land south of the Yangzi (Chang) River and reunify the different parts of the country that had begun to fragment by the late Eastern Han dynasty. "The young general Zhou" refers to Zhou Yu (175–210), who was the frontline commander of Sun Quan's forces at the Battle of Red Cliff responsible for defeating Cao Cao's forces.

SCENE 15

1. Su Qin (?–284 BCE) and Zhang Yi (c. 370–310 BCE) were famous political strategists of the Warring States period, and both were known for their sharp tongues. For more on Su Qin see scene 13, note 7.

2. Using red ink and brush to circle felicitous expressions or excellent thoughts was a common practice of teachers in traditional China. Therefore, when a teacher made many red circles on an essay, it meant that the teacher had highly praised it.

3. Officials dressed in either red or purple official robes depending on their rank in the bureaucracy. Here, waiting for red-robed officials to nod their heads means that the officials have not yet given approval of Zhang Zhongyou's promotion.

4. "Helping a tyrant to victimize his subjects" is an idiom that originally referred to those who helped King Zhou of the Shang dynasty (1105–1046 BCE) in tyrannizing his subjects. This expression was used later for anyone who became an accessary to a tyrant's crimes or, idiomatically, held the candle to the devil.

5. In *Zhuangzi* (36: "Lieyukou"), there is a story about a young man from a poor family who found a pearl in a river. His father said that his son must have gotten this pearl when the dragon of the river was asleep. This line may allude to this story.

6. In traditional China, it was a common practice to use a red card for auspicious events such as a wedding invitation or to report the news of an examination success. Such a practice is very popular in contemporary China, too. People still use red cards for expressing good wishes at holidays and for wedding invitations.

7. Fan Zhongyan (989–1052) was a prominent politician and literary figure in the Northern Song dynasty (960–1127). He was also a strategist and educator. After serving the central government for many years, he finally rose to the position of vice chancellor over the whole of the Song Empire. By mentioning Fan Zhongyan, Zhang Zhongyou intends to suggest that Fan Shi comes from a prominent clan, though in fact the only thing the two share is their last name. This kind of name-dropping was a common convention of traditional Chinese theater.

8. Ruan Xiaoxu (479–536) was famous for both literary talent and filial devotion. By the age of thirteen he was thoroughly versed in the Confucian Five Classics, and at twenty had lofty aspirations for himself. Nevertheless, he stayed away from worldly affairs and wrote a treatise on reclusion.

9. See scene 10, note 6.

SCENE 16

1. "Using the red thread to tie the feet of groom and bride" is a common expression in Chinese culture. It means "tie the knot" or "get married."

2. "Iceman" is another expression for a matchmaker; here, pun intended.

3. Emperor Gaozu (256 or 247–195 BCE), personal name Liu Bang, was the founder and first emperor of the Han dynasty (206 BCE–220 CE). He ruled until 195 BCE and was one of the few dynastic founders in Chinese history who originated from the peasant class. He is known for his dislike of scholars and behaved rudely toward them. When the learned scholar Lu Jia (240–170 BCE) tried to discuss the Confucian classics with him, the emperor brusquely replied: *I gained the throne on horseback, not by discussing books.* Lu questioned the emperor: *Your Majesty may have won the land on horseback, but can you rule it on horseback?* This conversation changed the emperor's attitude toward scholars. Soon after the first emperor of the Qin (259–210 BCE) founded the Qin dynasty, he responded to complaints that too many former officials of the now-vanquished kingdoms were given high positions at his court, by stripping many of their official titles and deporting them from the capital.

4. This tune, *zaojiaoji* 皂角儿 can also be written as *zajiaoer* 皂角儿 meaning "Black Little Corner."

5. "The Dream of the Southern Bough" (Nankemeng) is a Daoist allegory about the illusory nature of worldly gains. The story stems from a Tang classical tale, "The Story of Nanke Governor," by Li Gongzuo. It tells of a scholar named Chun Yufen drinking under an old pagoda tree and then falling asleep and having a dream. He had all of his worldly desires fulfilled in his dream: he passed the highest level of examination, became a high-ranking official at the imperial court, married a princess, and lived in luxury. But everything turned out to have been a dream, which he realized when he woke up.

6. See scene 10, note 9.

7. *Chiyi* is a container, made of either copper or leather, to hold wine. According to *Shiji* or *The Records of the Grand Historian*, when Fuchai, the king of Wu State, killed Wu Zixu (?–484 BCE), he used a leather *chiyi* to hold Wu's corpse. Later on, when Fan Li thought that he lost the trust of Goujian, the king of Yue, he called himself *chiyi zipi* or "leather bag" as a way to castigate himself. Obviously, *chiyi* is used for a subordinate who has offended an authority figure, and therefore receives a severe punishment on that account.

8. This line translates the idiom *kezhou qiujian*, which refers to a man who carved a mark on a drifting boat to find the place where a sword had fallen into the river. The idiom is usually used for people who tend to have fossilized ideas or concepts and are not able to adapt to new circumstances.

SCENE 17

1. "A hundred sons are playing in the spring" is a common theme of traditional Chinese painting. The earliest appearance of this theme is in *The Classic of Poetry* (*Shijing*), in which King Wen of the Zhou dynasty (1029–771 BCE) is described as having a hundred sons. In the patriarchal family system that prevailed in traditional China, having more sons meant having male heirs to continue the family lineage and provide a good life for parents when they are old. Here, "the painting of a hundred sons" is used to suggest that boatmen tend to have many children.

2. Mencius (c. 372–289 BCE) was the most famous Confucian philosopher after Confucius himself. When Mencius was three years old, his father passed away, leaving his mother to raise him alone. She was praised as an exemplary female figure; one of the most famous Chinese phrases about her life, "Mencius's mother moved three times," refers to a story about

moving their household three times—from a location next to a ceme-
tery to one next to a market, and eventually to one next to a school—in
order to provide the young Mencius with a good environment that would
exert salutary influence over his upbringing.

3. Breaking a willow branch to present it to a parting friend was a traditional custom, particularly popular during the Tang dynasty.

4. This alludes to a couplet from a poem by Du Mu, "Whereas the bright
moon still shines over the Four and Twenty Bridge, / where is the jade-
like person now to teach the flute?" For the complete poem, see scene 3,
note 10. Du Mu's original poem was written in memory of his old friend
Han Chuo; here, Yuhua suggests that what she feels for Jianyun is not
simply friendship, but a deep love.

5. Yan Yuan or Yan Hui (521–481 BCE) was Confucius's favorite student.
He is mentioned many times in *The Analects* for his love of learning and
virtuous conduct.

6. Cao Zhi (192–232), courtesy name Zijian, was Cao Cao's third son and a
prince of the state of Wei in the Three Kingdoms period (220–265). One
of the most accomplished poets of his time, his poetic style, which was
greatly revered during the Jin dynasty (317–420) within and the Southern and Northern Dynasties (420–589), came to be known as the Jian'an
style. Cao Zijian is regarded as a precocious genius for both his prose
and poetry. A story tells of him composing a poem in seven steps when
pressured by his elder brother.

7. Musical instruments, and especially drums, were used by plaintiffs to initiate accusations against wrongdoers. The advice to "beat drums to accuse
wrongdoers" is credited to Confucius himself (See *Analects* XI.17).

8. This refers to *Chunqiu*, or *The Spring and Autumn Annals*, a historical
work that was included as one of the Five Confucian Classics. The
Annals is the official chronicle of the state of Lu, and it covers a 241-year
period from 722 to 481 BCE. It is the earliest surviving Chinese historical text to be arranged in the form of annals. It gained the status of a
Confucian classic because it was traditionally regarded as having been
compiled by Confucius. It also spawned the "Spring and Autumn"
school of Confucian exegesis, whose adherents claimed that every single
word of the text possesses an allegorical or sub rosa meaning of either
praise or blame. Such subtle and indirect commentary was revered as an
effective style and model for Confucian criticism and moral judgment.

9. The literal meaning of "burning a rhinoceros-horn" is "to light things in
darkness." Its extended meaning is to understand thoroughly and to go
deeply into things.

10. This alludes to Wang Wei's (701–761) poem about parting from a friend who was on his way to China's western border to serve in a post guarding the frontier. The entire poem reads: "The morn rain of Wei Town has laid the light dust clean; /and willow trees around the inn look fresh and green. /A cup of farewell yet, oh you, I do entreat, / for West across Yang Pass, and friends but seldom meet."

11. The word translated as "official sweat" (*hanlinli*) puns with (Hanlin li), meaning "leaving as a Hanlin academician," which was the prestigious posting awarded to top-ranked graduates of the Ming and Qing dynasty metropolitan examinations—hence Cao Gechen's pleasure at hearing such an auspicious omen.

12. The three matrons are Buddhist nuns, female Daoist priests, and women fortunetellers, while the six hags include female women traffickers, women matchmakers, sorceresses, female brothel keepers, gynecological practitioners, and midwives.

13. "Silken cords" is *qingsi* in Chinese, which is a homophone for *qingsi* (feelings of affection, or the emotion of love). Therefore, "silken cords" as used here is a pun for affection and love.

14. In Chinese mythology, Mount Penglai or Penglai Island is a Daoist paradise. The paradise is said to be the abode of the Eight Daoist Immortals, or at least where they travel to hold banquets. Supposedly, everything on Mount Penglai seems white, while its palaces are made from gold and platinum, and jewels grow on trees. There is no pain and no winter; there are rice bowls and wine glasses that never become empty no matter how much people eat or drink from them; and there are magical fruits growing there that can heal any disease, grant eternal youth, and even raise the dead. Historically, the first emperor of the Qin dynasty (221–206 BCE), in search of the elixir of life, made several attempts to find the island where the mountain is located, but to no avail.

15. "Shake up the pillow and have a good sleep" is an often-used expression meaning to "sleep soundly without any worry." The maid uses this idiom here in a playful way.

SCENE 18

1. "Eight Min" or "Ba Min" refers to modern-day Fujian Province; the name is still in use today.

2. "The friendship of Gold and Orchid" means to form a deep and righteous friendship between two men whose combined force or sharpness can cut gold and whose shared expression is as fragrant as an orchid. The

earliest reference to this conception is in the following passage from
Zhouyi (Book of Changes), in "Xici shang" (The Appended Words): "If
two people share the same views, their combined sharpness can cut gold;
when two likeminded people talk, their words are as refined or fragrant
as an orchid."

SCENE 19

1. "Creating flowers with the brush" or "flowers blossom under one's brush"
   is an often-used expression describing one's skill in writing, or the beauty
   of someone's writing. This expression is still in use today.
2. The idiom "*qingzhu nanshu*" is used here. It means that one's crimes are
   so numerous that even if all of the bamboo slips (upon which crimes were
   inscribed) were used up to record them, they still wouldn't include every
   one the wrongdoings.
3. According to a passage in *Mencius*, Fengmeng learned archery from
   Houyi but later killed him, as Fengmeng wanted to be the preeminent
   archer in the kingdom.

SCENE 20

1. "Yellow Springs" refers to the netherworld.
2. According to the "Biography of Su Qin" in *The Records of the Grand Historian*, in his early years the famous statesman and strategist Su Qin
   traveled about seeking employment in different states during the Warring States period, but eventually returned home impoverished and
   empty-handed. He was therefore ridiculed by his family and relatives.
3. "Break the cauldrons and sink the boats" is a Chinese idiom, meaning
   to exert every effort to fight a last battle by cutting off all means of retreat.
   This idiom originally referred to a military strategy employed by the
   famous general Xiang Yu. See "The Annuals of Xiang Yu" in *Records of
   the Grand Historian*.
4. This refers to the story that Sima Xiangru wrote a message on the pillar
   of a bridge in the northern part of the city of Chengdu before he left
   for the capital. It read: "If I am not able to ride in a red carriage with
   four horses [indicating one's prominent social status and wealth], I will
   not pass this bridge." See Du Shuying, annotated *Lianxiang ban* (Beijing: Zhongguo shehui kexueyuan chubanshe, 2011), 108, n. 3.
5. This alludes to the famous line, "A jade-like beauty can be found among
   the books" from "Admonition to Study Poetry" (*Quanxue shi*) by Emperor

Zhenzong (986–1022) of the Song dynasty. This line, coupled with another line: "Golden mansions are to be found through the books" have been frequently quoted by parents, teachers, and officials to urge youngsters to study.

SCENE 21

1. According to legend, Yingzhou is a divine realm where Daoist immortals live. Here it is used as a metaphor for a place of high social status.
2. "Smelly skin-bag" is a Buddhist term used to refer to the human body. Here Yuhua uses it to sarcastically suggest that by ignoring her feelings, her father treats her life as worthless.
3. Du Liniang is the famously love-obsessed heroine in *The Peony Pavilion*.
4. The wild goose is conventionally used as a literary figure for a letter bearer.

SCENE 22

1. One *li* is about one-third of a mile or one-half of a kilometer.
2. Fan Li (536–448 BCE) of the Spring and Autumn period was a military strategist and statesman of the state of Yue. It is commonly believed that he was the one who found the legendary beauty Xi Shi and used her to distract Fuchai (c. 528–473 BCE), the king of Wu, from his duties in order to weaken that state. After Wu was destroyed by Yue, Fan Li sensed that Goujian (?–464 BCE), the king of Yue, distrusted him, and escaped together with Xi Shi by boat.

SCENE 23

1. "Climbing up a ladder of clouds" is a metaphor for succeeding in one's career, similar to climbing the social ladder.
2. The Moon Goddess is a metaphor for Yuhua (Miss Cao).
3. The steps in the Imperial Palace where the emperor held audience with the scholars of the Imperial Academy have carvings of turtles, hence "standing on the Giant Turtle's back" has become a figurative expression for taking the first place in the exam. Similarly, breaking off a cassia branch is also a metaphor for placing high on an exam. Since cassia trees were said to grow in the Moon Palace, by extension, receiving a cassia branch from the Moon Goddess indicates taking first place in an exam.

4. This refers to the fable of the snipe and the clam. When the snipe sticks its beak inside the clam, the clam snaps its shell shut. Neither budge because the clam refuses to open, knowing that would allow the snipe to use its beak to peck out the clam's body. Their deadlock enables a fisherman who passes by to capture them both.

SCENE 24

1. See scene 5, note 3.
2. This refers to the story of the musician Boya and his soulmate, Ziqi. After Ziqi died, Boya broke his instrument and never played again. See scene 6, note 18.
3. To be like a frog at the bottom of a well means to see only the little patch of sky above. From *Zhuangzi*, chapter 23 ("Qiushui," Autumn Waters).

SCENE 25

1. Qi Xi was a politician in the state of Jin during the Spring and Autumn period. When he was about to retire from the Jin court, the Duke of Jin asked him to recommend his successors. Qi first recommended Xie Hu, toward whom he had considerable enmity, and then later recommended his own son as the successor of Xie Hu. The moral of this story is that Qi Xi was able to place the concerns of the state before his own self-interest, such as personal relations or reputation. For the benefit of the state, he could promote someone whom he personally hated, and he was also not afraid of being condemned for partiality by recommending his own son. The story is taken from *Spring and Autumn Annals*. See Du Shuying's annotation in *Lianxiang ban*, p. 123, n. 3.

SCENE 26

1. In the original text the character 桃 (*táo*), literally translated as "peach" in the line "peach-sized characters," is used by the playwright to mock the candidate's limited literacy. She means to boast about her knowledge of Chinese characters, but ironically uses the expression "a few liters' worth" to describe the number of the characters that she has learned. Given the fact that the "peaches" are large in size and heavy in weight, "a few liters" of them cannot be many. Therefore, as a result of

this "boasting," she is actually admitting that she does not really know that much.

2. This refers to an anecdote from the Jian'an period. Chen Lin (d. 217) wrote an essay denouncing Cao Cao's enemy Yuan Shao. Cao Cao enjoyed reading the essay so much that a headache that had been bothering him went away immediately.

3. "Meng" here means Meng Haoran (c. 689–740), a famous landscape poet of the Tang dynasty. This line suggests that Meng's poetry has a tranquil quality that could be used to treat epilepsy.

4. Ban Zhao (here referred to by her alternate name, Ban Ji, 45–117, as in the original script) came from a family of historians who were active during the Eastern Han. *The History of the Han,* an epic work started by her father, was taken over by her brother, and finally completed by her hand.

5. The story of Red String took place during the Tang dynasty. Red String was the secretary of a General Xue, whose belligerent neighbor General Tian plotted to invade Xue's territory. Upon learning of this, Red String sneaked into Tian's bedroom at night and stole a golden box from his bedside. The next day Xue sent the box back to Tian, who was startled and called off his plans for aggression.

6. The story of Phoenix and the red leaf comes from the Tang. A gentleman named Jia was walking by the imperial moat one day and picked up a leaf that had floated out from the compound. On the leaf was inscribed a poem, written by Phoenix, the adopted daughter of a concubine. Jia was moved to tears by the poem. The emperor heard of this story and gave Phoenix to Jia in marriage.

7. Lady Su refers to Su Hui (fl. c. 350), the wife of Dou Tao, who was banished to the frontier. Lady Su wove a palindrome poem on a handkerchief expressing longing for her husband. The general in charge at the time heard of this, and was moved to pardon Dou Tao, permitting him to come home.

8. These are the three most famous Chinese historians: Zuo Qiuming (556–451 BCE) wrote *Zuozhuan* (the Zuo Commentary on the *Spring and Autumn Annals*); Sima Qian (c. 145–135 BCE) wrote *Shiji* (*The Records of the Grand Historian*); and Ban Gu (32–92) was one of the authors of *Hanshu* (*History of the Western Han*).

9. She confused Lady Su Hui (fl. c. 350) with the wife of Su Qin (d. 284 BCE), who did not greet her husband when he came home after a long absence. She kept on weaving at her loom, ignoring Su Qin because he was indigent at the time.

10. Both Zuo Fen (d. 300) and Xie Daoyun (fl. c. 400) were famous female literati known for their poetic talents.

11. Yu Xuanji (fl. 850) was a famous poet and Daoist nun during the Tang dynasty.

12. The jade tree and flowering orchid are both precious plants used as metaphors for exceptionally talented people. Here they refer to Jianyun and Yuhua.

SCENE 28

1. In Ming and Qing times, the Confucian texts used in the examinations were known as the Four Books and Five Classics. Zhou's faulty count here attests to his buffoonish ignorance of all things scholarly.

2. The expression "*daoji xiangying*" or "[in a hurry to] welcome a guest, one puts on his/her shoes backwards," is used to indicate the eagerness to meet someone.

SCENE 29

1. Literally the "God of Matchmaking."

2. This refers to the story of Cao Cao's Bronze Sparrow Tower (Tongquelou). During the Three Kingdoms period, Cao Cao built a magnificent tower named Bronze Sparrow, boasting that he would one day take the Qiao sisters, the wives of his opponents Sun Ce and Zhou Yu, and lock them away in his tower. As it turned out, this aim was never fulfilled. The use of this allusion here indicates that, try as they may, villains like Cao Cao will never succeed in breaking apart marriages destined by fate.

3. According to the penal codes of the Ming and Qing dynasties, scholars who held the *juren* title (conferred on those who passed the provincial level exam), were exempt from some forms of corporeal punishment.

4. The expression translated to refer to his exposed identity literally means "revealing the horse's hoof," which while not necessarily malign, has roughly the same sense of exposing evil intentions as the Western saying "show the cloven foot."

5. "Making another's wedding dress" is a figure of speech describing laboring for someone else's benefit. This line comes from a Tang poem by Qin Taoyu (fl. 880).

6. In imperial times, a bundle of bamboo slips was placed on the judge's desk in the courthouse, to be used ritually during the sentencing phase of a case. When the judge reached his decision, he threw a bamboo slip

out from his desk as he announced the sentence. The sharp clap of the slip striking the floor signified the irreversibility of the judge's final decision.

7. Dong Zhongshu (179–104 BCE) was a thinker and minister of the Han dynasty who was renowned for his Confucian scholarship.

8. He Wu (d. 3 CE) was a minister of the Western Han, who in spite of his high position was known for acting impartially and without malice toward someone who had slandered him in the past. Liu Kuan (120–185) was a minister of the Eastern Han, known for his lenience in sentencing criminals. It is recorded that when people received canings in his court, it was always with straw instead of staffs.

SCENE 30

1. Bo Le (fl. c. 650 BCE) was an expert equestrian who was exceptionally talented at selecting and taming horses.

2. Here "Luanfeng," or phoenixes, refers to talented scholars who come to take the examination.

3. "Although peaches and plums cannot speak, paths naturally form beneath them" is a figure of speech that comes from *Records of the Grand Historian*. Just like fruit trees that bear beautiful and tasty fruits will naturally attract many people, so do people with real potential. Here Shi Jian is using this to refer to the eventual fruition of his budding talent.

4. *Jinshi* scholars are ranked into three classes according to their performance in the final phase of the metropolitan examinations, known as the palace examination (*dianshi*).

5. In Chinese folklore, it was believed that some fish have the potential to turn into dragons through extraordinary means. This fish-to-dragon transformation is used as a figure of speech for turning around or changing one's fate, and in particular, for attaining status through success in the civil service examinations.

6. Zhong Jun (133–112 BCE) was a renowned statesman and diplomat of the Western Han. Jia Yi (200–168 BCE) was a famous statesman and poet also of the Western Han. Both achieved fame early in life and died young.

7. Ziqi was a young statesman from the Spring and Autumn period. It was recorded that he was appointed to be in charge of a province of the state of Qi at age eighteen. Later he became a byword for precocious youth. Here Shi Jian is apologizing for being "old."

8. Liang Hong was a hermit of the Eastern Han, who was known for turning down offers of marriage or jobs from powerful people, instead preferring his reclusive life.

9. Sima Xiangru (179–118 BCE) was a famous statesman and poet of the Western Han. Due to his tendency to speak directly to rulers and the powerful, he was often forced to go on the road to escape their wrath or find new employment. See scene 13, note 5.

10. "Old sword" is a metaphor for one's first wife. This comes from an anecdote of Emperor Xuan of the Han, who elevated his first wife, whom he had married before he ascended the throne, to the status of empress against his ministers' opposition. Here it refers to Shi Jian's engagement to Jianyun.

11. "Jade mirror" is a metaphor for a betrothal gift. Here it refers to a potential second engagement.

SCENE 31

1. "Gazing up at the Altair Star" is a reference to a famous line from a Tang poem about a woman's loneliness. The Altair Star is thought to be the spirit of the Herd Boy banished from his lover, the Weaver Girl. It symbolizes a lone lover separated from his beloved.

2. In traditional China, comparing women's eyebrows to mountains in the distance or to the moth's antennae are both high compliments.

3. In 283 BCE, the powerful state of Qin requested a piece of precious jade from Zhao, and Lin Xiangru was sent on the dangerous mission to take the jade to Qin and then bring it back to Zhao. Lin successfully completed the mission, and here Yuhua compares Jianyun to the jade, urging her to hurry up and return to her rightful place in their home.

4. Ice and jade are both considered objects of purity, and hence comparing them to father- and son-in-law is meant to describe ideal relations among in-laws.

5. Five-Flower Colors is an emblem made of special brocade allowed only for wives of high-ranking officials. The Seven-Perfumed Carriage is a carriage made of expensive aromatic wood. Both are symbols of high status.

SCENE 32

1. Both Shi Chong (d. 300) and Wang Kai were wealthy figures from the Eastern Jin known for their unprecedentedly extravagant lifestyles. See scene 6, note 14.

SCENE 33

1. This refers to the *Rites of Zhou,* one of the most revered ritual texts and included in the *Classic of Ritual.*
2. When clouds of five different colors gather, it is considered an auspicious sign.
3. Zhongshan literally means "Mid-Mountain."
4. The gold gauze wings and green ribbons refer to accessories on the hat worn by a high-ranking official. Here they are used as metonyms to contrast China's civilization with the Ryukyu Islands' lack thereof.
5. See note 3; the Chinese emperor conferred the name Zhongshan on the kingdom of the Ryukyu Islands.
6. A song that "lingers on the rafters" and the "Rainbow Skirt Dance" are both compliments. The former comes from an anecdote that dates back to the Warring States period, while the latter refers to Precious Consort Yang Yuhuan from the Tang dynasty, who was a talented dancer. In this play, both serve to contrast the splendor of Chinese civilization with the rusticity of the Ryukyu Islands.
7. Jade pendants hung on strings were commonly worn as accessories around one's belt, hence the sound of jade pendants striking against one another is used as an allusion to traveling.

SCENE 34

1. These lines refer to the first poem of the *Classic of Poetry,* a love poem that opens with an image of ospreys singing to one another on an islet.
2. This refers to an idiom that comes from a poem in the *Classic of Poetry* titled "Magpie's Nest." Turtledoves are a breed of bird that lacks the ability to build their own nests, and hence they often take over the nests of others birds, such as the magpie, by force. Here Yuhua compares herself to a new turtledove who took over the magpie's nest by pushing out the old turtledove, Jianyun.
3. The left side of the dining table is reserved for the guest of honor; here Yuhua leaves the left side of the bed empty for Jianyun.

SCENE 35

1. A long thin tablet held by a minister when having an audience with the emperor, used for notetaking.
2. Zhang Qian (164–114 BCE) was a Han dynasty diplomat famed for his epic journey to Central Asia via the Silk Road.

3. The title conferred on the king of the Ryukyu Islands.
4. This refers to the Han practice of marrying princesses to neighboring countries in order to form political alliances and thereby to prevent invasions or raids.

SCENE 36

1. This refers to the custom of throwing candies and trinkets onto the newlyweds' bed, as a sign of fertility and prosperity.
2. "Three phoenixes" is a conventional title given to three outstanding figures who live in the same period. Here it refers to the three newlyweds.

APPENDIX: MODES AND TUNES

1. Usually northern drama tends to have just one mode in each act whereas the southern drama can have up to three modes in the same act (scene).
2. Li Yu 李漁, *Lianxiang ban* 憐香伴 (Beijing: Zhongguo shehui kexue chubanshe, 2011), 36–42.

SELECTED WORKS ON LI YU AND SAME-SEX LOVE IN CLASSICAL CHINESE FICTION AND DRAMA

CHINESE SOURCES

Cao Xueqin 曹雪芹. *Honglou meng* 紅樓夢 (The Dream of the Red Chamber, or alternatively The Story of the Stone). 2 vols. Beijing: Renmin wenxue chubanshe, 2008.

Chen Sen 陳森. *Pinhua baojian* 品花寶鑑 (A Precious Mirror for Classifying Flowers). 2 vols. Beijing: Remin Zhongguo chubanshe, 1993.

Ding Bingren 丁秉仁. *Yaohua zhuan* 瑤華傳 (The Story of Yaohua). Kindle edition, 2018.

Du Shuying 杜書瀛. *Xikan renjian: Li Yu zhuan* 戲看人間: 李漁傳 (Playfully Seeing the Human World: The Biography of Li Yu). Beijing: Zuojia chubanshe, 2014.

Du Shuying 杜書瀛. "Li Yu shengping sixiang gaiguan" 李漁生平思想概观 (An Overview of Li Yu's Life and Thought). *Wen shi zhe* 文史哲 6 (1983): 17–23.

Fang Gang 方剛. *Tongxinglian zai zhongguo* 同性戀在中國 (Homosexuality in China). Changchun: Jilin renmin chubanshe, 1995.

Guben xiaoshuo jicheng bianweihui 古本小說集成編委會, ed. *Gelian huaying* 隔簾花影 (Shadows of Flowers behind the Screen). 2 vols. Shanghai: Shanghai guji chubanshe, 1990.

Hu, Siao-chen (Hu Xiaozhen) 胡曉真. "Cainü cheye wei mian—Qingdai funü tanci xiaoshuo zhong de ziwo chengxian" 才女徹夜未眠: 清代婦女彈詞小說中的自我呈現 (Self-Representation in Qing Women's *Tanci* Novels). *Jindai Zhongguo funü shi yanjiu* 近代中國婦女史研究 3 (1995): 51–76.

Hua Wei. 華瑋. "Ming Qing Funü juzuo zhong 'ninan' biaoxian yu xingbie wenti" 明清婦女劇作中"擬男"表現與性別問題 (The Problem of Women's Cross-Dressing and Gender Identity in the Ming and Qing). In *Ming Qing xiqu guoji yantaohui lunwenji* 明清戲曲國際研討會論文集 (Proceedings of the International Conference on Ming-Qing Drama), ed. Hua Wei and Wang Ailing 王愛玲. Taipei: Dawen yinshua, 1998.

Ji Dawei 紀大偉. *Tongzhi wenxueshi: Taiwan de faming* 同志文學史: 台灣的發明 (A Queer Invention in Taiwan—A History of Tongzhi Literature). Taiwan, Xinbeishi: Lianjing chuban, 2017.

Kang Zhengguo 康正果. *Chong shen fengyue jian: Xing yu Zhongguo gudian wenxue* 重審風月鑑: 性與中國古典文學 (Reexamining the Mirror of Wind and Moon: Sex and Classical Chinese Literature). Taipei: Maitian, 1996.

Li Mei 李梅. "Jin shinian Li Yu yanju pinge shuping" 近十年李漁研究品格述評 (A Review of the Characteristics of the Past Decade's Li Yu Studies). *Panzhihua xueyuan xuebao* 攀枝花學院學報 2 (2009): 90–93.

Li Yinhe 李銀河. *Tongxinglian yawenhua* 同性戀亞文化 (The Subculture of Homosexuality). Huhehaote: Neimenggu daxue chubanshe, 2009.

Li Yu 李漁. *Li Yu quanji* 李漁全集 (The Complete Works of Li Yu). Hangzhou: Zhejiang guji chubanshe, 1991.

Li Yu 李漁. *Lianxiang ban* 憐香伴 (The Fragrant Companions). Annotated by Du Shuying 杜書瀛. Beijing: Zhongguo shehui kexue chubanshe, 2011.

Li Yu 李漁. *Rouputuan* 肉蒲團 (The Carnal Prayer Mat). Kindle edition, 2021.

Li Yu 李漁. *Shi'er lou* 十二樓 (Twelve Towers). Kindle edition, Yiya chubanshe, 2018.

Li Yu 李漁. *Wusheng xi* 無聲戲 (Silent Operas). Hangzhou: Zhejiang guji chubanshe, 2018.

"Li Yu yanjiu lunwen lunzhu suoyin" 李漁研究論文論著索引 (The Index of Research Articles on Li Yu). In *Li Yu quanji* 李漁全集, vol. 20. Hangzhou: Zhejiang guji chubanshe, 1991.

Mao Feng 矛鋒. *Tongxinglian wenxue shi* 同性戀文學史 (The History of Homosexual Literature). Taipei: Hanzhong wenhua, 1996.

Shan Zai 善哉. "Funü tongxing zhi aiqing" 婦女同性之愛情 (Same-Sex Erotic Love Between Women). *Funü shibao* 婦女時報 1, no. 7 (June 1911): 36–38.

Shao Yuanyuan 邵媛媛. "Ku'er lilun shiyu xia jiedu *Lianxiang ban* zhong zhuyao nüxing juese de xingbie renzhi" 酷兒理論視閾下解讀《憐香伴》中主要女性角色的性別認知 (The Interpretation of Gender Identity of the Female Characters in *The Fragrant Companions* in the Perspective of Queer Theory). *Xiju zhijia* 戲劇之家 27 (2020): 4–5.

Shi Zhenlin 史震林. *Xiqing sanji* 西青散記 (Random Records of West-Green). Beijing: Beijing shi zhongguo shudian, 1987.

Suiyuan xiashi 隨緣下士. *Lin Lan Xiang* 林藍香 (The Three Women Named Lin, Lan, and Xiang). Annotated by Xu Ming 徐明. Beijing: Zhonghua shuju, 2004.

Tao Wu 檮杌. "Mo jing dang" 磨鏡黨 (The Mirror-Rubbing Gang). In *Shanghai funü nie jingtai* 上海婦女孽鏡台 (A Mirror of Shanghai Women's Sin), vol. 4, 65–70. Shanghai: Zhonghua tushu jicheng gongsi, 1918.

Pan Guangdan 潘光旦. *Feng Xiaoqing xing xinli biantai jiemi* 馮小青性心裡變態揭秘. (Revealing Feng Xiaoqing's Perversion in Sexual Psychology). Shanghai: 1927; Beijing: Wenhua yishu chubanshe, 1990.

Pan Guangdan 潘光旦, trans. *Xing xinli xue* 性心裡學. (The Psychology of Sexuality). Shanghai, 1946; Beijing Sanlian shudian, 1987.

Pan Guangdan 潘光旦. "Zhongguo wenxian zhong tongxinglian juli" 中國文獻中同性戀舉例 (Examples of Homosexuality in Chinese Documents). In *Xing xinli xue*, trans. Pan Guangdan, 516–547.

Pu Songling 蒲松齡. *Liaozhai zhiyi* 聊齋誌異 (Strange Tales in a Chinese Studio). 3 vols. Beijing: Renmin wenxue chubanshe, 1989.

Qiu Xinru 邱心如. *Bi sheng hua* 筆生花 (Flowers Generated from the Writing Brush). 3 vols. Taipei: Heluo, 1980.

Shen Fu 沈復. *Fusheng liuji* 浮生六記 (Six Records of a Floating Life). Beijing: Renmin wenxue chubanshe, 2018.

Weixing shiguan zhaizhu 唯性史觀齋主. *Zhongguo tongxinglian mishi* 中國同性戀秘史 (The Secret History of Homosexuality in China). Hong Kang: Yuzhou chubanshe, 1964.

"Xiandai xuezhe yanjiu Li Yu lunwen jingxuan" 現代學者研究李漁論文精選 (A Well-Chosen Collection of Li Yu's Studies by Modern Scholars). In *Li Yu quanji* 李漁全集. Vol. 20. Hangzhou: Zhejiang guji chubanshe, 1991.

Zhao Jingshen 趙景深. "Tongxing lian'ai xiaoshuo de chajin" 同性戀愛小說的查禁 (The Banning of a Novel about Same-Sex Love). *Xiaoshuo yuebao* 小說月報 20, no. 3 (1929): 611–612.

Zhao Ting 趙婷. "*Lianxiang ban* yu *Liaozhai zhiyi* zhong nü tongxianglian zhe renwu xingxiang yanjiu" 《憐香伴》與《聊齋誌異》中女同性戀者人物形象研究 (The Study of Lesbian Characters in *The Fragrant Companions* and *Strange Tales from a Chinese Studio*). *Pu Songling yanjiu* 蒲松齡研究 2 (2020): 71–78.

Zhou Zuoren 周作人 (Kai Ming 開明). "Ailisi de hua" 靄理思的話 (The Words of Ellis). *Chen bao fukan* 晨報副刊, February 23,1924.

ENGLISH SOURCES

Chang, Chun-she, and Shelley Hsueh-lun Chang. *Crisis and Transformation in Seventeenth-Century China: Society, Culture, and Modernity in Li Yü's World*. Ann Arbor: University of Michigan Press, 1992.

Chang, Dongshin. "Xiang Yong (Poems on Fragrance): A Translation of A Scene from Li Yu's *Lian Xiang Ban (The Fragrant Companion)*." *CHINOPERL Papers* 30, no. 1 (July 2011): 239–258.

Chang, Ivy I-chu Chang. "Queer Politics, Sexual Anarchism, and Nationalism: The Chinese Male Mother and the Queer Family in *He Is My Wife, He Is My Mother*." *The Drama Review* 58, no. 1 (Spring 2014): 89–107.

Chen, Chang. "The Intersection of Nationalism, Confucian Familism, and Queer in Katherine Hui-ling Chou's *He's My Wife, He's My Mother*." *Orbis Litterarum* 75, no. 4 (August 2019): 356–379.

Choy, Elsie. *Leaves of Prayer: The Life and Poetry of He Shuangqing, A Farmwife in Eighteenth-Century China*. Hong Kong: The Chinese University Press, 1993.

Dhawa, Huai Bao aka H. B. *Cross-Gender China: Across Yin-Yang, Across Cultures, and Beyond Jingju*. London and New York: Routledge and Taylor & Francis Group, 2018.

Fang, Fu Ruan. "Homosexuality." In *Sex in China: Studies in Sexology in Chinese Culture*, 107–143. New York: Plenum Press, 1991.

Fong, Grace S. "De/Constructing a Feminine Ideal in the Eighteenth Century: 'Random Records of West-Green' and the Story of Shuangqing." In *Writing Women in Late Imperial China*, ed. Ellen Widmer and Kang-I Sun Chang, 264–281. Stanford, CA: Stanford University Press, 1997.

Furth, Charlotte. "Androgynous Male and Deficient Females: Biology and Gender Boundaries in Sixteen-and Seventeenth-Century China." *Late Imperial China* 9, no. 2 (1988): 1–31.

Furth, Charlotte. *A Flourishing Yin: Gender in China's Medical History: 960–1665* (Philip E. Lilienthal Books). Oakland, CA: University of California Press, 1999.

Gilmartin, Christina K., Gail Hershatter, Lisa Rofel, and Tyrene White, eds. *Engendering China: Women, Culture, and the State*. Cambridge, MA: Harvard University Press, 1994.

Hanan, Patrick. *The Invention of Li Yu*. Cambridge, MA: Harvard University Press, 1988.

Hayden, George A. "Li Li-Weng: A Playwright on Performance." *CHINOPERL Papers* 9 (1980): 80–91.

Henry, Eric. *Chinese Amusement: The Lively Plays of Li Yu*. Hamden, CT: Archon Books, 1980.

Hinsch, Bret. *Passion of the Cut Sleeve: The Male Homosexual Tradition in China*. Berkeley: University of California Press, 1990.

Hinsch, Bret. *Women in Imperial China* (Asian Voices). Lanham, MD: Rowman & Littlefield reprinted edition, 2016.

Hua, Wei. "The Lament of Frustrated Talents: An Analysis of Three Women's Plays in Late Imperial China." *Ming Studies* 32 (April 1994): 28–42.

Huang, Martin. "*Qing* and Homoerotic Desire in *Bian er chai* and *Lin Lan Xiang*." In *Desire and Fictional Narrative in Late Imperial China*, 176–205. Cambridge, MA: Harvard University Asia Center, 2001.

Idema, Wilt, and Beata Grant. *The Red Brush: Writing Women of Imperial China*. Cambridge, MA: Harvard University Asia Center, 2004.

Kang, Wenqing. *Obsession: Male Same-sex Relations in China, 1900–1950*, Queer Asia series. Hong Kong: Hong Kong University Press, 2009.

Kile, S. E. "Sensational *Kunqu*: A Performance Review of the May 2010 Beijing Production of *Lian Xiang Ban* (Women in Love)." *CHINOPERL Papers* 30, no. 1 (July 2013): 221–228.

Kile, S. E. "Transgender Performance in Early Modern China." *Differences: Journal of Feminist Cultural Studies* 24, no. 2 (November 2013): 130–149.

Ko, Dorothy. *Teachers in the Inner Chambers: Women and Culture in Seventeenth-Century China*. Stanford, CA: Stanford University Press, 1994.

Li, Siu Leung. *Cross-Dressing in Chinese Opera*. Hong Kong: Hong Kong University Press, 2003.

Mann, Susan, and Yu-yin Cheng, eds. *Under Confucian Eyes: Writings on Gender in Chinese History*. Berkeley: University of California Press, 2001.

McMahon, Keith. *Misers, Shrews, and Polygamists: Sexuality and Male-Female Relations in Eighteenth-Century Fiction*. Durham, NC: Duke University Press, 1995.

Ng, Vivien W. "Homosexuality and the State in Late Imperial China." In *Hidden from History: Reclaiming the Gay and Lesbian Past*, ed. Martin Duberman, Martha Vicinus, and George Chauncey Jr., 76–89. New York: Meridian Press, 1989.

Pollard, David, trans. "Li Yu on the Theatre: Excerpts from *Pleasant Diversions*." *Renditions*, 72 (2009): 30–70.

Roddy, Stephen John. "Groves of Ambition, Gardens of Desire: *Rulin waishi* and the Fate of the *Portrait of Xiaoqing*." *Nan Nü: Men, Women, and Gender in Traditional China* 16, no. 2 (2014): 239–273.

Ropp, Paul S. *Banished Immortal: Searching for Shuangqing, China's Peasant Poet*. Ann Arbor: University of Michigan Press, 2001.

Ropp, Paul S. "'Now Cease Painting Eyebrows, Don a Scholar's Cap and Pin': The Frustrated Ambition of Wang Yun, Gentry Women Poet and Dramatist." *Ming Studies* 40 (Fall 1998): 86–110.

Sang, Tze-lan D. "Revising Premodern Chinese Female-Female Relationship." In *The Emerging Lesbian: Female Same-Sex Desire in Modern China*, 37–95. Chicago: University of Chicago Press, 2003.

Shen, Jing. "Chapter 7: An Ironic Perspective on Love Poeticized *Fengzheng wu.*" In *Playwrights and Literary Games in Seventeenth-Century China.* Plymouth, UK: Lexington Books, 2010.

Shen, Jing, and Robert E. Hegel, trans. *A Couple of Soles: A Comic Play from Seventeenth-Century.* New York: Columbia University Press, 2020.

Sommer, Matthew H. *Sex, Law, and Society in Late Imperial China.* Stanford, CA: Stanford University Press, 2000.

Starr, Chloe. "Shifting Boundaries: Gender in *Pinhua baojian.*" In *Men, Women and Gender in Early and Imperial China,* ed. Harriet T. Zurndorfer, 268–302. Vol. 1. Leiden: E. J. Brill, 1999.

Stevenson, Mark and Cuncun Wu, eds. *Homoeroticism in Imperial China: A Sourcebook.* London: Routledge, 2013.

Szekely, Lenore. "A Surrogate Hero: Generic Innovation and Reinventions of Masculinity in *Naihe Tian. CHINOPERL* Papers 39, no. 2 (December 2020): 111–127.

Szonyi, Michael. "The Cult of Hu Tianbo and the Eighteenth-Century Discourse of Homosexuality." *Late Imperial China* 19, no. 1 (1998): 1–25.

Van Gulik, R. H. *Sexual Life in Ancient China: A Preliminary Survey of Chinese Sex and Society from ca. 1500 B.C. till 1644 A.D.* Leiden: E. J. Brill, 1961.

Vitiello, Giovanni. "The Dragon's Whim: Ming and Qing Homoerotic Tales from the *Duanxiu pian.*" *T'oung Pao* 78 (1992): 341–372.

Vitiello, Giovanni. *The Libertine's Friend: Homosexuality & Masculinity in Late Imperial China.* Chicago: University of Chicago Press, 2011.

Volpp, Sophie. "The Discourse on Male Marriage: Li Yu's 'A Male Mencius Mother.'" *Positions* 2 (Spring 1994): 113–132.

Volpp, Sophie. "Four: Illusion and Allusion in *Nan wanghou*" and "Appendix: The Male Queen (A translation of Wang Jide's *Nan wanghou*). In *Theatricality in Seventeenth-Century China,* 129–172; 263–314. Cambridge, MA: Harvard University Press, 2011.

Wang, Ying. "Tragic Ending and Inversion in *The Tale of Orchid Dream.*" *Nan Nü: Men, Women and Gender in China* 13 (2011): 111–148.

Wang, Yun. *A Dream of Glory (Fanhua meng): A Chuanqi Play.* Qingyun Wu, trans. Hong Kong: The Chinese University Press, 2008.

Wu, Laura H. "Through the Prism of Male Writing: Representation of Lesbian Love in Ming-Qing Literature." *Nan Nü* 4, no. 1 (2002): 1–34.

Wu, Qingyun. "Daring to Dream: Wang Yun and Her Play *A Dream of Glory.*" *Renditions* 64 (August 2005): 83–95.

Xu, Peng. "The Essential Li Yu Resurrected: A Performance Review of the 2010 Beijing Production of *Lian Xiang Ban* (Women in Love)." *CHINOPERL Papers* 30 (2011): 229–238.

Zhang, Jie. "Watching Li Yu's Plays in Seventeenth-Century China." *Southeast Review of Asian Studies* 34 (2012): 4–24.

Zhou, Zuyan. *Androgyny in Late Ming and Early Qing Literature.* Honolulu: University of Hawai'i Press, 2003.

Zito, Angela, and Tani E. Barlow. *Body, Subject, and Power in China.* Chicago: University of Chicago Press, 1994.

Zurndorfer, Harriet T., ed. *Men, Women and Gender in Early and Imperial China*, vol. 1. Leiden: E. J. Brill, 1999.

INDEX

Major Plays of Chikamatsu, tr. Donald Keene 1961

Four Major Plays of Chikamatsu, tr. Donald Keene. Paperback ed. only. 1961; rev. ed. 1997

Records of the Grand Historian of China, translated from the Shih chi of Ssu-ma Ch'ien, tr. Burton Watson, 2 vols. 1961

Instructions for Practical Living and Other Neo-Confucian Writings by Wang Yang-ming, tr. Wing-tsit Chan 1963

Hsün Tzu: Basic Writings, tr. Burton Watson, paperback ed. only. 1963; rev. ed. 1996

Chuang Tzu: Basic Writings, tr. Burton Watson, paperback ed. only. 1964; rev. ed. 1996

The Mahābhārata, tr. Chakravarthi V. Narasimhan. Also in paperback ed. 1965; rev. ed. 1997

The Manyōshū, Nippon Gakujutsu Shinkōkai edition 1965

Su Tung-p'o: Selections from a Sung Dynasty Poet, tr. Burton Watson. Also in paperback ed. 1965

Bhartrihari: Poems, tr. Barbara Stoler Miller. Also in paperback ed. 1967

Basic Writings of Mo Tzu, Hsün Tzu, and Han Fei Tzu, tr. Burton Watson. Also in separate paperback eds. 1967

The Awakening of Faith, Attributed to Aśvaghosha, tr. Yoshito S. Hakeda. Also in paperback ed. 1967

Reflections on Things at Hand: The Neo-Confucian Anthology, comp. Chu Hsi and Lü Tsu-ch'ien, tr. Wing-tsit Chan 1967

The Platform Sutra of the Sixth Patriarch, tr. Philip B. Yampolsky. Also in paperback ed. 1967

Essays in Idleness: The Tsurezuregusa of Kenkō, tr. Donald Keene. Also in paperback ed. 1967

The Pillow Book of Sei Shōnagon, tr. Ivan Morris, 2 vols. 1967

Two Plays of Ancient India: The Little Clay Cart and the Minister's Seal, tr. J. A. B. van Buitenen 1968

The Complete Works of Chuang Tzu, tr. Burton Watson 1968

The Romance of the Western Chamber (Hsi Hsiang Chi), tr. S. I. Hsiung. Also in paperback ed. 1968

The Manyōshū, Nippon Gakujutsu Shinkōkai edition. Paperback ed. only. 1969

Records of the Historian: Chapters from the Shih chi of Ssu-ma Ch'ien, tr. Burton Watson. Paperback ed. only. 1969

Cold Mountain: 100 Poems by the T'ang Poet Han-shan, tr. Burton Watson. Also in paperback ed. 1970

Twenty Plays of the Nō Theatre, ed. Donald Keene. Also in paperback ed. 1970

Chūshingura: The Treasury of Loyal Retainers, tr. Donald Keene. Also in paperback ed. 1971; rev. ed. 1997

The Zen Master Hakuin: Selected Writings, tr. Philip B. Yampolsky 1971

Chinese Rhyme-Prose: Poems in the Fu Form from the Han and Six Dynasties Periods, tr. Burton Watson. Also in paperback ed. 1971

Kūkai: Major Works, tr. Yoshito S. Hakeda. Also in paperback ed. 1972

The Old Man Who Does as He Pleases: Selections from the Poetry and Prose of Lu Yu, tr. Burton Watson 1973

The Lion's Roar of Queen Śrīmālā, tr. Alex and Hideko Wayman 1974

Courtier and Commoner in Ancient China: Selections from the History of the Former Han by Pan Ku, tr. Burton Watson. Also in paperback ed. 1974

Japanese Literature in Chinese, vol. 1: Poetry and Prose in Chinese by Japanese Writers of the Early Period, tr. Burton Watson 1975

Japanese Literature in Chinese, vol. 2: Poetry and Prose in Chinese by Japanese Writers of the Later Period, tr. Burton Watson 1976

Love Song of the Dark Lord: Jayadeva's
  Gitagovinda, tr. Barbara Stoler Miller.
  Also in paperback ed. Cloth ed.
  includes critical text of the Sanskrit.
  1977; rev. ed. 1997

Ryōkan: Zen Monk-Poet of Japan, tr.
  Burton Watson 1977

Calming the Mind and Discerning the Real:
  From the Lam rim chen mo of
  Tson-kha-pa, tr. Alex Wayman 1978

The Hermit and the Love-Thief: Sanskrit
  Poems of Bhartrihari and Bilhaṇa, tr.
  Barbara Stoler Miller 1978

The Lute: Kao Ming's P'i-p'a chi, tr. Jean
  Mulligan. Also in paperback ed. 1980

A Chronicle of Gods and Sovereigns: Jinnō
  Shōtōki of Kitabatake Chikafusa,
  tr. H. Paul Varley 1980

Among the Flowers: The Hua-chien chi,
  tr. Lois Fusek 1982

Grass Hill: Poems and Prose by the Japanese
  Monk Gensei, tr. Burton Watson 1983

Doctors, Diviners, and Magicians of Ancient
  China: Biographies of Fang-shih, tr.
  Kenneth J. DeWoskin. Also in
  paperback ed. 1983

Theater of Memory: The Plays of Kālidāsa,
  ed. Barbara Stoler Miller. Also in
  paperback ed. 1984

The Columbia Book of Chinese Poetry: From
  Early Times to the Thirteenth Century,
  ed. and tr. Burton Watson. Also in
  paperback ed. 1984

Poems of Love and War: From the Eight
  Anthologies and the Ten Long Poems of
  Classical Tamil, tr. A. K. Ramanujan.
  Also in paperback ed. 1985

The Bhagavad Gita: Krishna's Counsel in
  Time of War, tr. Barbara Stoler Miller
  1986

The Columbia Book of Later Chinese Poetry,
  ed. and tr. Jonathan Chaves. Also in
  paperback ed. 1986

The Tso Chuan: Selections from China's
  Oldest Narrative History, tr. Burton
  Watson 1989

Waiting for the Wind: Thirty-Six Poets of
  Japan's Late Medieval Age, tr. Steven
  Carter 1989

Selected Writings of Nichiren, ed. Philip B.
  Yampolsky 1990

Saigyō, Poems of a Mountain Home, tr.
  Burton Watson 1990

The Book of Lieh Tzu: A Classic of the Tao, tr.
  A. C. Graham. Morningside ed. 1990

The Tale of an Anklet: An Epic of South
  India—The Cilappatikāram of Iḷaṅkō
  Aṭikal, tr. R. Parthasarathy 1993

Waiting for the Dawn: A Plan for the Prince,
  tr. with introduction by Wm. Theodore
  de Bary 1993

Yoshitsune and the Thousand Cherry Trees: A
  Masterpiece of the Eighteenth-Century
  Japanese Puppet Theater, tr., annotated,
  and with introduction by Stanleigh H.
  Jones Jr. 1993

The Lotus Sutra, tr. Burton Watson. Also in
  paperback ed. 1993

The Classic of Changes: A New Translation
  of the I Ching as Interpreted by Wang Bi,
  tr. Richard John Lynn 1994

Beyond Spring: Tz'u Poems of the Sung
  Dynasty, tr. Julie Landau 1994

The Columbia Anthology of Traditional
  Chinese Literature, ed. Victor H. Mair
  1994

Scenes for Mandarins: The Elite Theater of
  the Ming, tr. Cyril Birch 1995

Letters of Nichiren, ed. Philip B.
  Yampolsky; tr. Burton Watson et al.
  1996

Unforgotten Dreams: Poems by the Zen
  Monk Shōtetsu, tr. Steven D. Carter
  1997

The Vimalakirti Sutra, tr. Burton Watson
  1997

Japanese and Chinese Poems to Sing: The
  Wakan rōei shū, tr. J. Thomas Rimer
  and Jonathan Chaves 1997

Breeze Through Bamboo: Kanshi of Ema
  Saikō, tr. Hiroaki Sato 1998

A Tower for the Summer Heat, by Li Yu, tr.
  Patrick Hanan 1998

Traditional Japanese Theater: An Anthology
  of Plays, by Karen Brazell 1998

The Original Analects: Sayings of Confucius
  and His Successors (0479–0249),

by E. Bruce Brooks and A. Taeko Brooks 1998

The Classic of the Way and Virtue: A New Translation of the Tao-te ching of Laozi as Interpreted by Wang Bi, tr. Richard John Lynn 1999

The Four Hundred Songs of War and Wisdom: An Anthology of Poems from Classical Tamil, The Puranāṇūru, ed. and tr. George L. Hart and Hank Heifetz 1999

Original Tao: Inward Training (Nei-yeh) *and the Foundations of Taoist Mysticism*, by Harold D. Roth 1999

Po Chü-i: Selected Poems, tr. Burton Watson 2000

Lao Tzu's Tao Te Ching: *A Translation of the Startling New Documents Found at Guodian*, by Robert G. Henricks 2000

The Shorter Columbia Anthology of Traditional Chinese Literature, ed. Victor H. Mair 2000

Mistress and Maid (Jiaohongji), by Meng Chengshun, tr. Cyril Birch 2001

Chikamatsu: Five Late Plays, tr. and ed. C. Andrew Gerstle 2001

The Essential Lotus: Selections from the Lotus Sutra, tr. Burton Watson 2002

Early Modern Japanese Literature: An Anthology, 1600–1900, ed. Haruo Shirane 2002; abridged 2008

The Columbia Anthology of Traditional Korean Poetry, ed. Peter H. Lee 2002

The Sound of the Kiss, or The Story That Must Never Be Told: Pingali Suranna's Kalapurnodayamu, tr. Vecheru Narayana Rao and David Shulman 2003

The Selected Poems of Du Fu, tr. Burton Watson 2003

Far Beyond the Field: Haiku by Japanese Women, tr. Makoto Ueda 2003

Just Living: Poems and Prose by the Japanese Monk Tonna, ed. and tr. Steven D. Carter 2003

Han Feizi: Basic Writings, tr. Burton Watson 2003

Mozi: Basic Writings, tr. Burton Watson 2003

Xunzi: Basic Writings, tr. Burton Watson 2003

Zhuangzi: Basic Writings, tr. Burton Watson 2003

The Awakening of Faith, Attributed to Aśvaghosha, tr. Yoshito S. Hakeda, introduction by Ryūichi Abé 2005

The Tales of the Heike, tr. Burton Watson, ed. Haruo Shirane 2006

Tales of Moonlight and Rain, by Ueda Akinari, tr. with introduction by Anthony H. Chambers 2007

Traditional Japanese Literature: An Anthology, Beginnings to 1600, ed. Haruo Shirane 2007

The Philosophy of Qi, by Kaibara Ekken, tr. Mary Evelyn Tucker 2007

The Analects of Confucius, tr. Burton Watson 2007

The Art of War: Sun Zi's Military Methods, tr. Victor Mair 2007

One Hundred Poets, One Poem Each: A Translation of the Ogura Hyakunin Isshu, tr. Peter McMillan 2008

Zeami: Performance Notes, tr. Tom Hare 2008

Zongmi on Chan, tr. Jeffrey Lyle Broughton 2009

Scripture of the Lotus Blossom of the Fine Dharma, rev. ed., tr. Leon Hurvitz, preface and introduction by Stephen R. Teiser 2009

Mencius, tr. Irene Bloom, ed. with an introduction by Philip J. Ivanhoe 2009

Clouds Thick, Whereabouts Unknown: Poems by Zen Monks of China, Charles Egan 2010

The Mozi: A Complete Translation, tr. Ian Johnston 2010

The Huainanzi: A Guide to the Theory and Practice of Government in Early Han China, by Liu An, tr. and ed. John S. Major, Sarah A. Queen, Andrew Seth Meyer, and Harold D. Roth, with Michael Puett and Judson Murray 2010

The Demon at Agi Bridge and Other Japanese Tales, tr. Burton Watson, ed.

with introduction by Haruo Shirane
2011

Haiku Before Haiku: From the Renga Masters to Bashō, tr. with introduction by Steven D. Carter 2011

The Columbia Anthology of Chinese Folk and Popular Literature, ed. Victor H. Mair and Mark Bender 2011

Tamil Love Poetry: The Five Hundred Short Poems of the Aiṅkurunūṟu, tr. and ed. Martha Ann Selby 2011

The Teachings of Master Wuzhu: Zen and Religion of No-Religion, by Wendi L. Adamek 2011

The Essential Huainanzi, by Liu An, tr. and ed. John S. Major, Sarah A. Queen, Andrew Seth Meyer, and Harold D. Roth 2012

The Dao of the Military: Liu An's Art of War, tr. Andrew Seth Meyer 2012

Unearthing the Changes: Recently Discovered Manuscripts of the Yi Jing *(*I Ching*) and Related Texts,* Edward L. Shaughnessy 2013

Record of Miraculous Events in Japan: The Nihon ryōiki, tr. Burton Watson 2013

The Complete Works of Zhuangzi, tr. Burton Watson 2013

Lust, Commerce, and Corruption: An Account of What I Have Seen and Heard, by an Edo Samurai, tr. and ed. Mark Teeuwen and Kate Wildman Nakai with Miyazaki Fumiko, Anne Walthall, and John Breen 2014; abridged 2017

Exemplary Women of Early China: The Lienü zhuan *of Liu Xiang,* tr. Anne Behnke Kinney 2014

The Columbia Anthology of Yuan Drama, ed. C. T. Hsia, Wai-yee Li, and George Kao 2014

The Resurrected Skeleton: From Zhuangzi to Lu Xun, by Wilt L. Idema 2014

The Sarashina Diary: A Woman's Life in Eleventh-Century Japan, by Sugawara no Takasue no Musume, tr. with introduction by Sonja Arntzen and Itō Moriyuki 2014; reader's edition 2018

The Kojiki: An Account of Ancient Matters, by Ō no Yasumaro, tr. Gustav Heldt 2014

The Orphan of Zhao and Other Yuan Plays: The Earliest Known Versions, tr. and introduced by Stephen H. West and Wilt L. Idema 2014

Luxuriant Gems of the Spring and Autumn, attributed to Dong Zhongshu, ed. and tr. Sarah A. Queen and John S. Major 2016

A Book to Burn and a Book to Keep (Hidden): Selected Writings, by Li Zhi, ed. and tr. Rivi Handler-Spitz, Pauline Lee, and Haun Saussy 2016

The Shenzi Fragments: A Philosophical Analysis and Translation, Eirik Lang Harris 2016

Record of Daily Knowledge and Poems and Essays: Selections, by Gu Yanwu, tr. and ed. Ian Johnston 2017

The Book of Lord Shang: Apologetics of State Power in Early China, by Shang Yang, ed. and tr. Yuri Pines 2017; abridged edition 2019

The Songs of Chu: An Ancient Anthology of Works by Qu Yuan and Others, ed. and tr. Gopal Sukhu 2017

Ghalib: Selected Poems and Letters, by Mirza Asadullah Khan Ghalib, tr. Frances W. Pritchett and Owen T. A. Cornwall 2017

Quelling the Demons' Revolt: A Novel from Ming China, attributed to Luo Guanzhong, tr. Patrick Hanan 2017

Erotic Poems from the Sanskrit: A New Translation, R. Parthasarathy 2017

The Book of Swindles: Selections from a Late Ming Collection, by Zhang Yingyu, tr. Christopher G. Rea and Bruce Rusk 2017

Monsters, Animals, and Other Worlds: A Collection of Short Medieval Japanese Tales, ed. R. Keller Kimbrough and Haruo Shirane 2018

Hidden and Visible Realms: Early Medieval Chinese Tales of the Supernatural and the Fantastic, compiled by Liu Yiqing, ed. and tr. Zhenjun Zhang 2018

A Couple of Soles: A Comic Play from Seventeenth-Century China, by Li Yu, tr. Jing Shen and Robert E. Hegel 2019